THE ART OF STRATEGY

Strategy is best understood not as a science, but as an art – one of universal applications that transcend situation or historical context. The principles that were successful in war and politics through history can have real and demonstrable applications in business and management.

Here, professor of strategy Owen Hughes helps practitioners and students to draw those parallels and to develop a profound and holistic understanding of strategy that will help them plan for, and achieve, success. Describing strategy as an intersection of five facets – purpose, capability, will, terrain and tactics – Hughes draws from colourful and dramatic examples from history, and clearly demonstrates how these tactics might be applied in your own life and work.

This book is an ideal strategy text for any practitioner, lecturer or student who tires of familiar strategy frameworks with limited scope.

Owen E. Hughes is Adjunct Professor at RMIT University, Australia.

THE ART OF STRATEGY

Learning Creative Practices from the
Great Strategists of the Past

Owen E. Hughes

Routledge
Taylor & Francis Group
LONDON AND NEW YORK

First published 2021
by Routledge
2 Park Square, Milton Park, Abingdon, Oxon OX14 4RN

and by Routledge
52 Vanderbilt Avenue, New York, NY 10017

Routledge is an imprint of the Taylor & Francis Group, an informa business

© 2021 Owen E. Hughes

British Library Cataloguing-in-Publication Data
A catalogue record for this book is available from the British Library

Library of Congress Cataloging-in-Publication Data
Names: Hughes, Owen E., author.
Title: The art of strategy : learning creative practices from the great strategists
    of the past / Owen E. Hughes.
Description: Milton Park, Abingdon, Oxon ; New York, NY : Routledge, 2021. |
    Includes bibliographical references and index.
Subjects: LCSH: Business planning. | Strategic planning.
Classification: LCC HD30.28 .H8666 2021 (print) | LCC HD30.28 (ebook) |
    DDC 658.4/012—dc23
LC record available at https://lccn.loc.gov/2020049857
LC ebook record available at https://lccn.loc.gov/2020049858

ISBN: 978-1-138-31635-5 (hbk)
ISBN: 978-0-367-75773-1 (pbk)
ISBN: 978-0-429-45571-1 (ebk)

Typeset in Joanna
by Apex CoVantage, LLC

CONTENTS

1

THE ART OF STRATEGY

Introduction

There is much written and spoken about strategy, but much too that is misapplied, misappropriated and may even be misleading. In common usage, the word 'strategy' is often used for relatively low-level plans, or for events that are without real strategic importance, instances that are tactical at best. Strategy is bigger than this; it is more comprehensive, more inclusive, more important.

Strategy looks ahead. Strategy is essentially about creating a future; using data, information and judgment, or other influences that have effects and consequences for that future. Strategy is a way of thinking, an art rather than a science. It refers to the big picture, not the small picture, the ultimate aim, the overall purpose, the very reason for being. Lower-level plans do have their utility and should not be discounted altogether; they are, however, of much greater utility when part of, but subservient to, an overarching strategy.

Creating and curating the future does not mean that strategy is akin to fortune-telling, futurology or magic. Done well, strategy is about the balance of probabilities, about being judicious. It is grounded and pragmatic.

Rather than finding certainty in foreseeing the future, strategy is about creating a manageable set of possible futures for an organization or individual bearing in mind constraints of time, information uncertainty, organization and competence. The presence of a strategy 'suggests an ability to look up from the short term and the trivial to view the long term and the essential, to address causes rather than symptoms, to see woods rather than trees'.[1] While the future cannot be foretold with exactitude, there are ways in which prior events, stories, theory, understandings of situation and context can be drawn upon so that the best choice is made despite inherent uncertainty.

There are many different aspects of strategy and different formulations as to what might be important. There are innumerable theorists of strategy, far too many to be mentioned or used. There are theorists of strategy, historians of strategy, users of strategy, menus of strategic plans and much more.[2] The basic argument here is that strategy is best understood in a simple model as the intersection of five facets, five aspects that impinge on strategy – purpose, capability, will, terrain and tactics. In brief, as all are detailed later: purpose is the ultimate aim of a strategy; capability the resources that can be brought to bear; will is the human factor to decide to proceed or not; terrain is the field of conflict; and tactics the lower-order actions aimed at bringing about the strategic purpose. It is argued that successful strategy occurs when these five facets – PCWTT – work together in a mutually reinforcing way, although there are, of course, situations where deficiencies in one facet can be overcome by superiority in another.

If there is misalignment – if, for instance, tactics are inconsistent with the overall purpose, or if capability and will cannot overtake constraints of terrain – a strategy is likely to fail. In some situations, different facets may be emphasized more than others. Terrain may not be a salient issue in some cases, capabilities and will may be equivalent between possible adversaries. But purpose is far more important than the other four facets; if purpose – the first facet – is unclear or unachievable, the outcome is bound to be poor even if other facets are strong.

An obvious question is how to illustrate this model of strategy, how to extrapolate from a particular aspect to a more general case. In what follows, the facets of strategy are illustrated by looking at events and situations that enable lessons can be drawn. If strategy is universal – an approach applicable to any context from business to government even to war – then examples can be chosen from events for which information is available.

Instances used here are selected and are chosen by how they relate to a particular theoretical point. There are many possible examples. The ones chosen here illustrate the PCWTT model in some way pointing to aspects of strategy. They are mostly high-level instances of international conflict and war for which information and historical discussion are readily available. Some illustrate a particular facet of the model – George Washington in the American Revolution is a case study in purpose; Julius Caesar for will – while others illustrate several facets. Some examples appear several times here. For instance, aspects of Japanese naval strategy in World War II have lessons for all five facets of the PCWTT model. Overall, though, the examples chosen are representative of a larger universe of strategy rather than being definitive or comprehensive.

Using examples such as these is not unusual. Military leaders often refer to history, for instance, Washington's Fabian strategy referred to the Roman general Quintus Fabius Maximus Verrucosus in combatting Hannibal's invasion of Roman Italy two thousand years before. In turn, Washington's leadership is used and celebrated in studies of business a further two hundred years later.[3] Many business leaders, notably in the 1990s, gained much from the wisdoms of Sun-tzu from even further back in history. Machiavelli enlivens his work with examples from his own time but also Roman times. Alexander the Great is often cited in terms of business strategy,[4] even if time and a lack of information may make the lessons somewhat problematic and even anachronistic. Instances and events such as these are when strategy is at its most raw; elemental cases with serious consequences. It is argued here that lessons can be drawn about strategy from such stories, as strategy is a universal concept applicable to any sector.

What is strategy?

Strategy is one of those words everyone knows and uses, but often not that precisely. The relevant Shorter Oxford definitions of strategy are 'the art of a commander-in-chief; the planning and direction of the larger military movements and overall operations of a campaign; . . . the art or skill of careful planning towards an advantage or a desired end' and 'in game theory, business theory etc, a plan for successful action based on the rationality and interdependence of the moves of opposing or competing participants'. The word derives from the Greek *strategus* (or *strategos*), meaning 'a commander-in-chief, general, or chief magistrate at Athens and in the

Achaean league', and is a combination of *stratos*, which meant 'army' (or more correctly an army spread out over the ground), and *agein*, meaning 'to lead' (*Shorter Oxford Dictionary*). The Greek word for strategy and its distinction from tactics goes back at least as far as the Emperor Justinian in the sixth century CE,[5] although Freedman argues that the word only came into general use at the start of the nineteenth century.[6]

These definitions all involve planning and, implicitly, this means planning for some future event or desired condition. The 'art of a commander-in-chief' points to higher order thinking than the day-to-day, while 'the larger military movements and overall operations of a campaign' reinforce the idea that strategy is a higher-order function. And, 'the art of careful planning towards an advantage or desired end' neatly summarizes how strategy is used here. Strategy is purposive thought and action towards a desired end, as Freeman argues:

> The essence of strategy is the effort to gain and retain the initiative, and to minimize the effects of chance. Strategy unites foresight and determination. It combines capabilities with opportunities to achieve broad, predetermined ends through skillful maneuver that minimizes costs.[7]

There is much in this view. Strategy is used to minimize chance and costs, while combining ideas of capability, opportunities and predetermined ends brings in much of the PCWTT model used here. A general argument is that strategy is best seen as a way of thinking and should not be confined to one field or another. Despite this general point, though, there are distinct usages in military strategy, in game theory and business. These are to be looked at even as strategy is to be seen as a unified concept.

Military strategy

The military usage of strategy is where the term derives and where it is still much used. For Clausewitz, a Prussian general, historian and theorist from the early nineteenth century:

> Strategy is the employment of the battle to gain the end of the War; it must therefore give an aim to the whole military action, which must be in accordance with the object of the War; in other words, Strategy

forms the plan of the War, and to this end it links together the series of acts which are to lead to the final decision, that, is to say, it makes the plans for the separate campaigns and regulates the combats to be fought in each.[8]

Strategy is a higher function linking the separate campaigns, which also need to be part of the object of the war itself. Like all strategy it is about the relationship of ends to means and achieving a result. It is purposive, deliberate and goal-directed. It is not random. As resources are always limited, strategy allows for prioritization in order to best pursue whatever the overall objective might be.

From this we derive the useful distinction between strategy and tactics, with strategy referring to the overall conduct of a conflict as opposed to tactics, the day-to-day conduct of operations. Clausewitz makes this distinction quite clearly, arguing that 'tactics teaches the use of armed forces in the engagement; strategy the use of engagements for the objects of the war'.[9] While there is a difference it may be of level rather than kind; tactics and strategy should be aligned, with strategy the overall goal and tactics the means employed to get there.

Strategy and tactics are not always aligned. It is not unknown for a tactical battle or series of battles to be lost but for the overall strategy to prevail. During the American Revolution, as will be discussed later (chapter 2), George Washington was renowned for losing battle after battle, for running away, and for failure. He should be seen, however, as a strategist of genius and his undoubted mistakes of tactics should not take away from this more general point. Despite losing many of the battles he found himself in, he maintained the clear purpose of keeping an army in being and ultimately prevailed.

Not all generals regard strategy as crucial for warfare. US Civil War General William Tecumseh Sherman said of strategy: 'What is strategy? Common sense applied to war. You've got to do something. You can't go around asking corporals and sergeants. You must make it out in your own mind'.[10] But Sherman does himself a disservice here; his work as a general shows quite outstanding strategic ability. The march of his army through Georgia with limited logistic support from Atlanta to the sea (see chapter 6) was his own initiative. Both his commanding general, Ulysses S. Grant, and President Lincoln were somewhat sceptical beforehand and needed to be persuaded. In the event the march through Georgia was a brilliant move and probably shortened the war substantially and with few casualties.

Strategy is about achieving a purpose, with military strategy being about achieving a military purpose. As Earle argues:

> Strategy deals with war, preparation for war, and the waging of war. Narrowly defined it is the art of military command, of projecting and directing a campaign. It is different from tactics – which is the art of handling forces in battle – in much the same way that an orchestra is different from its individual instruments.[11]

This view is quite consistent with the separation of strategy and tactics set out by Clausewitz, but there is an even higher level of strategy termed 'grand strategy' pitched at the very survival of nation-states.

Grand strategy incorporates military strategy but adds much else besides. Earle argues that, as society and war have become more complicated, strategy has 'of necessity required increasing consideration of non-military factors, economic, psychological, moral, political, and technological'.[12] Strategy then becomes 'the art of controlling and utilizing the resources of a nation – or coalition of nations – including its armed forces, to the end that its vital interests shall be effectively promoted and secured against enemies, actual, potential, or merely presumed'.[13] As Earle adds, this more expansive view of strategy is sometimes known as grand strategy; this more expansive view quite understandable given that he was writing during World War II when these wider factors were certainly in play.

Grand strategy is about national well-being, including non-military interests, the interplay of nation-states and their competition and cooperation to serve national ends. It is meta-strategy, higher than military strategy alone. As Kennedy argues,

> The crux of grand strategy lies . . . in *policy*, that is, in the capacity of the nation's leaders to bring together all of the elements, both military and non-military, for the preservation and enhancement of the nation's long-term (that is, in wartime *and* peacetime) best interests.[14]

Where in earlier decades or even centuries, conflicts were narrowly confined to the military forces of contending parties, major conflicts at least since Napoleon have involved entire communities, military and civilian. Also, there have been long running strategic contests between ideologies and cultures that have not necessarily involved direct conflict in the military sense. The Cold War of the 1950s and 1960s, for instance, was a fierce strategic contest that did not involve direct military conflict between the key protagonists; the Soviet Union and the United States.

Even without any direct conflict, grand strategy requires the articulation of both policy goals and interim objectives, as well as a definition of power that extends well beyond the use of the military. As Freeman argues:

> Grand strategy unites military and diplomatic strategy. It integrates all elements of national power in policies calculated to advance or defend national interests and concerns in light of anticipated trends and events. Grand strategy is directed at the achievement of the greatest gain at the least military, political, economic, and cultural cost to the state and the nation. Grand strategy commonly aims at the achievement of a state's objectives without the uncertainties and expense of war. It seeks to ensure conditions that will produce victory when war occurs.[15]

Military strategy and grand strategy do tend to blur together. Grand strategy is mostly about the interaction of nation-states in all its aspects – military, diplomatic, economic. While military strategy is still crucial, this higher level of strategy 'is that which so integrates the policies and armaments of the nation that the resort to war is either rendered unnecessary or is undertaken with the maximum chance of victory'.[16] Grand strategy includes population, industrial capacity and potential, infrastructure, education and training. Even cultural interaction can have strategic consequences through the use of soft power.[17]

Strategy in business

Strategy is a term much used in business, both in studies of business and in practical application by businesses of all sizes. An analogy between warfare and business was made as long ago as Socrates who reportedly compared the duties of a general and a businessman 'and showed that both utilise plans to use resources to meet objectives'.[18] Clausewitz, too, saw war as analogous to business, arguing that

> Rather than comparing [war] to art we could more accurately compare it to commerce, which is also a conflict of human interests and activities; and it is still closer to politics, which in turn may be considered as a kind of commerce on a larger scale.[19]

For Clausewitz, then, war, commerce and politics are all quite close to each other as interactions of humans and their interests.

Strategy is about choice, about choosing a path based on available information, that should lead to a better outcome, however that might be defined. This is clearly applicable to business where choices may need to be made about preferring one course of action or another. Choices could include: investing in one opportunity or a different one; allocation of internal resources; shutting down or starting up; and the pluses and minuses of following one course of action or another. The judicious application of strategic thinking can assist in making the optimal choice between alternatives. This is not to say that strategic planning or management is perfect and always leads to better outcomes in every circumstance; rather, it is that the probability of overall benefit is higher than managing without a long-term view.

Business strategy as a discipline starts in the 1960s and has been central to intellectualization of business since.[20] Standard definitions of strategy within the business literature include: 'the determination of the long-run goals and objectives of an enterprise, and the adoption of courses of action and the allocation of resources necessary for carrying out these goals[21]; 'the plan enabling a company to gain, as efficiently as possible, a sustainable edge over its competitors'[22]; and 'a pattern of resource allocation that enables firms to maintain or improve their performance'.[23] Implicitly or explicitly, all these see strategy as the way of improving performance compared to competitors. The strategic tasks of devising a plan, allocating resources and measuring achievement of goals compared to the long-term plan, holding managers accountable for performance and discarding activities that do not contribute to the overall plan are such familiar parts of business that it is hard to imagine other ways of organizing.

Strategy in its business sense is seen by Andrews as

> the pattern of decisions in a company that determines and reveals its objectives, purposes or goals, produces the principal policies and plans for achieving those goals, and defines the range of businesses the

company is to pursue, the kind of economic and human organization it is or intends to be, and the nature of the economic and non-economic contribution it intends to make to its shareholders, employees, customers, and communities.[24]

Merely by changing a few words —company, shareholders, customers – this definition could well be about military strategy. Businesses do carry out their operations with the longer term in mind. They employ means to an end and can draw on concepts of military strategy to achieve such an end. Competitors may be regarded as foes to be defeated, or at least, bypassed; market share can be seen as territory to be captured; and internal organizational structures could be reconfigured for efficiency to best advance strategic goals.

Business strategy is often seen as starting with the organization's *mission*, followed by an *environmental scan* involving the familiar SWOT analysis – strengths, weaknesses, opportunities and threats – then, finally, an *action plan*. For instance, Grant argues there are four common factors for strategy: goals that are simple, consistent, and long term; profound understanding of the competitive environment; objective appraisal of resources; and effective implementation.[25] Such formulations are quite useful even if mission or goals could be considered lower level than purpose.

The analogy with military strategy could be extended further. Porter uses the term 'competitive strategy' for business competition, and this framework is widely followed. He starts out with a definition relating to ends and goals:

> Competitive strategy is a combination of the *ends* (goals) for which the firm is striving and the *means* (policies) by which it is seeking to get there . . . Some firms use terms like 'mission' or 'objective' instead of 'goals' and some firms use 'tactics' instead of 'operating' or 'functional policies'. Yet the essential notion of strategy is captured in the distinction between ends and means.[26]

Informed by research into firms, Porter describes what he calls the five forces driving industry competition. These are: rivalry among existing firms; bargaining power of buyers; the threat of substitute products or services; bargaining power of suppliers; and the threat of new entrants.[27] Porter argues that:

> An effective competitive strategy takes offensive or defensive action in order to create a *defendable* position against the five competitive forces. Broadly, this involves a number of possible approaches:
>
> - Positioning the firm so that its capabilities provide the best defense against the existing array of competitive forces;
> - Influencing the balance of forces through strategic moves, thereby improving the firm's relative position; or
> - Anticipating shifts in the factors underlying the forces and responding to them, thereby exploiting change by choosing a strategy appropriate to the new competitive balance before rivals recognize it.[28]

Porter's arguments about competitive strategy and about the strengths and weaknesses in an industry are quite military in tone and content, with such ideas as seeking a defensible position against competitors, choosing strategic positions against competitors and the like.

A remaining point is the extent to which business strategy is separable from other kinds of strategy. Studies of business strategy are often limited and tend to be laudatory, even hagiographic, about leaders. Information as to failure or even success is frequently opaque or not useful. The extent of competition is also more questionable as businesses may collude as well as compete, but this is hardly likely in military strategy. There are differences in terms of lethality – that is, competitors in business do not generally set out to kill off their competitors. The lives of protagonists are not at stake; their material well-being may be at risk, but bodily survival is not. Some companies or their leaders may talk as if they are in a war, a war of survival. But this is not really the case for the individuals involved.

Business as war is at best an imperfect analogy, although strategy remains a useful tool for business. Certainly, there are ample opportunities in business to use data, to use facts to support inference, and tools of path analysis or scenario building, and, in the end, judgment is required, judgment that points to strategy as art rather than science. The stakes in business may not be as high as in war or grand strategy, but the thought processes are certainly analogous and relevant.

Normal management processes may be adequate for ordinary operations, but it is also necessary, from time to time, to reassess the fundamental reason the organization exists, what it is trying to do and where it is going. This is not to say that a strategy needs to be inflexible or fixed for all time or irrelevant for the work of an organization. Strategy has become embedded into business – government, too – as without it there is randomness attached to what an organization does. Its strategic purpose should be clear.

Strategy as game theory

In some circles, notably parts of economics, strategy means game theory.[29] For Schelling:

> The term 'strategy' is taken from the theory of games, which distinguishes games of skill, games of chance, and games of strategy, the latter being those in which the best course of action for each player depends on what the other players do. The term is intended to focus on the interdependence of the adversaries' decisions and on their expectations about each other's behaviour. This is not the military usage.[30]

While game theory may not be the military kind of strategy as Schelling notes, strategic games do follow the same principles – players try to gain advantage to pursue a purpose.

As developed in the 1950s, game theory was used to model the behaviour of individual actors in bargaining situations such as nuclear war, arms control and deterrence. The very idea of deterrence relies on the other party behaving rationally if faced with a disparity of resources. Game theory goes beyond this in working out scenarios and associated probabilities for various actions. Ideas such as zero-sum and non-zero-sum games – such as the 'prisoners' dilemma' – derive from game theory. If one party acts in a certain way, what should the counter response be? How can an action be anticipated?

There are some circumstances in which game theory could be used in wider strategy. For instance, Schelling points to the need to understand irrationality as well the varieties of rationality. Even though the Japanese attack on Pearl Harbor could be seen as irrational in taking on another power with vastly more resources, there should have been greater understanding at the time in America that pushing the Japanese into an impossible position might well lead to the response that did occur.

Public sector strategy

As military strategy and grand strategy are generally seen as within the scope of governmental action they could be seen as strategy for and about the public sector. In addition, though, recent decades have seen concepts of strategy applying more widely to ordinary government operations. More governments and their agencies demand strategic intent and action as parts of what they do, deriving from the apparent success of strategic thinking in business over recent decades. While in many ways analogous to the use of strategy in the private sector, there are aspects of public sector strategy – of the non-military kind – that are somewhat different. Public agencies are organized by mandate, a legislative restriction as to organizational scope.

Public value is another highly useful way of looking at strategy in the public sector. An open question for both strategic planning and strategic management is that around the ultimate purpose of any public sector organization, what it is trying to achieve. Moore argues that the purpose should be the creation and maintenance of 'public value', a commodity analogous to the private value that is created in the private sector.[31] Moore posits a 'strategic triangle' linking at the three corners: legitimacy and support; operational capacity; and public value. Public value comes from alignment of the three points of the triangle. Agencies seek to create public value but are aware of the need to consider their authorizing environment – the source of legitimacy and support – as well as their own capacity and capability. Consideration by the public manager of the three points of the triangle helps focus on what the organization is aiming to do in a strategic sense; imbalance in the three sets of linkage may threaten its future.

Strategy in the public sector is analogous to that in the private sector, but its differences are significant. As Bryson argues:

> Together mandates, mission, and values indicate the public value the organization will create and provide the social justification and legitimacy on which the organization's existence depends. Public and non-profit organizations are externally justified. This means that they are

chartered by the state to pursue certain public purposes, and their legitimacy is conferred by the broader society. These organizations must find ways to show that their operations do indeed create public value, or they risk losing the social justification for their existence.[32]

Strategy in government needs to be practical, based on evidence and on extrapolation of existing into possible futures. Strategy should not be static or overly abstract. It is, or should be, a guide to action even as Bryson states that strategic planning is no panacea.[33]

A person, an organization or an army may act without a sense of strategy and may even succeed to some limited extent. However, the focus of strategy can reduce costs of all kinds by being more focused on a result. Without strategy any organization is without direction. Day-to-day activities do not add up to any coherent goal. Ideally, all activities undertaken help to further specified objectives and beyond them contribute to the overall organizational purpose whatever it may be.

A unified framework: the five facets of strategy

Thus far we have looked at several distinct usages of strategy. Business, international relations and game theory use the term but do so somewhat differently, even if all are about the relationship between goals and means. The argument now is that there is a unified model of strategy; that strategy is an art and a science applicable to various contexts and situations. Rather than being quite separate, business strategy, military strategy, grand strategy and other kinds are all related, sub-categories of a wider concept. Strategy is not only about war, even if its manifestations can be seen most easily in that context.

It is argued here that strategy has five interlinked, but separable facets – purpose, capability, will, terrain and tactics. The term 'facet' is used to emphasize that each are parts of a whole, that they are not sequential or linear ideas where one simply follows another. Each facet relates to all the others. Strategy is best seen as the interplay of these five facets – in some situations one might be dominant, sometimes another. While a strategy might exist without one or another facet being important in that particular case, if they are in harmony the strategy is likely to work better. For instance, undertaking a clear purpose with vague tactics is unlikely to work well, being thoroughly imbued with will but lacking in resource capability is similarly not going to work well. Ideally, the facets of strategy need to be aligned.[34]

1. **Purpose:** Purpose is about why we do something, its ultimate goal. Standard works on strategy always start with a word denoting such an overarching goal or objective – usually 'mission' or 'vision'. It is argued here that the best word for a higher goal in English is 'purpose'. Purpose is clearly higher than 'mission', more about fundamentals, more about the very *raison d'être* of an organization, venture or situation. 'Mission' implies a more limited day-to-day task – for instance, 'your mission for today is' when referring to a day's events or a day's task. 'Vision' may be used more often now, but suffers from an overly inflated view of leadership and inspiration.

2. **Capability:** Capability refers to the assets held by a protagonist that can be deployed to a contest and what it can do as a consequence of having and holding these assets. In addition, capability is expressly comparative in that it requires reference to a competitor. No party can be totally capable in everything, but can be relatively capable compared to someone else. Capability is related to the SWOT analysis used in other treatments of strategy but is a better term.

3. **Will:** Will involves having the strength of character, the firmness, the decisiveness, to undertake an action. It is about commitment, deciding to proceed or not. The other facets of strategy may all be present, but, without the will to move ahead, an organization is not going to move. Will does involve some of the more personal aspects of strategy, including leadership as the manifestation of will.

4. **Terrain:** Terrain refers to the field, area or arena where a contest is to take place. In most contexts thinking about terrain is about factors that are relevant but beyond human control such as geography or physical conformation, the land and the sea, the elements, the seasons and the weather. Terrain is argued to be more precise than the environmental scan as used in standard strategy.

5. **Tactics:** Tactics are day-to-day actions that aggregate to an overall purpose and strategy. Tactics could be in the form of action plans or some other kind of subsidiary points, events or actions that aggregate

into the purpose and that assist in bringing about that larger purpose. Tactical actions that are inconsistent with purpose delay and may cut across a desired strategic outcome.

Each of these facets is explained further in following chapters. A standard sequence can be that purpose, capability and will take place logically prior to action, while terrain and tactics impinge how an action is carried out once it has been decided to proceed. But even if terrain and tactics occur later, a strategy still needs to take them into account in the early stages as they impinge on the practicality of purpose, capability and will. Similarly, capability affects purpose for obvious enough reasons – that is, even considering a course of action requires an assessment of capability. Terrain and tactics similarly affect purpose. Will is about commitment, but still requires clear and logical consideration of purpose, capability, terrain and tactics.

The five facets of strategy

Seeing strategy as a set of headings, a mnemonic or acronym is not novel. The PCWTT model is but another. Even if it does not lead to a neat acronym, the five facets used here – purpose, capability, will, terrain and tactics – are chosen as the best words to encapsulate their respective areas. Why are there five facets? There could simply be three, aim or purpose, resources and actions, but this leaves out external factors of terrain or environment as well as the will or leadership point as argued here. As noted earlier, Porter talks of five forces for competitive strategy. There could be ten as outlined by Bryson for public sector strategy, but this is likely too large a number. There could be seventeen, as argued by Gray, although a number of these could be aggregated into more inclusive terms rather than separated.[35] But rather than searching for five words to make an acronym it is more the case that the five chosen are the most appropriate for the question at hand. However, even as there is no particular reason for choosing five facets here, two of the theorists used here – Sun-tzu and Clausewitz – also nominate five.

Around the fifth century BCE the Chinese philosopher Sun-tzu wrote one of the earliest extant formulations of strategy.[36] It is not certain whether or not there was such a person, but the words have survived and offer great insight into strategy and tactics. Sun-tzu refers to five factors for structuring warfare known to successful generals, and arguably relevant to strategy more generally: the first is termed the Tao, the second Heaven, the third Earth, the fourth generals, and the fifth the laws. In more detail:

> 'The Tao' causes the people to be fully in accord with the ruler. [Thus] they will die with him; they will live with him and not fear danger. Heaven encompasses yin and yang, cold and heat, and the constraints of the seasons. Earth encompasses far or near, difficult or easy, expansive or confined, fatal or tenable terrain. The general encompasses wisdom, credibility, benevolence, courage, and strictness. The laws [for military organization and discipline] encompass organization and regulations, the Tao of command, and the management of logistics. There are no generals who have not heard of these five. Those who understand them will be victorious; those who do not understand them will not be victorious.[37]

The five facets of the PCWTT model do draw from these. The factors Sun refers to as Earth and Heaven relate to terrain, the laws, organization and logistics could be read as capability, and the wisdom and credibility of the general, along with 'the Tao causes the people to be fully in accord with the ruler', relate to will and leadership in the PCWTT model.

The factors set out by Sun-tzu form a simple calculus leading to success or failure. As he argues:

> If one who finds that the majority of factors favor him will be victorious while one who has found few factors favor him will be defeated, what about someone who finds no factors in his favor? If I observe it from this perspective, victory and defeat will be apparent.[38]

Victory comes from possession of the five factors and defeat comes from their absence. If the majority of the factors are favourable, success is bound to follow where an absence of the factors means defeat.

Two millennia after Sun-tzu, Clausewitz set out what he called five elements of strategy – 'the moral, physical, mathematical, geographical, and statistical elements'. Some are related to those of Sun-tzu, others are rather different:

The first class includes all that can be called forth by moral qualities and effects; to the second belong the whole mass of the military force, its organization, the proportion of the three arms, etc., etc.; to the third, the angle of the lines of operation, the concentric and eccentric movements in as far as their geometrical nature has any value in the calculation; to the fourth, the influences of country, such as commanding points, hills, rivers, woods, roads, etc., etc.; lastly, to the fifth, all the means of supply.[39]

Clausewitz goes on to argue that strategy involves all of these and that they are 'intimately connected with each other in every single operation of War'.[40] There is some commonality between these views and those of Sun-tzu. The emphasis on matters of terrain, for instance, and supply and logistics, and capability. What Clausewitz calls 'moral forces' could be read as Sun-tzu's 'Tao of the ruler'; both contribute to the ideas of 'purpose' or perhaps as a combination of purpose and will in the PCWTT model.

The PCWTT model here could be seen as drawing on others or as merely a refinement of the standard model of strategy: 'purpose' could be taken as meaning 'mission'; 'capability' and 'terrain' as components of standard SWOT analysis, while 'tactics' could be considered as related to action plan. But 'purpose' is a much stronger word than 'mission'; an organization's *purpose* is more fundamental than its immediate mission. Also, 'capability' is more focused than SWOT, as capability can be compared to other parties on particular aspects. An organization's capability in terms of, say, the skills of workers can be compared to others; fixed assets can be measured. Also, what is often called 'the environment' in the standard model of environmental scan is rather nebulous, with boundaries that are unclear. Terrain is rather more specific, meaning the field where the contest is to take place. Tactics, too, is a better word than 'action plans', although tactics would often include plans for action. Tactics include those day-to-day, lower-level actions, including missions, that crucially, need to aggregate to the overall strategy. Tactics that are inconsistent with the established strategy do not assist in helping to achieve the defined purpose. Adding will to the other four facets is also realistic in that an organization or leader may have everything in place but still be unwilling to take the next step and act.

There are a few other general points about strategy to look at before more detailed discussion of each facet and its examples in separate chapters.

These are: strategy is serious; strategy is realistic; strategy and stratagem are different from each other; and the role of chance and fortune in strategy.

Strategy is serious

Clausewitz sees strategy and war as rational and realistic extensions of policy. He argues that in the final analysis the undertaking of war is for political purposes. He argued that war is an extreme but natural extension of policy – 'war is nothing but the continuation of policy with other means'. It is a serious business and not to be undertaken lightly.

Sun-tzu argues that the exercise of strategy in war is a serious exercise, it is not frivolous. Under the heading 'Initial Estimations, Sun argues that 'Warfare is the greatest affair of state; the basis of life and death, the Way [Tao] to survival or extinction. It must be thoroughly pondered and analysed.'[41] There is an implicit warning here that strategy should not be resorted to lightly, on a whim or without reason. Sun-tzu notes, 'Those who do not thoroughly comprehend the dangers inherent in employing the army are incapable of truly knowing the potential advantages of military actions.'[42] As Sun-tzu argues:

> If it is not advantageous, do not move. If objectives cannot be attained, do not employ the army. Unless endangered do not engage in warfare. The ruler cannot mobilize the army out of personal anger. The general cannot engage in battle because of personal frustration. When it is advantageous, move; when not advantageous, stop. Anger can revert to happiness, annoyance can revert to joy, but a vanquished state cannot be revived, the dead cannot be brought back to life. Thus the enlightened ruler is cautious about it, the good ruler respectful of it. This is the Tao for bringing security to the state and preserving the army intact.[43]

For Sun-tzu the ultimate aim is to win at minimal cost or, even better not fighting at all. As he argues:

> Ultimate excellence lies not in winning every battle but in defeating the enemy without ever fighting. The highest form of warfare is to attack strategy itself; the next to attack alliance; the next to attack armies. The lowest form of war is to attack cities. Siege warfare is a last resort.[44]

Not only is war serious, it will eventually be over, as 'No country has ever profited from protracted warfare'.[45] Even if seemingly obvious, this is a point of some profundity. Not only will the conflict be over, but the certainty that it will eventually end needs to constrain, should constrain, how the conflict is to be carried out. This reality means that all participants need to look ahead to likely scenarios after the conflict is over and to manage the conflict accordingly. Each needs to be behave in such a way as to not be counterproductive to the peace that will inevitably follows, as Freeman argues:

> Peace requires the revision of relationships with former adversaries. The enlistment of erstwhile enemies in a stable post-war balance of power buttresses peace. War is properly conducted to shape the peace to follow.[46]

Seen this way, war is about peace, about what can be achieved in the peace that will one day follow conflict and this, in turn, means that the way the war was carried out should not poison the longer-run relationships. This lesson can be seen quite clearly in the Pacific War.

As discussed later (chapter 6), along with other failures of Japanese strategy in World War II more generally, their actions during the conflict, their very behaviour, made the time after the war even more difficult than it might have been. As Paine argues:

> Japan's brutality proved singularly counterproductive. If the goal was empire and autarky, making the colonies ungovernable by leaving the colonial population no alternative but resistance indicated a stunning lack of perception. Everywhere the Japanese went, they alienated those whom they encountered. They conducted serial diplomacy with the United States, Germany, China, and Russia, alienating each in turn. Their cruelty in China transformed a fractured people into a lethal enemy.[47]

It is a salutary lesson that war is actually about the peace that follows, and, consequently, that behaviour during the conflict can affect the peace and relationships afterwards. Decades later, Japanese relations with other nearby nations are still affected by its behaviour during World War II; not that there was a war, but that how it acted during that war was so extreme.

Memories are long. Japan lost the war, and struggled after 1945 to have as significant a role in the peace that it should have had considering its population and economy.

Strategy is realistic

Strategy does need to challenge the future; it does need to extend the present state into desired directions, but still it must be realistic. A strategy that is wildly unrealistic, one that is based on overly optimistic views of capability, is highly likely to fail. In practice, drawing an exact line between being bold and being unrealistic is not easy, but it is part of being a strategist. Realism is a contested concept, but in the current context it may be seen as formulating a strategy that is within the bounds of probability. Relying on the unlikely is unrealistic. For instance, it is unrealistic to imagine that sheer will can overcome a lack of capability. It may be within the bounds of possibility to assume this, but not within the bounds of probability.

Realism owes much to Machiavelli, 'the first important political realist',[48] and his kind of realism is the foundation of one of the key schools of international relations, most often contrasted with utopianism or idealism. To Carr, one of the key tenets of the realist philosophy implicit in Machiavelli is that 'history is a sequence of cause and effect, whose course can be analysed and understood by intellectual effort, but not (as the utopians believe) directed by 'imagination'.[49] What happens is grounded in reality, not in imagination or mysticism. Above all, Machiavelli is logical and at least partly secular, both aspects unusual in that age. Although a role is given to 'fortune' or luck, an at least equal role is given to personal effort, arguing that 'in order that our free will not be extinguished, I judge it to be true that Fortune is the arbiter of one half of our actions, but that she still leaves the control of the other half, or almost that, to us'.[50] Missing from Machiavelli are appeals to the gods. It is, at base, secular and realist in that sense. Fortune or fate or even God do not do everything – a person can to some extent control their own fate.

Freedman argues Machiavelli is essentially empirical and that

> Political survival depended on an unsentimental realism rather than the pursuit of an illusory ideal. This meant paying attention to conflicts of interest and their potential resolution by either force or trickery. But

guile and cunning could not create their own political legacy: the foundation of states still lay in good laws and good armies.[51]

Realism can be contrasted with idealism, or utopianism, even though in some circumstances a neat distinction is hard to make. But the general point that survival depends on unsentimental realism is a valid one, as is the need for good laws and good armies. It was a revolution in thinking that individuals could make their way by their own efforts – a far cry from notions of predestination and preordination – and implicitly challenged the authority of the church. Machiavelli tells us not how things should be, but merely explains what to do if we seek certain ends. He is a realist, a 'strikingly modern thinker who paved the way for a science of politics'.[52]

Machiavelli also had a realistic if somewhat bleak understanding of people and their motivations:

> For one can say this generally of men: that they are ungrateful, fickle, pretenders and dissemblers, evaders of danger, eager for gain. While you do them good, they are yours, offering you their blood, property, lives, and children, as I said above, when the need for them is far away; but when it is close to you they revolt.[53]

Machiavelli had been let down many times by other people, notably when he tried to raise a militia army in Florence in 1512 to defend the city from the Medici. Perhaps Machiavelli possessed a better understanding of the weaknesses of people rather than their strengths.

Benner argues that Machiavelli is deeply ironic and, rather than lauding the self-interested behaviours of princes, clearly prefers republican government and good laws:

> When we listen to his own voice, instead of trusting too much in his 'Machiavellian' reputation, we begin to see a strong character, irrepressibly friendly yet often at odds with his fellow citizens, with a steely determination to change the corrupt world he lived in – and a belief that any individual, however weak or downtrodden, could do their bit to change things for the better. Throughout his life, he urged people to see themselves as free agents who could always hope to influence the course of events.[54]

Strategy should be realistic; an unrealistic strategy risks failure. Strategy needs to be based on logic and data, on cool assessment of the probability of success. It need not necessarily be completely secular. Strategy could conceivably be conducted for a religious purpose; however, the steps that follow are unlikely to be as successful if they are fantasies, not based on empiricism or logic, at least when compared with an alternative more realistic approach. A complete realism may not be possible as at some point there needs to be some kind of ideal, some kind of view of a better society that animates protagonists. The point really is to allow for this but also for the steps and the process to be informed by facts, by science and by reliable theory, as opposed to chance, voices in the air, phantasms or other kinds of mysticism.

Strategy and stratagem

A stratagem is different from a strategy; while it can be part of a strategy it is more often akin to a tactical manoeuvre. It is more about an artifice, a piece of trickery, a cunning ploy that may help achieve an immediate goal, but most often one that is low level and tactical rather than strategic. Sun-tzu has many examples of stratagem, using deception to trick or fool an adversary. The key is simply a matter of doing the opposite of what is expected:

> Warfare is the Way [Tao] of deception. Thus although [you are] capable, display incapability to them. When committed to employing your forces, feign inactivity. When [your objective] is nearby, make it appear as if distant, when far away create the illusion of being nearby. Display profits to entice them. Create disorder [in their forces] and take them. If they are substantial, prepare for them; if they are strong avoid them. If they are angry, perturb them; be deferential to foster their arrogance. If they are rested, force them to exert themselves. If they are united, cause them to be separated. Attack where they are unprepared. Go forth where they will not expect it. These are the ways military strategists are victorious. They cannot be spoken of in advance.[55]

As Freedman notes, Sun-tzu described relatively simple conflicts, in which bold moves left an enemy helpless or dissolving into disorder.[56] A retreat can be feigned to lure an enemy to a prepared position. A 'Parthian shot' refers to the ability of the Parthian warriors to fire arrows backward at a pursuing enemy. These are stratagems rather than strategies, although, if successful, a series of stratagems can have some impact. In more recent times of machine-age conflict, stratagems are less likely to be resorted to or to be effective.

In World War I the Royal Navy deployed Q-ships, merchant ships of seemingly innocent appearance that could quickly drop their camouflage and fire back when attacked by surfaced submarines. After some early successes they became ineffective once unrestricted submarine warfare commenced in 1917, while an attempt to reinstate the idea in World War II was a complete failure – 'a wasted effort and an inexcusable episode'.[57] On the other hand, prior to the D-Day landings in Normandy a series of elaborate deceptions were employed to convince the Germans that the landings would take place at Calais. The deceptions were so successful that even after the landings the German army held back believing that Normandy was only a feint.

Deception can be useful in limited circumstances but is not necessarily crucial. Clausewitz argues that stratagem 'implies a concealed intention', has 'nothing in common with means of persuasion, of self-interest, of force, but a great deal to do with deceit'.[58] As such a general should not be taken in by deception. He adds that resort to stratagem is resorted to more by those in a position of weakness, that 'the more helpless his situation, the more everything presses towards one single, desperate blow, the more readily stratagem comes to the aid of his boldness'.[59]

The role of chance

No strategy can be perfect and great strategies can fall apart by events that were not foreseen. Randomness and even luck can derail any strategy; events can overtake even the best prepared. Even if the greatest possible effort is expended on considering all eventualities a strategy still can fail. Clausewitz notes that 'war is the province of chance', adding that 'in no sphere of human activity is such a margin to be left for this intruder'.[60] And, as nineteenth century Prussian General von Moltke said, 'No plan of operations ever survives the first collision with the main body of the enemy', adding that strategy was little more than a series of expedients.[61]

To the calculations of a known and unknown quantity, one's own and the enemy's will, will also come third factors that escape all foresight:

weather, sickness, railroad accidents, misunderstandings, and delusions, and all the effects which man may call luck, fate, or God's will, but which man neither creates not rules.[62]

Von Moltke allows for fate or fortune to affect outcomes but still argues for purposive action and not simply relying on chance, arguing that 'the conduct of war does not lapse into blind, arbitrary action' and that 'a calculation of probabilities shows that all those chance happenings are just as often to the detriment or advantage of the one side or the other'.[63] The supreme commander must work out what is reasonable and, in effect, make their own luck. As von Moltke argues:

> Success, above all, obviously determines the reputation of a supreme commander. How much of this is really earned is extraordinarily difficult to determine. Even the best man falls against the irresistible power of circumstances, and even the average man must endure this power. Nevertheless, in the long run only the intelligent have good luck.[64]

It could be regarded as luck that during the Battle of Midway, the US Navy dive-bombers arrived above the Japanese aircraft carriers just at the point they were vulnerable due to rearming and refuelling operations underway at that time (see chapter 6). But it could also be the years of preparation, better ship design and the sheer professionalism of senior officers, notably Admiral Spruance, that led to an action-filled six minutes when three Japanese carriers were sunk – and a fourth a little later – thereby changing the course of the Pacific War. The calculation of probabilities, as von Moltke puts it, clearly favoured the US in the longer run and the stunning victory at Midway brought forward the inevitable; Spruance and the other US commanders merely seized the chances that came their way that day.

Seeking the perfect should not be the enemy of the good; thinking ahead and acting according to the balance of probabilities are still likely to be far better than acting randomly or being passive and reactive. Even if chance is recognized as a possibility in any action, relying on chance or luck is another matter altogether. The probability of success is low. That random events will occur is certain enough, but they need to be taken into a strategy as far as is possible. Overly elaborate plans that take no possibility of diversion, and that do not allow lower level commanders to use their initiative, can be easily thrown off course by chance. Some measure of flexibility is required in devising successful strategy.

Conclusion

The PCWTT model outlined here – purpose, capability, will, terrain and tactics – draws from some of the classic writers on strategy. A question remains as to the best way to illustrate these five facets of strategy. It is argued that, as an art rather than a science, strategy is perhaps best shown by stories and cases from situations where actors were faced with making strategic decisions.

A recent newspaper article about lessons for business leaders from politicians, citing Bismarck, Franklin Roosevelt and Winston Churchill, noted that three qualities that any executive or entrepreneur might usefully acquire were 'clear strategic goals, flexibility in tactics and an ability to inspire others'. The story added, 'Bosses should read more history books'.[65] Typically, they do not. However, if strategy is seen as a universal phenomenon, as a way of thinking rather than a mechanical process applying to one area alone, its lessons can be drawn from any strategic situation. There are instances of historical events that can be used as illustrations for the facets of strategy. Examples are drawn here from a number of events and many great writers from Sun-tzu to Machiavelli, Napoleon and many more, including aspects of World War II.

Past events, past stories, can be analysed; learnings may be able to be gleaned from specific circumstances. Past events are an inevitable part of current culture. For instance, a marathon race refers to the Greek runner Pheidippides running some 40 kilometres from Marathon to Athens to report victory against Persia in 460 BCE. Even if the story may be apocryphal it shows how the past is still with us all. Washington's trials and tribulations at Valley Forge are still with us; Pearl Harbor is a constant presence 80 years on. Writers such as Sun-tzu, Machiavelli and Clausewitz are still used for their insights.

Lessons can be drawn from the past, from historical circumstances, and applied to more recent instances, as Luecke argues:

> Many of the best and most interesting lessons for business people are actually found outside the corporate domain, in the worlds of generals, clergy, revolutionaries, and adventurers. Among these we find events and human struggles where leadership, daring and the skills of

artful management made a difference, often between life and death. The fact that the stakes were so high makes the lessons that much more vivid.[66]

As will be seen, lessons about strategy can be drawn from instances over hundreds of years – even thousands, as will be seen – where a strategic choice needed to be made. In many of these instances – Wellington in the Peninsular Campaign, Julius Caesar, the insights of Machiavelli, Japanese naval strategy in World War II – wider lessons can be found. Bose draws lessons from the campaigns of Alexander the Great,[67] even though the historical distance must cast some doubt as to exactly what happened back then. Even if the past is to a large extent unknowable, it is still possible to draw lessons from it. As Luecke argues,

> Today our ability to lead others in important undertakings, to manage organizations, to deal with human conflict and change and to avoid repeating the foolish mistakes of our predecessors is probably no greater than was that of people who lived hundreds – or thousands – of years ago.[68]

An understanding of the past should be a requirement for leadership of any kind. This should mean a working knowledge of the past insofar as it affects the role being undertaken.

Strategy is about a simple question, 'What do we do next?' It is about the methods that can be brought to bear, the choices that can be made from the many that are available, the principles and theories that can be drawn on, so that the path chosen is the best in the circumstances. Freeman argues:

> The essence of strategy is the effort to gain and retain the initiative, and to minimize the effects of chance. Strategy unites foresight and determination. It combines capabilities with opportunities to achieve broad, predetermined ends through skilful maneuvre that minimizes costs.[69]

Strategy is serious. It may be the greatest game, but it is also important for the futures of other people, hundreds, thousands or even millions of them. It is argued here that the five facets of strategy are: purpose, capability, will, terrain and tactics. Each of these will now be looked at in more detail.

Notes

1   Lawrence Freedman, *Strategy: A History* (Oxford: Oxford University Press, 2013), p. ix.

2   Beatrice Hauser, *The Evolution of Strategy* (Cambridge: Cambridge University Press, 2010); Freedman, *Strategy*.

3   Mark McNeilly, *George Washington and the Art of Business: The Leadership Principles of America's First Leader* (Oxford: Oxford Scholastic, 2008).

4   Partha Bose, *Alexander the Great's Art Of Strategy: The Timeless Leadership Lessons Of History's Greatest Empire Builder* (New York: Gotham).

5   Hauser, *Evolution of Strategy*, p. 4.

6   Freedman, *Strategy*, p. 72.

7   Chas W. Freeman, *Arts of Power: Statecraft and Diplomacy* (Washington, DC: United States Institute of Peace Press, 1997), p. 71.

8   Carl von Clausewitz, *On War*, edited by Anatol Rapoport (Harmondsworth: Penguin, 1968), p. 241.

9   Ibid., p. 128.

10 Burke Curtis, *Sherman's March* (New York: Random House, 1980), p. 299.

11 Edward Mead Earle, 'Introduction' to Edward Mead Earle (ed.), *Makers of Modern Strategy: Military Thought from Machiavelli to Hitler* (Princeton, NJ: Princeton University Press, 1943), p. viii.

12 Ibid.

13 Ibid.

14 Paul Kennedy, 'Grand Strategy in War and Peace: Toward a Broader Definition', in Paul Kennedy (ed.), *Grand Strategies in War and Peace* (New Haven, CT: Yale University Press, 1991), p. 5.

15 Freeman, *Arts of Power*, pp. 71–2.

16 Edward Mead Earle, 'Introduction' to Edward Mead Earle (ed.), *Makers of Modern Strategy: Military Thought from Machiavelli to Hitler* (Princeton: Princeton University Press, 1943), p. viii.

17 Joseph S. Nye Jr., 'Public diplomacy and soft power', *The Annals of the American Academy of Political and Social Science*, 616, 2008, pp. 94–109.

18 John R. Montanari, Gregory A. Daneke and Jeffrey S. Bracker, 'Strategic Management for the Public Sector: Lessons from the Evolution of Private-Sector Planning', in Jack Rabin, Gerald J. Miller and W. Bartley Hildreth (eds), Handbook of Strategic Management (New York/Basel: Marcel Dekker, 1989).

19 Clausewitz, *On War*, p. 149.

20 Alfred D. Chandler Jr., *Strategy and Structure: Chapters in the History of Industrial Enterprise* (Cambridge, MA: MIT Press, 1962).

21 Ibid.

22 Kenichi Ohmae, *The Mind of the Strategist* (New York: McGraw-Hill, 1982).

23 Jay. B. Barney, *Gaining and Sustaining Competitive Advantage*, 4th edn (Harlow, UK: Pearson Education, 2014).

24 Kenneth Andrews, *The Concept of Corporate Strategy* (Homewood, IL, R.D. Irwin, 1980), p. 18.

25 Robert M. Grant, Contemporary Strategy Analysis, 6th edn (Oxford: Blackwell, 2008), pp. 7–9.

26 Michael E. Porter, *Competitive Strategy* (New York: The Free Press, 1980), p. xvi.

27 Ibid., p. 4.

28 Ibid., p. 30.

29 Avinash Dixit and Barry J. Nalebuff, *Thinking Strategically: The Competitive Edge in Business, Politics and Everyday Life* (New York: W.W. Norton, 1991).

30 Thomas C. Schelling, *The Strategy of Conflict* (London: Oxford University Press, 1963), p. 3.

31 Mark Moore, Creating Public Value: Strategic Management in Government (Cambridge, MA: Harvard University Press, 1995).

32 John M. Bryson, *Strategic Planning for Public and Nonprofit Organizations*, 4th edn (San Francisco: Jossey-Bass, 2011), p. 117.

33 Ibid., p. 19.

34 Moore, *Creating Public Value*.

35 Colin Gray, *Strategic Studies: A Critical Assessment* (New York: Greenwood Press, 1982).

36 There are many translations of Sun-tzu's *The Art of War*. The one used most here is Ralph D. Sawyer (ed. and transl.), *The Seven Military Classics of Ancient China* (New York: Basic Books, 2007).

37 Sun-tzu, *The Art of War*, in Ralph D. Sawyer (ed. and transl.), *The Seven Military Classics of Ancient China* (New York: Basic Books, 2007), p. 157.

38 Ibid., p. 159.

39 Clausewitz, *On War*, pp. 249–50.

40 Ibid., p. 250.

41 Sun-tzu, *The Art of War* (Sawyer edn), p. 157.

42 Ibid., p. 159.

43 Ibid., p. 184.

44 Sun-Tzu, *The Art of War*, translation, commentary and introduction by John Minford (London: Penguin, 2002), pp. 14–15.

45 Sun-tzu, *The Art of War* (Sawyer edn), p. 159.

46 Freeman, *Arts of Power*, p. 64.

47 S.C.M. Paine, *The Wars for Asia, 1911–1949* (Cambridge: Cambridge University Press, 2012), p. 214.

48 E.H. Carr, *The Twenty Year Crisis, 1919–1939* (Basingstoke: Palgrave, 2001), p. 62.

49 Ibid., p. 62.

50 Peter Bondanella and Mark Musa (ed. and transl.), *The Portable Machiavelli* (Harmondsworth: Penguin, 1979), p. 159.

51 Freedman, *Strategy*, p. 50.

52 Ross King, *Machiavelli: Philosopher of Power* (New York: Harper Perennial, 2009), p. 237.

53 Bondanella and Musa, *The Portable Machiavelli*, p. 131.

54 Erica Benner, *Be Like the Fox: Machiavelli's Lifelong Quest for Freedom* (London: Allen Lane, 2017), p. xxi.

55 Sun-tzu, *The Art of War* (Sawyer edn), p. 158.

56 Freedman, *Strategy*, p. 45.

57 Arthur Marder, 'The Influence of History on Sea Power: The Royal Navy and the Lessons of 1914–1918', *Pacific Historical Review*, 41, 4 (1972), p. 429.

58 Clausewitz, *On War*, p. 274.

59 Ibid., p. 276.

60 Ibid., p. 140.

61 Daniel Hughes (ed.), *Moltke on the Art of War: Selected Writings* (New York: Random House, 2009).

62 Ibid.

63 Ibid.

64 Ibid.

65 *The Economist*, 25 August 2018.

66 Richard Luecke, *Scuttle Your Ships Before Advancing and Other Lessons from History on Leadership and Change for Today's Managers* (New York: Oxford, 1994), p. 9.

67 Bose, *Alexander the Great*.

68 Luecke, *Scuttle Your Ships*, p. 4.

69 Freeman, *Arts of Power*, p. 71.

2

PURPOSE

Introduction

The starting point for any strategy needs to be its purpose, what it is trying to do. Purpose is not about a short-term goal or a medium-term goal, but an ultimate goal or aim. Clarity of purpose is fundamental to any strategy, at any place and at any time. What is the longer-term goal that other actions or ideas are to lead towards? What is the ultimate aim that the organization or person is trying to achieve? A purpose that is vague, unclear or unachievable is, unsurprisingly, unlikely to be achieved.

Purpose is what we do, why we exist, what are we trying to do, what is our reason for being. A person or organization can meander their way through the days. They can respond on a short-term basis to short-term forces that are at play, but this kind of action could be considered purposeless or directionless unless it has an underlying consistency provided by clarity of purpose. The question needs to be asked, 'what does success look like?' or 'if I pursue a particular course of action how will this help advance my ultimate purpose?'

For some individuals, the pursuit of the game itself or the pursuit of glory might be personal motivations of purpose, but these may not be strategic, or about strategy in the larger sense of trying to achieve an overarching purpose. The pursuit of glory in other strategic situations may be regarded as essentially irrational or, at best, a short-term action for a personal benefit in terms of pride, self-worth or regard by others.

There are examples in what follows that illustrate the idea of purpose. There are other instances of purposeless behaviour, of follies carried out either without an overarching direction or with a purpose so unrealistic as to be unachievable. Four cases will be looked at here. To start with, George Washington's strategy in the Revolutionary War exemplifies eventual success after much failure by maintaining focus on the overall purpose. An instance of an absence of clear purpose can be seen in the short career of Alexander the Great. This is an example of it not being clear what the purpose was, what he was trying to do – or at the very least a purpose that is not clear more than two millennia later. A more detailed case is that of the Japanese naval strategy in World War II, starting with Pearl Harbor. There was a strategic purpose, but it is argued to be both unclear and unachievable. The cost was the near devastation of Japan and the loss of millions of lives there and elsewhere in Asia. An additional and sobering example is that of the start of World War I, when a massive conflict appeared to happen either without purpose or, at the very least, where the protagonists' early goals were lost as the conflict became ever larger and with little prospect of either success or even ending.

The meaning of purpose

The first meaning for 'purpose' in the *Shorter Oxford Dictionary* is, as a noun, 'the reason for which something is done or created or for which something exists'. The second meaning is 'a person's sense of resolve or determination' as a noun, and, as a verb, 'have as one's intention or objective'. Purpose is described as being of Middle English origin from Old French *porpos* then *proposer*. The close link to 'propose' points to some future intent; a proposal being an intended action put forward, but which may or may not be endorsed for action.

The first dictionary meaning listed – the reason for which something is done or created or for which something exists – points to the very fundamentals of strategy. The French phrase *raison d'être* – 'reason for being' – is particularly useful in setting out what strategy is about. The reason for being is more fundamental than an immediate goal. It goes to the heart of the matter, the core, the very reason that an organization exists or the very essence that is to be explored.

Depictions of strategy often refer to 'mission' or 'mission statement' in setting out the goals for a course of action. While worthy in some circumstances, 'mission' is a lower-order function and is most often tactical rather than strategic. It usually refers to a separable event with an expressed aim, but one that is contained by time and space. For instance, 'today's mission is to fly to France'. If the flight to France goes ahead, the mission is completed; it is a separable event constrained by time and space. The intent of such an event may be for reasons of strategy and ideally a number of missions will assist in the furtherance of strategy when aggregated. But the strategic purpose is above that more tactical level where the term 'mission' really belongs.

Some kind of direction or aim or intention is a fundamental requirement of any directed action. It is commonplace in business strategy to use the term 'mission'; sometimes the term 'vision' is used in its place. 'Purpose' is argued here to be a higher-level function than either 'mission' or 'vision' or any other word in English when referring to motivation or direction.

In business, some organizations speak of 'vision statements', with these seen as statements of the future, of where the organization is going. But a wish or a dream need not have any basis in reality. Some organizations have 'purpose statements', but this does not add much to the idea of vision statement other than, perhaps, as a source of shared inspiration. A strategic purpose is more basic, elemental. It provides an organization its reason for being, its *raison d'être* as said before; its very survival. These meanings are clear enough and certainly point to higher levels of ambition than a mission or vision.

The need for clear purpose in terms of strategy seems obvious enough but finding out exactly what is to be achieved can be quite difficult. Individuals, organizations or even nation-states sometimes set out on ventures that were never likely to be successful. For Sun-tzu, 'the skilful strategist defeats the enemy without doing battle, captures the city without laying siege, overthrows the enemy state without protracted war'.[1] Such an ultimate aim may be difficult, but it certainly provides focus on purpose.

Focus on the ultimate purpose:
George Washington's revolution

The way that events transpire can sometimes seem to have been inevitable, that the way to victory was always going to happen. But even taking due regard to the tendency that history is for winners, and written by the winners, clear focus on purpose can lead to the desired outcome.

A great example of purpose, and maintaining clear focus on that regardless of setbacks, is that of George Washington during the American Revolutionary War. Despite numerical inferiority where it counted, despite overwhelming naval inferiority, poor training and equipment, the colonists achieved their independence. The colonial strategy prevailed over the British strategy, mainly because of clearer purpose and better appreciation of what success should look like.

As commanding general of the Continental Army, Washington has received a mixed set of reviews, both at the time and later, and is often regarded as a military failure. Some of his tactical decisions were indeed poor and the tactic, eventually adopted, of running away from possible battles was a source of great frustration to the British and their Hessian mercenaries. But a more considered response is that Washington was a strategist of genius in keeping the overall purpose crystal clear and following tactics that were consistent with carrying out that purpose despite what seemed to be a position of weakness in terms of resources. Washington may have lost most of the battles he was ever in, but still he won the war by maintaining focus despite several years of adversity.

In hindsight, the American Revolutionary War appears to be a fraternal conflict that could and should have been avoided. But once fighting started there is a sense of inevitability in much of what followed. Relatively minor compromise earlier on might have obviated conflict altogether, with most of the intransigence on the British side, most notably from King George III personally. The British Parliament was far from united about pursuing a war with some key figures, including William Pitt the Elder and Edmund Burke, speaking against punishing the American colonies. The great Scottish economist Adam Smith supported independence for the American colonies.

Early conflicts around Boston from April to June 1775 – Concord, Lexington, Bunker Hill – showed that the colonists would not give up without a fight. The British held Boston, but their occupancy did not extend far into the countryside. An uneasy truce ensued for some nine months. However, when the Americans dragged cannon from Fort Ticonderoga in the winter and emplaced them on Dorchester Heights overlooking the town and harbour, the British hold on Boston became untenable. Rather than risk another costly fight attacking entrenched positions up a hill as at Bunker Hill, the British gave up Boston and in March 1776 withdrew to Halifax. At this point an honourable peace could have been agreed, with the British giving up their American colonies while maintaining close economic and social links. Instead, the British government decided to greatly reinforce the navy and army in North America and gathered an invasion fleet of several hundred ships, with more than 30,000 soldiers on board, including mercenaries from the German state of Hesse.

By July 1776, the British navy under Admiral William Howe was in a position to land the army led by his brother Richard anywhere along the east coast. It chose New York to be the starting point of what became a crucial campaign along the Hudson River. More than 30,000 British soldiers and Hessian mercenaries set up camp on Staten Island. Washington had already moved much of the Continental Army to New York, having anticipated that the British would go there next. Despite New York being essentially indefensible against maritime attack, Washington decided to defend the city. As it turned out, this was a costly error.

The Howe brothers had been against war in America and had hoped, vainly, that the appearance of such a large force would drive the colonists to settle. It did not. Indeed, if anything, the existence of such a large invasion force led to an inevitability that it would be used. And on 22 August 1776, with any prospect of compromise now over, more than 20,000 British and Hessian troops crossed the harbor from Staten Island, and thus began what became known as the Battle of Long Island.

Much went wrong for the Americans in that battle, with fixed positions being bypassed, high casualties, poor leadership, and some troops running away. The reality was that, at this stage, American troops were outclassed by disciplined troops from Europe. American prepared positions in Brooklyn were outflanked by General Howe's forces using a minor road instead of the one they had been expected to use. Washington managed to get the remaining troops across the East River into Manhattan in the dark and in a heavy fog.

The tactical success of escaping into Manhattan could not disguise the fact that the conflict on Long island had been disastrous for the colonists. As McCullough argues:

> It had been the first great battle of the Revolution, and by far the largest battle fought in North America until then. Counting both armies and the Royal Navy, more than 40,000 men had taken part. The field of battle ranged over six miles, and the fighting lasted just over six hours. And for the Continental Army, now the army of the United States of America, in this first great test under fire, it had been a crushing defeat.[2]

Further conflicts took place in Manhattan, with occasional successes but greater losses, then Washington withdrew across a narrow bridge into the countryside of New York state, eventually crossing the Hudson River into New Jersey in November. A much diminished American army survived the winter of 1776/7 in New Jersey and Pennsylvania.

It is at this time, a time of adversity, following reverse after reverse and with a decidedly smaller army, that Washington's greatness as a strategist becomes evident. Set-piece battles in the European mode had been tried and failed given American weaknesses in men and equipment. Playing to British strengths in trying to hold territory vulnerable to maritime forces would lead to failure. The whole conflict needed to be thought about anew.

In a letter to John Hancock, written after the Battle of Long Island, Washington concluded that 'on our side the war should be defensive' and that 'we should on all occasions avoid a general action or put anything to the risque unless compelled by necessity'. He resolved to keep his army in being, but it would be a 'retreating army', defending what it could, yielding when it must, keeping the field and watching for an opportunity when 'a brilliant stroke could be made with any probability of success'.[3] The strategy would become Fabian, alluding to that of the Roman general Quintus Fabius Maximus, who had fought Hannibal during his invasion of Italy (218–201 BCE). Fabius had prevailed eventually by retreat, by delay and avoiding large battles. The American war against Britain would have to become 'a war of attrition, with the major emphasis on preserving the Continental Army and stalling until it was in sufficient condition to fight'.[4]

In the prevailing circumstances, this was entirely the best strategy. So long as the American army existed the war would not be over, and the greatest priority for Washington was avoiding any circumstance where the army could be lost. The terrain and the weather assisted, as did support from much – not all – of the population. And it was a source of great frustration to the British and their German mercenaries that Washington would not fight but kept retreating. As McPherson argues,

> Washington traded space for time; he retreated when necessary in the face of a stronger enemy; he counterattacked against isolated British outposts or detachments when such an attack promised success; above all he tried to avoid full-scale battles that would have risked annihilation of his army and defeat of his cause.[5]

This was a brilliant strategy, dictated by adversity but brilliant nonetheless.

By contrast, the British strategy in North America was unclear and internally contested to the point of real weakness. George III did not want to lose his American colonies, but beyond that policy in London was unclear. The American colonies had existed for more than 150 years. They were prosperous, its people were well educated and the standard of living probably higher than in Britain. Britain's population was around eight million, but the colonies were far from insubstantial at some 2.5 million. This was not a mere West Indian sugar island rebelling against the Crown, nor could it be treated as such, and there was real opposition to punitive action in the British Parliament. At times, the war was not prosecuted as thoroughly as it might be, as, at higher levels, there was some hope of an eventual settlement. Strategic success for Britain was ill defined.

On the ground, too, the British faced real problems in utilizing all their ships and thousands of men to effect. Even if they had the advantages of command of the sea and greater resources, they could not really define what success would look like. There was an asymmetry in aims, as Holmes and Evans argue:

> On the one side was a power which enjoyed almost unfettered command of strategic communications, but faced a clash of strategic priorities as what started as a struggle in North America became a world war, and enjoyed no unanimous domestic support . . . On the other

was a new nation, which declared its independence in 1776 . . . [Its army's commander] Washington may not rank as a great tactician . . . but he had a better understanding of the real nature of the war than his opponents.[6]

In adverse circumstances, the Continental Army could retreat still further into the hinterland and remain a force in being. The British army could not garrison every town, and for all its size the British navy could not institute a complete blockade along the coast. The colonial settlements were 'so decentralized that the capture of a city or large town meant little'.[7] Even the capture of the then capital Philadelphia in 1777 did not greatly assist the British as the Congress simply departed for other towns in Pennsylvania. And as a largely agrarian society the Americans could not be starved into subjugation by denying it maritime trade. The British strategy was unclear; its attempts to fight a European war in America a failure, and its attempts to win over the population inept.

Washington's greatest understanding was that the war was a political contest. Winning meant winning the political battle not by gaining territory or resources or by holding towns and cities. The political battle included winning over potential allies. As long as the army was kept together and making only occasional gains, the possibility existed of European intervention, notably from France. At the end of 1776, Washington won a small-scale but politically important victory at Trenton in the Christmas snow, followed by another at Princeton in January. These showed that the Revolution was not over and helped persuade France to join the conflict. Even if Trenton and Princeton were minor battles, to the extent they helped persuade France to join in they were crucial to the overall outcome. Washington's strategic purposes were constant: to win independence by maintaining American resolve to continue the war; by preserving an American army in being; and by raising the cost of the war to the enemy.[8]

Washington's travails contain too many mistakes to be considered a brilliant application of force, leading from victory to victory. But the story of the Revolutionary War is a great example of focus on ultimate purpose. As McCullough says of Washington:

He was not a brilliant strategist or tactician, not a gifted orator, not an intellectual. At several crucial moments he had shown marked indecisiveness. He had made serious mistakes in judgment. But experience had been his great teacher from boyhood, and in this his greatest test, he learned steadily from experience. Above all, Washington never forgot what was at stake and he never gave up.[9]

This single-minded focus on purpose was more important than battles. Washington did make mistakes. Initial tactics and even strategy could have been better, and there should have been greater support from the Continental Congress. But after the disaster that was New York, Washington showed he was a brilliant strategist in keeping the overall purpose clearly in the front of his mind and tailoring tactical responses to that strategy.

It seems odd that avoiding conflict would be the best strategy and that the party with the least in the way of resources should be able to prevail. For Washington and for Fabius two millennia earlier, there were other points on their side. Both had most of the population on their side, and both knew the terrain and how to use it to best advantage; their adversaries were far from home. Most of the supplies for the British army and navy in North America had to be carried across the Atlantic and both Washington and Fabius were able to at least partly deny access to resources from their lands. For Washington, as long as the army existed it could retreat into the wilderness and it was of no great moment that Britain controlled the sea. Running away and running away again was a brilliant strategy for the circumstances and times. The wisdom of a strategy of retreat was not well understood, and Washington was heavily criticised for retreating just as Fabius had been. Washington was not averse to the idea of a grand battle, as occurred at Yorktown in 1781, but the strategy required caution.

Paine argues that the Chinese response to Japanese invasion in the 1930s had its parallels in the events of the Revolutionary War. She argues:

> China's response to conventional defeat – an insurgency in order to outlast the enemy – was not original, but time honored. The United States won its independence from Britain using this strategy. At that time American forces lost virtually every major conventional engagement, but they delivered a costly insurgency, convinced the French and others to intervene, and, relying on French conventional land and especially naval forces, won at Yorktown, by which time the British government, propelled by elections, refused to waste any more money on the insurgency, and the thirteen colonies gained their independence.[10]

In times of adversity, Mao's army retreated further into the interior, re-emerging only when ready. Fabius, Washington and Mao had in common a clear belief in their political path, and it was this, in the end, that provided the purpose and enabled them to eventually prevail. The most important point for all of them was to not be placed in a position where they could lose it all in some grand, glorious battle. In 216 BCE, the Roman army had been annihilated by Hannibal's army at Cannae as Paullus and Varro – Fabius's replacements – attempted and failed at one big battle aimed at driving Hannibal from Italy. Washington could not afford another Cannae. The political contest required that Washington not place himself in a position where he could lose, and this he did brilliantly by maintaining clear focus on the ultimate purpose.

Even though clear purpose could exist and still fail, the focus that a strategy offers does allow for a greater likelihood of eventual success.

Alexander's purpose

The short but stellar career of Alexander the Great has been used as far back as the Romans to illustrate lessons about strategy.[11] There are some problems with this. Much of what actually occurred during the short career of Alexander the Great is rather uncertain and separating myth from reality is less than straightforward. There is an absence of first-hand accounts, and the most comprehensive stories were written some four hundred years later. That there was such a person is undoubted; the real question is what was he trying to do, what was the purpose? It is not entirely clear that there was a clear purpose, or at least one that can be readily understood more than two millennia later.

Alexander was the son of King Philip II of Macedonia, who had built up the Macedonian army and forced the unification of Greece. Philip had aimed at conquest to the east but was assassinated before starting out. Surviving dynastic issues, Alexander succeeded his father, becoming leader at age twenty. After putting down a revolt at Thebes in Greece, Alexander continued to pursue the Persian venture. Greece and Persia were long-time rivals; Persia, under Xerxes, had invaded Greece within historical memory and rivalry continued. However, Persia was vulnerable. Local rulers – satraps – were controlled by Darius to only a limited extent; the loyalty of local populations to their distant rulers may not have been great.

After Alexander had secured Greece as a base and built up a navy for control of the sea, he was able to move on to Persia, invading in 334 BCE. After defeating the Persians at the Battle of Granicus, Alexander diverted south to march through Syria then Egypt, founding the town that still bears his name. Returning to Mesopotamia, Alexander finally defeated the Persians through battles that included Issus and Gaugamela. Darius was captured and the Persian empire was then controlled by Alexander. Alexander and his army set off further to the east through present-day Iran, Bactria, Afghanistan and Pakistan and into India. Eventually he was prevailed upon to return to the west and reluctantly agreed, only to die, aged 32, upon reaching Babylon.

For most of his conquests, Alexander relied on his reputation and conquering without fighting. Typically, he would appear with his army outside a town and say that if the town surrendered the people and soldiers would be spared, but if they resisted they would all be slaughtered. For the most part this tactic succeeded. While these were quite remarkable achievements in a short time, there are differing views as to what Alexander was trying to do.

Fuller argues that Alexander set out to create a new empire. He speaks of Alexander's impulse to eliminate, not merely defeat, hostile armies, and argues that he was generous to defeated armies. His policy aim was to pacify rather than antagonize his enemy so as to limit the number of battles he would have to fight. If fighting was necessary, Alexander's armies were better than their opponents. To Fuller, Alexander's battles followed a typical pattern:

> brilliant adaptation to local, often unfavourable, terrain (all his battles were fought at or near rivers); generalship – courage at the head of the companion cavalry; and stunning cavalry charges focused on a concentrated spot in the enemy line that aimed to turn the dazed enemy onto the spears of the advancing phalanx.

Fuller adds:

> Alexander's aim was not to bring Darius to terms, it was to appropriate his empire, and, were his conquest to be of profit to him, he had not only to defeat the Persian army but win his acceptance in the eyes of the Persian peoples . . . Alexander's aim was conquest, and at the minimum expenditure of force and the minimum dislocation and damage of the Persian empire: his policy limited and moderated his policy.[12]

There are some issues with the Fuller view. For a start, while the Macedonian armies were very good there were no technological or tactical advances that could not be readily emulated by others. Also, the Persian army included a large number of Greek mercenaries, presumably well versed in Macedonian ways of making war. Also, if the aim was to set up a great empire, taking the place of Darius, there is the question of what kind of empire – and what empire means in that time and place.

Another view of purpose is that there was personal motivation for Alexander, notably when, after defeating Darius, he kept going further east and the whole enterprise seemed aimless and even irrational. Martin and Blackwell take issue with the point that Alexander seemed to behave irrationally, and argue that 'it makes no sense to use the term "irrational" for purposive human action, that is, action aimed at a goal'.[13] They argue:

> If anything seems clear about Alexander, it is that he thought deeply about his actions, and he always acted with a purpose. In that fundamental sense, categorizing him as lacking rationality is itself an intellectually empty reproach. Alexander, like every other human being, made choices from a complex mixture of reasoning and emotion. He was a complex, even contradictory personality, which seems a given of human nature.[14]

This comment is apposite as far as it goes. Martin and Blackwell add:

> Competition defined Alexander's life. He dedicated his three decades, above all, to the challenge of going beyond all others in excellence and of winning the ultimate reward, a superhuman status that no human being had ever achieved. Alexander longed to become unique by becoming the best, and the religious concepts of his time convinced him that he could earn that fabulous distinction, that he could become not only, like the Achilles of Homer's Iliad , 'the best of the Greeks,' but the best of everyone, ever, anywhere, at any time.[15]

If correct this would suggest that the sole motivation was personal, and personal glory at that. However, there are some problems with seeing Alexander as a clear thinking and acting strategist.

If it was clear that Alexander was following a purpose, what was it, and why did no one know what it was even at the time? A significant set of events followed when his men threatened mutiny and Alexander had to turn back. It appears that his soldiers did not know what his purpose was either. Some who spoke up were punished and even killed. They wanted to go home after being on campaign for almost ten years. And it was on the way back from India that Alexander became ill and died.

Mary Beard addresses motivation in a more nuanced way. She writes, 'Closely related to the basic issue of how far we can admire Alexander's career is the question of what he was attempting to do', and lists several possibilities: 'a civilizing mission . . . to bring the lofty ideals of Hellenic culture to the benighted East'; a 'compulsive and unsatisfiable yearning'; even a 'rather more literary sense of identification with the heroes of Homer's *Iliad*'. She goes on to argue,

> A rather more down-to-earth view would see him starting out as simply a follower of his father, who at the time of his assassination had already launched a limited series of military operations in Asia Minor; success went to Alexander's head and he simply didn't know where to stop.[16]

Beard adds:

> Even more significant is the character and the cultural background of the surviving ancient accounts of Alexander's life. It is repeatedly said that these accounts were all written much later than the events they described. True; but more to the point is the fact that they were all written under the Roman Empire against the background of Roman imperialism . . . They are bound to have seen this story through a Roman filter, to have interpreted and adjusted what they read in the light of the versions of conquest and imperial expansion that were characteristic of their own political age.[17]

The Romans could then claim to be the inheritors of Alexander and that their empire followed in his footsteps. It is noticeable that it was during Roman times that Alexander advances to celebrity.

The very idea of an Alexandrian empire analogous to the British empire or even the Roman empire is somewhat tenuous. Empire requires communication, empire requires effective occupation, empire requires administration. The Romans were much better at all of these. To the extent that there was a Persian empire at all before Alexander, it was as a set of satrapies with relatively loose attachment to the centre. Alexander did change the over-lordship, but little else; he had 'not fought to change, but to take over'.[18] But to what end is not explained. As Fox argues:

> The one perceptible change in government, apart from minor alterations in the satrapal boundaries, was that satraps had gradually lost the right to issue their own silver coins. This continuity is not a criticism, for against the unalterable facts of time, distance and native tradition, deep change in the empire would have been either naïve or irresponsible.[19]

The very idea of creating an empire is rather doubtful given that there would have been formidable obstacles to making it real.

The distance and the paucity of records has not stopped those arguing about Alexander and strategy. Partha Bose uses Alexander as an exemplar of strategy, saying:

> As Philip and Alexander demonstrated . . . strategy is about the deploy-ment of geographic, economic, social, interstate, political and behav-ioural realities to achieve a broader set of objectives. For them it wasn't domination of Greece, it was domination for a purpose: to lead Macedonia and Greece together in a quest for domination over and subjugation of Persia.

Bose, too, argues that Alexander aimed to set up an empire involving dom-ination of the known world by Macedonians and Greeks, essentially in the same way as the Romans did later. This account goes too far in ascribing a strategy and doing so anachronistically. Overall, it is interesting that what Alexander was trying to do remains so unclear. His legacy was minimal and the long-term effects slight, all resulting from what can be seen as an unclear purpose.

Vague purpose and overreach: Japan in the Pacific

Following a strategy that is overly ambitious or unachievable is not likely to end well. An unfettered dream about the future can be out of step with any likely outcome, but strategy needs to be reasonably realistic. It needs to be achievable even if its purpose has an element of stretch; an unachievable strategy is folly – and expensive. Being bold is fine in theory, but a strategy needs to be grounded by the laws of probability and feasibility. This is demonstrated well by Japanese naval strategy in World War II.

At 7.55 am on Sunday 7 December 1941, Japanese planes from a strike force of six aircraft carriers attacked the US naval base at Pearl Harbor in Hawaii. The attack came as a surprise to the Americans. Even as tensions with Japan had been rising, it was not thought conceivable that a strike could be made so far from their home base. Neither was it thought imaginable that Japan would attack the United States, a state with far greater economic power, and to do so without warning and without a declaration of war.

The attack on Pearl Harbor was part of a more complicated but coordinated strategy that sent invasion fleets south from Japan to the Philippines, Indochina, Malaya and the Dutch East Indies. The idea of attacking Pearl Harbor was to neutralize the American fleet to then allow Japan a free hand in the conquest of South East Asia where oil and other resources could be found. While superficially successful – at least for a time – the attack on Pearl Harbor should be seen as a massive strategic error, one so large as to be used to show how any action for unclear purpose is not likely to work. Indeed, it could be argued that the entire war against the US was strategically flawed and would inevitably result in disaster for Japan. Moreover, the inevitability of failure from a long war was known and understood in Japan even before the venture started.[20]

The Pearl Harbor attack was only part of a wider conflict in Asia. The occupation of Manchuria by the Japanese army from 1931 and the later extension into other north-eastern parts of China coincided with a febrile atmosphere within Japan. With growing militarism, civilian politicians were bypassed and the military became the government with the army dominant over the navy. Civilian politicians and any others suspected of opposition to war were targeted for assassination by roving groups of fanatical officers.[21] However, the army's war in China was not going well. China's vast size and terrain worked against the Japanese army, as did opposition from the Nationalist forces of Chiang Kai-Shek and the Communist forces of Mao Tse-Tung, at least when they were not fighting each other.

The US had been unhappy with the Japanese invasion of China, especially after the capture of Beijing, Shanghai and Nanjing in 1937, with the taking of Nanjing notable for its displays of Japanese brutality. The US had attempted to exert diplomatic pressure against the Japanese to withdraw from parts of China. In July 1941, the US adopted economic sanctions against Japan, including an oil embargo. Japan feared being excluded from oil supplies and realized that, as the United States had commenced rearming, its superior resources would become more significant as the months and years progressed. Time was considered to be of the essence.

With their backs to wall, with the military as the government, with threats from the United States, it is perhaps unsurprising that the Japanese did something to secure resources, even though 'what it was now planning bordered on the incredible – and the absurd'.[22] Negotiations between Japan and the United States persisted for several months leading up to December 1941, but were not carried out in good faith. At the exact time of the Pearl Harbor attack, negotiations were still continuing in Washington. Not only had the Japanese diplomats – Ambassadors Nomura and Kurusu – negotiating with US Secretary of State Cordell Hull been kept uninformed about the plan to attack Pearl Harbor, they were 'told to continue diplomacy in a deliberate attempt to deceive and mislead the other side'.[23]

It was claimed later that the intention was for a message breaking off negotiations to be delivered to the US just before the attack itself, but a delay in decoding within the Japanese Embassy led to this only being completed after the attack had started. As Paine argues:

> Tokyo had ordered Nomura and Kurusu to see Hull at 1.00 pm, shortly before the first bomb was to be dropped on Pearl Harbor. Because the diplomatic communications, consisting of fourteen parts was late in being typed up for delivery, the two Japanese diplomats were shown into Hull's office at 2.20 pm., utterly unaware that their country had already attacked the United States.[24]

The cable in question did not in any case declare war, only break off negotiations, meaning that the idea all along had been to begin the attack before war was declared and to do so without the knowledge of the Japanese negotiators in Washington.

The key questions in terms of strategy are: what was the Japanese purpose in the attack on Pearl Harbor; and how could such a purpose be achieved? It appears that the Japanese aim in attacking Pearl Harbor was to buy themselves a year or two of freedom to act in the Pacific without US interference and to then sue for peace, retaining some of their gains. But this purpose was totally flawed as the way the war started meant that achieving any kind of negotiated outcome was simply not possible. No American president could have settled for less than unconditional surrender by Japan due to the surprise attack before war was declared.

The Japanese may have seen the American trade embargo as an outrageous provocation, a threat to their way of life. On being pushed into an impossible position, as they saw it, the Japanese lashed out, but to their ultimate, and predictable, detriment. As Wohlstetter argues:

> Our own standards, as we have observed them in military and State Department documents, reckoned the risks to the Japanese as too large, and therefore not likely to be taken. They were too large. But they were going to be taken. And we missed this apparently illogical connection because we did not include in our reckoning any consideration of the alternative of 'gradual exhaustion,' the danger of encirclement and defeat without having struck a single blow'.[25]

War became 'an inevitability', but one 'without an obvious route to victory' for Japan.[26] The attack on Pearl Harbor merely aimed at removing the US Navy as a significant player while the simultaneous strikes at Indochina, the Philippines and the Dutch East Indies would aim at gaining resources needed at home and for the war in China. Japan would have a free hand in China and South East Asia and then, in peace negotiations, keep their gains. Pearl Harbor was not a prelude to invasion of US territory, merely a raid.

The overall idea, the purpose, in so far as there was one, was for a limited war, just like the earlier Japanese wars against Russia and China at the turn of the century — 'a war that they could initiate and then limit its conduct and aims'.[27]

> The long-term aim . . . was to wear down enemy resolve and means of fighting until the enemy, tiring of struggle and losses, came to terms with the pointlessness of the conflict and the reality of Japanese conquests. The Japanese did not envisage being able to bring about the total defeat of Britain and the United States, but they calculated that the British and Americans, with their (in Japanese eyes) low resolve, would be forced to accept the fait accompli rather than fight on with little hope of success.[28]

The enterprise rested on the premise that Japan could not win a long war but could only make the war so costly that the other side would negotiate a favourable peace. As Freedman argues,

> The Americans never had any doubt that they would win an eventual war and had explained clearly to the Japanese why this was so. This why they kept on pushing the Japanese, and it was why they got caught by surprise when the Japanese decided they could take it no more'.[29]

But the very act of a surprise attack doomed any notion of a negotiated peace and this meant that any idea of a limited war was untenable. President Roosevelt later declared the ultimate war aim of the United States to be nothing less than unconditional surrender. There could be no negotiation whatsoever with someone who would attack without warning, attack without a declaration of war, someone who could enter into a war hoping for a negotiated settlement having disobeyed international rules on the conduct of war. Japan had declared itself a pariah state and would be treated as one.

In the immediate aftermath, US President Franklin Roosevelt declared that 7 December 1941 was a day that would 'live in infamy', and American public opinion immediately changed in favour of war. A few days later Hitler declared war on the US. Japanese attacks continued on the Malay Peninsula. On 10 December 1941, the British battleships HMS *Repulse* and *Prince of Wales* were sunk by Japanese aircraft near Singapore, further reinforcing the obsolescence of that class of ships. The US territories of Guam and Wake Island were captured the same month, as were Hong Kong, Thailand, the Philippines and Borneo. The British fortress of Singapore surrendered in February 1942, to a much smaller Japanese force.

However, after the initial flurry of action from the Japanese, new attacks and conquest virtually ceased within a few months or, rather, became bogged down in Burma, the Solomons and New Guinea on land and at sea. The war in China was going nowhere too. The naval Battle of the Coral Sea in May 1942 was a tactical victory for Japan but a strategic victory for the US and its allies. It also marked a turning point as the associated Japanese invasion force heading to Port Moresby in Papua was forced to turn back, never to try again. The Solomons were invaded by the Japanese in May 1942, but as early as August that year US Marines were engaged in driving the

Japanese out of Guadalcanal and beginning three years of pushing back the Japanese from the islands it had captured in the first few months. Within six months of Pearl Harbor, the seemingly inexorable Japanese advance had virtually ended.

The early objectives of the US in the Pacific were to hold the line, keep communications open between the West Coast, Hawaii and Australia, then push back along the island chain pointing towards Japan. Unrestricted submarine warfare commenced immediately and was crucial in implementation of American strategy. Its submarines imposed a rate of attrition that was in the end unbearable for Japan. Over the course of the war, for the loss of 52 submarines there were sunk more than a 1,100 Japanese merchant ships – almost five million tons – and many naval craft including seven aircraft carriers.[30] Mounting losses of ships meant that it became close to impossible to send resources to the far-flung Japanese possessions, and, additionally, the resources of South East Asia – the ostensible reason for fighting – were also denied to Japan.

Tactical aspects of Pearl Harbor and the Pacific War will be looked at later (chapter 6), but the overall aims were so far removed from Japan's available or potential capability that they were unachievable. The plan was wildly impractical and its assumption of psychological superiority and greater will was simply unfounded. It gravely underestimated US resolve – indeed, that resolve was greatly enhanced by the very manner of the war starting with 'Remember Pearl Harbor' becoming a rallying cry for the American forces. A better understanding of the United States and its longer-term ability to achieve its own purposes may have provided a more achievable outcome. As Willmot argues:

> If the Japanese were correct in their view that psychological rather than material factors were the decisive elements of war, then the Pearl Harbor attack ensured their defeat; the war was lost already. After 7 December the Americans would never have accepted anything less than either total victory over Japan or total defeat at her hands; after the attack there could never be any question of a compromise or a negotiated peace. The war had to be fought to a finish.[31]

Japanese Naval Commander-in-Chief Admiral Yamamoto had not wanted war with the Americans, at least initially. A year earlier, in September 1940, he had said, 'If I am told to fight regardless of the consequences, I shall run wild for the first six months or a year, but I have utterly no confidence for the second or third year.'[32] This comment ended up being remarkably prescient, in that following the Battle of Midway, almost exactly six months after Pearl Harbor, the naval war was effectively over, although no one realized it at the time. Furthermore, the folly of attacking the US was known in Japan. As late as September 1941, while planning for Pearl Harbor was going on, Admiral Yamamoto had warned the naval general staff that 'A war with so little chance of success should not be fought.'[33] Yamamoto had been to the US, had some understanding of its resource potential and was less inclined than others to disparage its will.

The Battle of Midway marked the turning point of the entire Pacific naval war. The US Navy regained superiority and it would not lose it again as its naval forces continued their rapid build-up. The US Navy lost one aircraft carrier in the battle but that was readily replaced – one arrived at Pearl Harbor the day after the battle – along with new planes and pilots. Many more were to follow. On the other side, the Imperial Japanese Navy 'would never recover their losses: four fleet carriers, one heavy cruiser, over 250 aircraft and 3,000 men, including many irreplaceable aircrew',[34] a number of them experienced pilots from the attack on Pearl Harbor. The ability of the Japanese Navy to threaten US territory or to expand further virtually ceased. Even by this early stage, the resource differentials of the two main protagonists were becoming evident.

In the final analysis, Pearl Harbor was a monumental strategic error. Japan could only win if the Americans lacked or lost their will or were vastly inferior in warrior spirit; to believe either was to be woefully ill informed. Such views were delusional; they were simply wrong. Japanese war aims were vague and unachievable – little more than unjustifiable assumptions that an attack would cause such morale problems for the Americans that they would sue for peace. The opposite happened. An attack prior to war being declared galvanized American public opinion and led to an unleashing of American industrial capacity. US morale was enhanced and any prospect of a negotiated peace settlement became illusory. Given the level of isolationism in the US still prevalent in 1941, it may well have been possible for Japan to have attacked the British and Dutch colonial possessions without an American intervention,[35] although part of the Japanese calculation may have been that the Americans would not stay out for long. These points should have been considered in strategic discussions before embarking on their venture.

To make the folly even worse, many of the Japanese leaders knew they could not win a long war. As Wohlstetter argues:

> It is interesting to observe now that Japanese and American estimates of the risks to the Japanese were identical for the large-scale war they had planned, as well as for the individual operations. What we miscalculated was the ability and willingness of the Japanese to accept such risks. As Ambassador [to Japan] Grew had said, 'National sanity would dictate against such an event, but Japanese sanity cannot be measured by our own standards of logic.'[36]

Even if the Japanese found themselves pushed into a corner, and even if they then felt that all they could do was strike back, the way that was chosen was naïve in the extreme. As Tuchman notes, 'Whether from ignorance, miscalculation or pure recklessness, Japan gave her opponent the one blow necessary to bring her to purposeful and determined belligerency.'[37] Attacking the United States was unwise enough, especially given that the resource disparity was appreciated and the long-term outcome known to be doubtful at best. But to attack Pearl Harbor without a declaration of war was sheer folly, a 'strategic imbecility'[38] and a profound under-appreciation of what would now become the purpose for its enemy and underpin its resolve in getting there. As Prange notes, 'Win, lose or draw at Pearl Harbor, by arousing the full might of the United States, the Japanese lost before they had fairly started.'[39]

It was all a great gamble and one largely bereft of strategy. Much of what happened as a result was predictable enough unless wildly unrealistic assumptions were made that Japanese will alone could overcome any shortfall in resource capability. And the result was tragic. As Paine argues:

> Japan went to war to secure resources, first in Manchuria, then in China south of the Great Wall, and finally throughout the Pacific theater. It sought resources to ensure prosperity at home. Yet each phase of the escalation made Japan more not less resource dependent, burdened rather than strengthened the home economy, and expanded rather than decreased Japan's list of enemies. Japanese leaders proved singularly incapable of cutting losses, so in the end they bet all and lost all. In the process, from 1931 to 1945, Japanese actions caused the deaths of 17.2 million people throughout Asia.[40]

That so many people would die as the result of flawed strategy and flawed purpose was sheer tragedy for much of Asia and for Japan itself.

Conflict without purpose

Even if strategy is generally seen as purposive, rational and achievable, it is sobering that there are instances of conflicts without clear goals that made the key participants worse off. If strategy is to be about politics, how can instances occur where there is an apparent absence of political goals?

Perhaps all wars – the highest points of grand strategy – are pointless, but there is usually some kind of purpose, something that at least one of the parties is attempting to do that will provide some kind of benefit. Remember that Sun-tzu says that strategy is not to be undertaken lightly and Clausewitz speaks of wars having political aims. A sobering reality is that many conflicts have been entered into without clear aims, and once started could not be stopped. Good strategy requires careful assessment of purpose, taking into consideration the other facets of capability, will, terrain and tactics, as argued here. But what if this is not done, what if major conflicts have been entered into that appear purposeless as well as pointless?

A classic instance of such a conflict is World War I. More than a hundred years later, that war's origin and purpose are surprisingly unclear. The existence of a series of interlocking and secretive treaties between European countries was certainly problematic, as shown by the relatively low-level event of the assassination of Franz Ferdinand in Sarajevo leading to one country then another taking up their positions agreed by treaty. And five weeks later, almost before anyone knew it, Europe was at war. But why?

Many of the usual explanations for war do not really fit this case. There was no overwhelming political dispute between different ideologies or dynasties. Wars for territory were already looking obsolete by 1914 and, in any case, World War I did not seem to have a pressing territorial imperative on the part of its participants. After the war France did regain Alsace-Lorraine which had been lost in the war of 1870 between Prussian-led Germany and France, but that was no rationale for the conflict of World War I. For Germany to try to emulate the colonies of Britain and France was naïve if it was even a serious consideration. The German colonies in Africa and Asia were very small and insignificant for its economy.

Germany was a rapidly rising power in terms of its economy, larger than Britain's by 1910, and its population and traditions had enabled the creation of a large and capable army. It did appear to offer a challenge as a rising power.

Allison argues that there is a 'Thucydides trap' between rising powers and declining powers that leads to war historically. World War I is one of the examples used. He argues that 'the growth of the German navy and its geographic proximity to Britain posed a unique existential threat' and that

> The mistrust and fear that that Germany's naval program provoked in the British provoked in the British contributed to London's identification of Berlin as its primary enemy. And once this concept took hold, it shaped Britain's views of Germany's other actions. While Britain faced many rivals, only Germany was capable of disrupting the European balance and building naval capabilities that could imperil Britain's survival.[41]

Allison argues that, for Britain, when Germany invaded France in 1914 'war seemed preferable to the prospect of Germany achieving dominance on the Continent and then threatening Britain's survival'.[42] While a possible explanation, it is hard to see 1914 as confirmation for the Thucydides trap thesis given there was so much else going on.

For a start, any rivalry was multi-party rather than between Britain and Germany alone; Russia was allied with France and France with Britain and so on. This also means that the rising power thesis needs to take account of the all the nations involved as well as their actual or potential allies. Britain and Germany might have been rivals but no more than France or Russia, or Austria-Hungary. Indeed, Germany was somewhat surprised that Britain went to war when it did. All of these powers could make a case that they were being threatened by rising powers, but some became allies instead of following the Thucydides trap.

By 1914 the naval race was no longer a serious policy issue and rivalry between Germany and Britain was not as great as that between Germany and the other continental powers. It was quite clear on both sides of the North Sea that, along with its highly favourable geographical position, Britain could easily outbuild the Germans in battleships for the foreseeable future. Even if the German Navy had aspired to compete with Britain in naval terms, it had given up the fight several years earlier. But the naval scares of the previous decade did lead to public opinion staying against Germany, given the emotional attachment of the British public to its navy.

There are literally thousands of views about World War I and its start. Rather than seeing any one cause or any one player as having started it, a better case is that there was no clear purpose, no clear cause at all. Keegan argues that 'politics played no part in the conduct of the First World War worth mentioning', and

> Germans, French, British and Russians found themselves apparently fighting war for war's sake. The War's political objects – difficult enough to define in the first place – were forgotten, political constraints were overwhelmed, politicians who appealed to reason were execrated, politics even in the liberal democracies was rapidly reduced to a mere justification of bigger battles, longer casualty lists, costlier budgets, overflowing misery.[43]

Perhaps the societies themselves sought war and were fighting for its own sake. As it went on, though, they found out the cost. Perhaps the very lack of purpose by any party caused the war to be prolonged. After little more than the first month, the German advance was halted inside France and trenches constructed from the mountains bordering Switzerland to the sea. There both armies remained for the next three years with attempts at breakthroughs halted at horrendous cost in casualties and other resources.

The Brodies too maintain that World War I was without purpose. As they argue:

> The First World War demonstrated that the twentieth century had put into the hands of each great nation a war machine of greater power than any known before. This change was accompanied, however, by a near-collapse of the forces previously serving to limit war, including that of common prudence. All rational concern with the proper political aims of war seems to have been suppressed. World War I was the purposeless war which no one seemed to know how to prevent, and which, once begun, no one seemed to know how to stop. Politically, the world it brought in its wake was in many respects a worse place than before.[44]

Clausewitz had argued that war should have clear political goals, but this was one war where the calculation was missing. As Heuser argues of World War I:

> While Clausewitz's view that no one in his right mind should ever start a war without a clear idea of what he wants to achieve is praiseworthy, the reality of the First World War was different. But then, this was not an age of enlightenment and rationality, but one which prided itself in its irrational passions and emotions, its xenophobic nationalism and its glorification of war.[45]

The irrationality, the glorification of war even by the wider population worked against any idea that strategy only should be undertaken for clear goals. War may have been different than in Clausewitz's time, but the need for well-defined objectives and a consistent strategy was still essential. It was not there in this case.

A hundred years after World War I, despite literally thousands of accounts, there still appears to be no definitive reason that war occurred in 1914, no definitive purpose. As Clark argues:

> The outbreak of war in 1914 is not an Agatha Christie drama at the end of which we will discover the culprit standing over a corpse in the conservatory with a smoking pistol. There is no smoking gun in this story; or, rather, there is one in the hands of every major character. Viewed in this light, the outbreak of war was a tragedy, not a crime.[46]

It is a salutary lesson that such a conflict can occur without discernible overall strategy and that more than a century later there is such dispute as to what it was all about. As Clark comments, 'One thing is clear: none of the prizes for which the politicians of 1914 contended was worth the cataclysm that followed.'[47] Millions of casualties incurred during the conflict, both military and civilian, followed by the Spanish influenza outbreak, assisted in its spread by the war, that killed many more. And to what end? As Clark argues: 'The protagonists of 1914 were sleepwalkers, watchful but unseeing, haunted by dreams, yet blind to the reality of the horror they were about to bring into the world.'[48] Seemingly without conscious design, each step on the path to war had followed the one before. But to what purpose? As Clark adds:

> "Ah, if we only knew." That was the best the German Chancellor could offer even when a colleague pressed Theobald von Bethmann Hollweg, he could not explain how his choices, and those of other European statesmen, had led to the most devastating war the world had seen to that point. By the time the slaughter of the Great War finally ended in 1918, the key players had lost all they fought for: The Austro-Hungarian Empire dissolved, the German Kaiser ousted, the Russian tsar overthrown, France bled for a generation, and England shorn of its treasure and youth. And for what? If we only knew.[49]

World War I started and ended without purpose, it seems. The old order was cast aside, but the litany of mistakes did not end there, as the overly punitive treatment of Germany and subsequent economic disruption led seemingly inexorably to World War II in Europe.

If there were any purposes in this war, they were subsumed into an inability to bring it all to an end. Even if there is no certainty around the start of World War I, it should have been possible to come to some agreement to end the conflict earlier than it was. Any war aims, such as they were, could not be achieved by any party, it seemed, but stasis prevailed. The sheer scale of the dead and injured seemed to preclude any diplomacy to end the futile conflict.

It could be argued that all participants were worse off. What a waste. What a massive failure of diplomacy and leadership. There should have been more thought about consequences, more analysis, more reflection before senseless, purposeless slaughter. The so-called statesmen who presided over their national affairs prior to World War I betrayed their own people in their meandering and stumbling towards a pointless war.

The Weinberger-Powell doctrine

The circumstances in which one nation could justifiably go to war with another have preoccupied philosophers for centuries. Such thinking continued from Greek and Roman times through to Thomas Aquinas and to the

League of Nations and the United Nations in more recent years. The Dutch philosopher Hugo Grotius set out principles of just war in the sixteenth century in what became one of the foundations of international law. Of course, as international law is not binding and consists only of agreements that some parties may choose to ignore the whole regime is hardly definitive.

In the era immediately after the Vietnam War, the United States military and foreign policy establishment engaged itself in much soul-searching about the role of its military in international affairs, most noticeably the circumstances in which military forces could or should be used to intervene or start foreign wars. As the US held overwhelming power at the time it possessed the *capability* of intervention but wanted some clarification as to *purpose*. A lesson it had drawn from the Vietnam War was that, in a democracy, using the military without public support was unlikely to be effective. The defence establishment sought some kind of constraint on the adventurism of political leaders in getting it into meandering conflicts with unclear aims. Clearly, the military did not want to find itself engaged in costly foreign conflicts that did not have the broad support of the public.

Caspar Weinberger, defense secretary during the Reagan presidency, set out his position in a speech at the National Press Club in November 1984 in which he outlined a number of tests to be applied when weighing the use of US combat forces abroad.[50] Commitment of forces was to be for occasions deemed vital to the national interest; the commitment of armed forces should be wholehearted with the clear intention of winning; and there should be clearly defined political and military objectives and how they might be achieved. The crucial point was that 'before the U.S. commits combat forces abroad, there must be some reasonable assurance we will have the support of the American people and their elected representatives in Congress'. For Weinberger, the commitment of US forces to combat should be a last resort and if the country was unwilling to commit the forces or resources necessary to achieve its objectives, they should not be committed at all. Weinberger argued that 'we must have in mind objectives that are clearly defined and understood and supported by the widest possible number of our citizens', and that those objectives 'must be vital to our survival as a free nation and to the fulfillment of our responsibilities as a world power'.[51] Weinberger argues here for more effort to be expended on clarifying objectives, on setting purpose, exactly what should have been done prior to World War I or by the Japanese in the Pacific.

The Weinberger Doctrine later became the 'Weinberger-Powell' doctrine or, more often and with some minor modification, the 'Powell Doctrine' after General Colin Powell, chair of the US Joint Chiefs of Staff and later secretary of state. Weinberger's six questions became Powell's eight questions for consideration prior to engaging in the use of military force.

1. Is a vital national security interest threatened? 2. Do we have a clear attainable objective? 3. Have the risks and costs been fully and frankly analyzed? 4. Have all other nonviolent policy means been fully exhausted? 5. Is there a plausible exit strategy to avoid endless entanglement? 6. Have the consequences of our action been fully considered? 7. Is the action supported by the American people? 8. Do we have genuine broad international support?[52]

Never again did Powell want the US to be drawn into a long and unwinnable conflict such as the Vietnam War he had fought in. Each of the questions needed to be answered with an unequivocal 'yes' prior to commitment of military force. Additionally, if the answer to all questions was in the affirmative, then the US should use its full force to resolve the issue as quickly as possible.

As it turned out, the Powell-Weinberger doctrine had its failings even as it may have prevented some interventions notably in Latin America in the 1980s. The US intervention in the first Gulf War in 1990/91 could be justified under the Powell Doctrine as its allies Kuwait and Saudi Arabia had been invaded. But the second Gulf War in 2003 would not have passed many of the eight Powell questions. Indeed, the world saw the unedifying appearance of the same Powell – now the US secretary of state – appearing before the United Nations showing the evidence that Saddam Hussein possessed weapons of mass destruction. Later it was ascertained that nearly all the intelligence Powell presented to the world in his speech was false.[53] Even some analysts within the CIA had reservations about its accuracy. Powell and British foreign secretary Jack Straw later claimed they were opposed to the invasion of Iraq and overthrow of Saddam Hussein, but their leaders President George W. Bush and Prime Minister Tony Blair disregarded their advice.[54]

The reality has been that many wars have not undergone the kind of thorough analysis that Powell set out. If this set of requirements were met, by the United States and other countries, fewer wars might result and those that remained would be seen as having clear purpose, adequate resources and support from the public and allies. Powell's eight questions or something like them could be used more widely, particularly if applied reasonably dispassionately. Of course this is difficult to do if the overly optimistic and overly enthusiastic are in charge.

It is hard to see a single straight 'yes' to any of Powell's questions if carried out by the Japanese prior to the Pacific war. To undertake a strategy that ends up risking too much is irresponsible leadership and a betrayal of the citizenry reliant on their leaders. Hotta argues of Japan in World War II that 'Some leaders were misguidedly hopeful, but *none* were confident of Japan's ultimate victory.'[55] She also argues that

> The leaders ultimately succumbed to a destructive – and self-destructive – course in the name of maximizing Japan's chance of survival and self-preservation in the short term and, more ambitiously, building an Asia for Asians under Japan's leadership in the long term. Neither the short-term nor the long-term goals were ever realizable because the planning for them was not realistic.[56]

If, as she says, none of the Japanese leaders were confident of victory, why did they go ahead? All knew that the strategy was risky and that the very existence of the state they led was at stake. And still they went ahead.

Conclusion

Conflicts attract many kinds of players with many kinds of motivation including national survival, quest for territory, individual glory, venality and sheer folly. To be truly strategic is to be calculating, not impulsive, and to act with a clear but achievable goal in mind. Actions need to be for a purpose. Even if purpose is the most important of the five facets, there are instances of unclear or vague purpose that were far from being purposive. Even with the caveat of circularity – a failure must have been insufficient consideration of purpose – or of history being written by the winners, it does appear evident that a lack of clarity does lead to poor outcomes or unintended consequences at best. Strategic contests are serious and must be approached that way as so much is at stake.

The undertaking of a strategy should require purpose and that purpose should be clear and realistic. Washington's purpose in 1776 was both clear and achievable, with clear political aims. The British purpose was to bring its rebellious colonies to heel, but to what end? Despite their greater resources, the British did not seem to be able to work out what success would mean.

In retrospect, World War I seems quite pointless in terms of any of the participants having a purpose that was in any way realistic or achievable. And the example of Japan in World War II points to purpose that was so unrealistic as to be quixotic. Any serious calculation of resources would show this and not simply because the Japanese did lose and history is against them as a result. There was never any prospect of success in a long war, and while many of the Japanese leaders knew that, they were unable or unwilling to speak up. On the other side of the Pacific War the US could easily answer yes to all the Powell questions once it was attacked without warning. Even if the Powell questions set a high bar, there is little dispute on the righteousness of the US participation in World War II. And once there was a clear purpose the other facets including superior capability came into play to an inevitable outcome.

Purpose is the most important of the five facets, but it is also the hardest to do well. The instances here show the need for clear thought, for thorough analysis prior to any kind of action. Events may proceed without this step but often lead to adverse consequences that should have been foreseen.

Notes

1   Sun-Tzu, *The Art of War*, translation, commentary and introduction by John Minford (London: Penguin, 2002), p. 16.

2   David McCullough, *1776* (New York: Simon & Schuster, 2005), pp. 178–9.

3   George Washington, Letter to John Hancock, 6 September 1776, in David Hackett Fischer, *Washington's Crossing* (New York: Oxford University Press, 2004), p. 102.

4   Ron Chernov, *Washington: A Life* (New York: Penguin, 2010), p. 208.

5   James M. McPherson, *Battle Cry of Freedom: The Civil War Era* (New York: Ballantine, 1988), p. 337.

6   Richard Holmes and Martin Marix Evans (eds), *Battlefield* (Oxford: Oxford University Press, 2006), p. 269.

7   Paul Kennedy, *The Rise and Fall of the Great Powers* (London: Unwin Hyman, 1988), p. 117.

8   Fischer, *Washington's Crossing*, p. 372.

9   McCullough, *1776*, p. 293.

10   S.C.M. Paine, *The Wars for Asia, 1911–1949* (Cambridge: Cambridge University Press, 2012), p. 196.

11   Partha Bose, *Alexander The Great's Art Of Strategy: The Timeless Leadership Lessons Of History's Greatest Empire Builder* (New York: Gotham, 2004).

12   J.F.C. Fuller, *The Generalship of Alexander the Great* (New Brunswick, NJ: Rutgers University Press, 1960), p. 284.

13   Thomas R. Martin and Christopher W. Blackwell, *Alexander the Great: The Story of an Ancient Life* (Cambridge: Cambridge University Press, 2012), p. 180.

14   Ibid.

15   Ibid., p. 181.

16   Mary Beard, 'Alexander: How Great?' *New York Review of Books*, 27 October 2011.

17   Ibid., p. 52.

18   Robin Lane Fox, *Alexander the Great* (London: Penguin, 2004), p. 428.

19   Ibid., p. 428.

20   Eri Hotta, *Japan 1941* (New York: Vintage Books, 2013).

21   John Toland, *The Rising Sun: The Decline and Fall of the Japanese Empire 1936–1945* (New York: Modern Library, 2003).

22   Kennedy, *The Rise and Fall of the Great Powers*, p. 303.

23   Hotta, *Japan 1941*, p. 281.

24   Ibid., p. 279.

25   Roberta Wohlstetter, *Pearl Harbor: Warning and Decision* (Redwood City, CA: Stanford University Press, 1962), p. 354.

26   Lawrence Freedman, *The Future of War: A History* (London: Penguin, 2017), p. 65.

27   H.P. Willmot, *Empires in the Balance* (Annapolis: Naval Institute Press, 1982), p. 74.

28   Willmot, *Empires in the Balance*, p. 74.

29   Freedman, *The Future of War*, p. 65.

30   Willmot, p. 140.

31   Ibid., p. 141.

32   Samuel Eliot Morison, *The Rising Sun in the Pacific: History of United States Naval Operations in World War II*, vol. III (Champaign, IL: University of Illinois Press, 2001).

33 Hotta, *Japan 1941*, p. 20.

34 John Hughes-Wilson, *On Intelligence* (London: Constable, 2016), p. 156.

35 Barbara W. Tuchman, *The March of Folly: From Troy to Vietnam* (London: Abacus, 1985), p. 37.

36 Roberta Wohlstetter, *Pearl Harbor: Warning and Decision* (Redwood City, CA: Stanford University Press, 1962), p. 354.

37 Tuchman, *The March of Folly*, p. 37.

38 Morison, *The Rising Sun in the Pacific*.

39 Gordon W. Prange (with Donald M. Goldstein and Katherine V. Dillon), *Pearl Harbor: The Verdict of History* (Harmondsworth: Penguin, 1986), p. 498.

40 Paine, *The Wars for Asia*, pp. 219–20.

41 Graham Allison, *Destined for War: Can America and China Escape Thucydides's Trap?* (New York: Houghton Miflin Harcourt, 2017), p. 81.

42 Allison, *Destined for War*, p. 81.

43 John Keegan, *A History of Warfare* (New York: Vintage, 1994), p. 21.

44 Bernard Brodie and Fawn McKay Brodie, *From Crossbow to H-bomb* (Bloomington: Indiana University Press, 1972), p. 172.

45 Beatrice Heuser, *The Evolution of Strategy* (Cambridge: Cambridge University Press, 2010), p. 119.

46 Christopher Clark, *The Sleepwalkers: How Europe Went to War in 1914* (New York: Harper Perennial, 2014), p. 561.

47 Ibid.

48 Ibid., p. 562.

49 Graham Allison, *Destined for War: Can America and China Escape Thucydides's Trap?* (New York: Houghton Miflin Harcourt, 2017), p. xi.

50 Caspar W. Weinberger, 'The Uses of Military Power', National Press Club, Washington, DC, 28 November 1984.

51 Ibid.

52 Stephen M. Walt, 'Applying the 8 Questions of the Powell Doctrine to Syria', *Foreign Policy*, 13 September 2013.

53 *New York Times*, 16 July 2020.

54 Ibid.

55 Hotta, *Japan 1941*, p. 11.

56 Ibid., p. 287.

3

CAPABILITY

Introduction

Capability is that facet of strategy focusing on resources and the marshalling and effective deployment of such resources so that the strategy can be carried out. It is hard to even imagine a strategy that can exist without resources, without capability. Any player, business or organization needs resources that can be brought to bear on a given situation; these resources allow them to operate, to move ahead, and for their strategy to be successful.

Resources are needed in order to prevail in a contest. Usually if one party has greater capability, if it can deliver this in a timely way, it is more likely to prevail. While there might be occasional exceptions, the 'balance of capabilities of the contending parties decides the outcome if both are equally determined'.[1] Of course, will and determination, or favourable terrain or tactics, may overcome a small capability disadvantage, but are unlikely to be able to overcome a large capability disadvantage. And if both parties are equally determined, the one with the greater capability is far more likely to prevail than not.

The resources for grand strategy and armed conflict are wide-ranging in nature, involving finance, industrial production, training, human resources more generally, weapons, information and intelligence, fixed assets and infrastructure. Even the very ideas of organization and efficiency in deployment and logistics provide for greater capability when used well. Superiority in resources is not an end in itself; resources need to be delivered as needed. A contestant could have overwhelming advantage in resources but be unable to get them to the right place at the right time.

Capability needs to include potential resources as well as those currently at hand. Total capability should be seen as the sum of current resources plus those potential relevant resources that can be brought to bear over some defined period of time. An army might be small but have the ability to greatly increase its size very quickly; factories can be turned from civilian products to making armaments; domestic infrastructure – railways, roads, buildings – can be sequestered for military use. Comparing capability requires much more than merely adding up the resources immediately available.

As the five facets of strategy are related and dependent on each other, it follows that some activities may overlap two or more facets. By definition, a fortress could be considered to be a constructed and fixed building that provides a resource for its occupiers. However, rather than discuss this as part of capability, it is to be left to the later chapter on terrain (chapter 6). The rationale is that a fortress involves creating an artificial terrain favourable to its defenders or using the existing terrain to advantage but enhancing it. Similarly, the quality of leadership could be seen as an asset, as a capability. The development of leaders, including the system that rewards or punishes, could be regarded as a resource as well and as part of capability. Much of the discussion on leadership, however, is left until later as a part of will (chapter 4).

Capability defined

Capability is defined as 'the quality of being capable', and, in turn, the relevant meanings of 'capable' are 'able to take in; having sufficient room or capacity', 'having the ability, power or fitness for some specified purpose or activity', also 'having general capacity, intelligence, or ability; competent; gifted' (New Shorter Oxford). Although the two words are obviously related, capacity is an amount, a space and a more limited concept than capability. Capability has a connotation of ability and competence rather than merely a physical amount available; the power or ability to do something is more action-oriented than having or possessing a space. 'Resources' or 'capacity' are related to capability but are not as comprehensive in terms of meaning.

Freeman argues that in terms of national power,

> Capabilities are capacities for action to reward or punish other states. They may be military, economic, political, or cultural. Capabilities are influence with observable consequences. They vary in mass, relevance, impact, irresistibility, and sustainability.[2]

These points are highly relevant in understanding capability. *Mass* includes: military mass – 'a concentration of forces capable of overwhelming the opposition; economic mass – the strength of the economy; political mass 'consists of dominant persuasiveness' and cultural mass – 'represented by intellectual preeminence'.[3] The *relevance* of a capability relates to how it 'can be brought to bear on the issues in dispute' and the balance of capabilities must 'be assessed by reference to capabilities and vulnerabilities bearing on the issues between them'. *Impact* refers to the level or degree 'of an injury or inducement'; *irresistibility* refers to the extent 'a capability cannot be countered or offset'; and *sustainability* is about how much time and effort can be invested' to reinforce capabilities or to exhaust them'.[4] All these contribute to national potential, as Freeman adds:

> The extent to which national potential can be realized reflects the organizational, industrial, and technological proficiency of a society. National potential is ultimately determined, however, by the degree to which a society's political system allows its state to concentrate and apply national skills and resources quickly in a struggle.[5]

It is interesting that the final point is on the strength and robustness of the political system. A more general case could be made that rather than leadership or national economy or chance and circumstance, recent conflicts have been between political systems with the eventual winner the society with the more robust political system. Of course, there might be an element of winner's bias here – the winner must have been more able to harness capabilities. It is not so much the kind of political system, the point is more about the ability of a political system to harness resources and, presumably, maintain the tacit or expressed support of the society to do so.

Capability is relative

There can be no fixed standard of capability, no simple binary choice between either capable or not capable in the abstract. Capability is neither static nor able to exist as an absolute value. Capability is always comparative, always relative to some other party, to some other real or possible contestant.

In business strategy, Porter refers to 'a realistic appraisal of each competitor's capabilities' as the final step in competitor analysis and points to the need to be realistic in making an appraisal of capability.[6] This is a crucial point. In any kind of strategy being overly optimistic in assessment of capability is problematic. So, too, is an under-assessment. As discussed later (chapter 4), Union Civil War General George McClellan continually over-estimated the strength of his opponents, even when he had far greater numbers on his own side. Porter also argues that competitive strategy 'involves positioning a business to maximize the value of the capabilities that distinguish it from its competitors'.[7]Again what we have here is the notion that capability – or capabilities in this instance – are expressly comparative to other competitors.

Sun-tzu's discussion of capabilities is expressly comparative, too. As he asks, 'when making a comparative evaluation',

> Which ruler has the Tao?
> Which general has greater ability?
> Who has gained [the advantages of] Heaven and Earth?
> Whose laws and orders are more thoroughly implemented?
> Whose forces are stronger?
> Whose officers and troops are more thoroughly trained?
> Whose rewards and punishments are clearer?[8]

These are all questions of capability and open to comparison. The strength of forces is a matter of numbers, but also a suggestion of competence. The implementation of laws and orders and the training of officers and troops are all matters of capability. Also, 'which general has greater ability?' could refer to the training of leaders, their selection and the personnel management systems that enable the talented to be recognized, rewarded and promoted.

Resources are obviously crucial for any conflict and for any strategy. There may be instances where smaller numbers of participants or fewer assets have been able to defeat a better-resourced foe. But these are rare. Tactical successes in war by smaller armies may be but brief interludes in a lengthier conflict where sheer numbers do lead to an outcome favouring the party with greater capability. For instance, the Confederate defeat of a Union Army twice its size at Chancellorsville in May 1863 led to overconfidence as to Southern fighting qualities and to the subsequent loss by the South at Gettysburg two months later. The Union possessed far greater resources and, provided that its political leaders could stay firm, in the end those greater resources would count. Early successes gained by Japanese forces in the invasion of South East Asia were followed by increased and eventually overwhelming resources directed at a Japanese defeat. In both instances, admirable fighting qualities and outstanding leadership in deployment of forces only delayed the inevitable once superior resources were well deployed.

Prior to World War II the Japanese appeared to have greater military capability than the United States in terms of numbers of soldiers, ships and aircraft. A mere adding up of resources at December 1941 would conclude that Japan possessed more and better resources in its army and navy than the US, suggesting that Japan might well prevail in a conflict. However, the US had superior *potential* productive capability once it could be drawn upon as it had a much bigger population and economy. Its relative war potential was estimated to be more than ten times that of Japan.[9] Factory production could readily be moved from, say, production of passenger vehicles for the domestic market to trucks, tanks, guns and ammunition for the military.

As was well known in Japan, the US military disadvantage was closing rapidly. The US had recently started an arms build-up mainly due to uncertainty about the war in Europe. Even if the US was not yet formally part of the European war, Japanese leaders could see the day approaching when the far greater potential capability of the US in terms of population and industrial economy would mean they would be at a substantial resource advantage against Japan. The very fear of future disadvantage may have led to the Pacific War starting when it did; perhaps the Japanese were motivated to strike early while they were still competitive in capability.

Overall resources

It is obviously advantageous to possess superior resources in a comparative sense. More people, more money, better equipment all offer advantages. The phrase 'sinews of war', coined by Roman orator and statesman Cicero (106–43 BCE), is used sometimes to refer to the money and equipment needed to wage a war. Strategic materials can include weapons, but much more than that in terms of capability – transport, food supply, communications and money.

Clausewitz refers to those matters that form part of the combat, including marches and camps but also other subjects that 'belong to the maintenance' including 'subsistence, care of the sick, the supply and repair of arms and equipment'.[10] Such resources need to be gathered and supplied. Capability includes the obvious points of human resources, money and equipment. Others include: physical assets such as buildings, roads, port facilities, airfields along with less tangible assets such as intelligence, including espionage and administrative and organizational competence. Infrastructure includes the stock of fixed assets – roads, buildings, energy supplies, communication systems – needed for the operation of an enterprise or economy. Some kinds of infrastructure may be privately owned in some countries, such as building stock or the electricity, communications, gas and oil; others may be governmental. But all are societal assets that government can use if needed.

During the US Civil War, the Northern states held a major advantage in many resources, but despite this being quite evident from the start, it still took five years for its resources to be brought to bear and be decisive. The Confederacy had only one-ninth the industrial capacity of the Union and, before the war, the Northern states manufactured more than 90 per cent of the nation's firearms, cloth, pig iron and boots and shoes.[11]

An infrastructure differential can have a real impact on the capability of antagonists. And with the Civil War highly dependent on railroads – the first major war that was – the Union side possessed more than twice the density of railroads and several times the mileage of canals and macadamized roads.[12] Slave labour produced cotton as the South's major export, but cotton exports were curtailed with the Union's naval blockade, greatly reducing Confederate overseas trade. Southern leaders seemed to believe that Britain would intervene in the war to regain supplies of cotton for its mills, but this was never realistic given the ban on slavery in the British empire and the ongoing work of the Royal Navy to stop the slave trade from Africa. The South was able to gain some minor resource benefit from operating on interior lines, but combined with its resource scarcity at the start, there was an inexorable strangling of its economy and reduction in its capability. The economy of the South began to fall apart even earlier than its losses in battle.

The US Civil War pointed to the great importance of organization in modern war, notably in the related spheres of logistics, communications and transportation. Furthermore, as the North was dragged into a conflict of attrition due to early disappointments, so did resources and their effective deployment become even more important. The North possessed the resources but found it hard to deploy them effectively, but once the North became better organized, the outcome was inevitable. Consequently, victory in the Civil War (as in the two world wars of the twentieth century) 'went to the side with the largest population, the most durable financial system, and the greatest industrial capacity'.[13]

The resource gap was even starker in World War II, with far greater resources eventually being able to be deployed by the Western allies compared to Germany, Italy and Japan. Prior to World War II, defence spending in the United States was far less than in other powers. In 1937, only 1.5 per cent of US national income was spent on defence compared to 28.2 per cent by Japan and 23.5 per cent by Germany, but the relative national income is in the other direction, with Japan's national income (in $US) at four billion, Germany 17 billion, France 10.2 billion, the British empire 22 billion and the United States 68 billion.[14] Before commencing its rearming, Kennedy estimates that the US held 41.7 per cent of the world's relative war potential, with another 10.2 per cent for the UK, its future ally, compared to 14.4 per cent for Germany, 3.5 per cent for Japan and 2.5 per cent for Italy.[15] It is notable in these figures that all the Axis powers were far behind the US and UK, and it is remarkable that the Japanese would start a war with the US. As Kennedy argues:

> Japan, counting only its frontline aircraft, warships, and army divisions and seeing them strong, had chosen to attack a country that had ten times its economic power (in terms of GDP) but which had not yet mobilized for total war. When that country was fully energized,

the defeat of Japan would come, because America had no reason to compromise.[16]

Resources do count in the longer run. The Japanese belief was that they could prevail in a short sharp war followed by negotiation. Even they did not see a future for themselves in a long war in which superior resources would overwhelm them and were unable to respond when it did become a long war.

Resource capability is crucial for strategy but needs to be looked at in a wider sense, as van Creveld argues:

> Strategy, like politics, is said to be the art of the possible; but surely what is possible is determined not merely by numerical strengths, doctrine, intelligence, arms and tactics, but, in the first place, by the hardest facts of all: those concerning requirements, supplies available and expected, organization and administration, transportation and arteries of communication.[17]

All these points refer to additional aspects of capability, not merely capacity or numbers of troops. While possessing resources provides an advantage, there is much to be gained by such mundane matters as administration, organization and the delivery of goods and services to where they are needed.

Finance

Any activity of government requires money; money buys people, goods and services. This need for money is especially the case for any kind of military and for any conflict. Alexander minted silver coins as he ventured east. Greek and Roman soldiers were paid in coins, and that pay helped develop their economies. Medieval monarchs needed money to pay soldiers and mercenaries. This led to innovation in taxation and public finance generally and the military was historically until recently the largest user of revenue.

From the sixteenth to at least the end of the eighteenth century, the mercantilist system in Europe aimed at keeping gold and silver bullion inside the nation for the express purpose of paying for soldiers and sailors. Silver and gold from the Americas funded the Spanish armies in Europe and the Eighty Years War. Imposing taxation on their American colonists before the American Revolution was thought warranted by the British government to help pay for the garrisoning of British troops in the American colonies to fight the Indians and to help pay for the war against the French that had ended in 1763. Even for this purpose, taxation without representation was intolerable to the American colonists and led to their revolution.

Most wars until the end of the eighteenth century were relatively small in scope, affecting military professionals more than the whole society and undertaken for many reasons – dynastic, religious, commercial and territorial. For some it was rather a game and, with some exceptions, did not involve many people or cost much money. However, the long conflict between France and much of the rest of Europe between 1792 and 1815 – broken by one year of peace after the Treaty of Amiens in 1802 – was different in kind and can be seen as the beginning of modern warfare, in which conflict engulfs the whole society.

Revolutionary France signalled the beginning of mass armies, raised by conscription; more than twenty years of conflict followed involving much greater mobilization of whole societies. The Napoleonic Wars involved many kinds of conflict, including 'a conflict between competing economies'.[18] Of course, economic matters were behind many other conflicts, between Britain and Spain over colonies, for instance, but the long conflict with Napoleonic France was about entire economic systems. This economic conflict was something new in warfare; as Kennedy argues, 'more than ever before, in this war . . . economic factors intermeshed with strategy'.[19]

For much of the time, France was dominant on land within Europe and while its conflicts there were similar in kind as previous wars, they were of a much greater scale. Britain was superior at sea, really for the whole period, but was dominant and unchallenged after the Battle of Trafalgar in 1805. Its naval strength also enabled its superiority in trade and commerce related to trade. Having failed to invade Britain – never a realistic prospect – Napoleonic France sought to attack British trade.

In November 1806, Napoleon promulgated the Berlin Decrees aimed at cutting British trade with the continent of Europe, in what was termed the Continental System. With this, as Knight argues:

> Napoleon set out to attempt to control the whole of the European coastline in order to implement what was in effect a restructuring of

Europe. French military and political expansion followed this escalation of economic warfare very closely. The emperor was not attempting to starve Britain, for there were too many alternative sources of supply; rather, he was attempting to destroy the British economy by blocking trade with the Continent.[20]

Britain responded by intensifying its blockade of European ports. Some parts of the British economy suffered as they were dependent on trade with Europe, but the French economy suffered still more. Its growth was slower than Britain's and the walls of the Continental System became permeable. Smuggling was rife, further benefiting the British economy and hurting the French. Customs revenue – a key source of taxation – in the French empire fell to 20 per cent of its 1806 level by 1809.[21] British trade actually expanded, bringing greater prosperity followed by even more money being able to be raised for the war effort through taxes and loans.[22]

Despite being smaller in population than France, Britain was able to finance its war so well that it could also subsidize European powers in joining Britain in one or other of the coalitions against France. Overall, Britain gained out of its economic warfare with Napoleon both at the time and in the years that followed. As Knight argues, 'The foundations of military victory . . . lay in the industrial capacity' of a number of workers in the economy from makers of weapons to farmers, shipbuilders, merchant seamen, even civil servants, and 'they were all needed as much as the tens of thousands of young soldiers and seamen who resisted, survived and finally overcame the threat from Napoleon'.[23]

Britain was better organized and financed than France during the Napoleonic wars with France. Although Napoleon brought in substantial administrative reform, it was not sustained or sustainable as too much depended on the whims of one person.

In the aftermath of the Napoleonic Wars, Britain's economy based on trade and empire thrived compared to the rest of Europe and did so for much of the following century. If what happens in the peace after a war is the real question as to who was the winner, Britain certainly won this one. It could even be argued that Britain's prosperity in the nineteenth century, and even the early adoption of industrialization, owed much to the financing of the French and Napoleonic wars.

Logistics

Capability includes not only possessing adequate resources, but also being able to get them where and when they are needed. This is the art of logistics and defined as 'the practical art of moving armies and keeping them supplied'.[24] There are circumstances where one combatant has had far greater resources but could not get them where they were needed and at the time when they are needed. During the US Civil War, the Northern states held a major advantage in resources, but found it difficult to use their overwhelming resources to best advantage.

World War II was another conflict where logistics were crucial and where Britain and its allies held a major advantage by their command of the sea. Particularly in the Pacific, this was 'a war of logistics . . . a war of distances, advance bases, and was a strategy driven and constrained by logistics'.[25] As noted in chapter 2, the Japanese could not supply their conquests or use them for resources. After the first few months of 1942, they not only could not hold their territory, they could not supply it either with its maritime marine decimated by Allied submarines.

One of the aspects of Japanese folly in attacking the United States was that its adversary possessed far greater resources. In a massive industrial war, dependent on machines, resources and the delivery of them were crucial in the longer run, as Harrison argues:

> A war of attrition developed in which the opposing forces ground each other down, with rising force levels and rising losses. Superior military qualities came to count for less than superior GDP and population numbers. The greater Allied capacity for taking risks, absorbing the cost of mistakes, replacing losses, and accumulating overwhelming quantitative superiority now turned the balance against the Axis. Ultimately, economics determined the outcome.[26]

Having resources is one thing but getting them to the best place at the best time is often another. In the North African campaign, Montgomery at El Alamein enjoyed a superiority of resources even if many of the supplies had been delivered via the Cape of Good Hope. The Germans, on the other hand, found much difficulty merely crossing the Mediterranean. As Paine argues:

> Rommel lost not for want of good soldiers or generalship, but for want of adequate supplies, sunk at sea before they could reach him. For

Asia, President Roosevelt supported Guadalcanal, a tropical nightmare, which was bad for all sides, but worse for the Japanese, again because of an inferior ability to protect their logistical lines by sea to supply their men on land.[27]

As soon as the United States joined Britain and the Soviet Union in World War II the resource equation swung away from Nazi Germany. Getting those resources to where they could be effective was far from simple, however. Starting nine months prior to Hitler declaring war on the United States in December 1941, American resources were deployed to assist Britain through the Lend-Lease scheme. Vast quantities of guns, trucks, planes, tanks and fuel were delivered to the Soviet Union as well as Britain.

As early as 1942 the Soviets began to demand a second front be opened in Western Europe through an invasion of France. This was not easy to do due, at least in part, to insufficient logistical capability, notably shipping and landing craft. By summer 1942 few US resources had been delivered to Europe. And by summer 1943 there were still major shortages of resources such that the British argued that it was too early to be able to cross the English Channel, land in Europe and sustain that effort. It was eventually agreed that by summer 1944 the resources would be in place for the landings that then occurred in Normandy on D-Day, 6 June. Even then, despite the vast resources deployed – 2,700 ships plus 1,900 landing craft with 130,000 soldiers, 2,000 tanks and 12,000 other vehicles in the first wave[28] – the logistical issues around crossing the English Channel meant the day was still risky. Earlier would most likely have been disastrous,

Logistics is a pivotal part of capability. Organization generally is an asset; processes, procedures, and administrative competence can be crucial in determining outcomes but require substantial effort.

Equipment

The equipment used by military forces is an obviously important part of capability even though it may be more often evenly matched rather than one side having a great advantage over the other. Normally the differential is not that large as, if one side develops a technical edge, it may be emulated by others. But there are times when the level of technology provides an advantage for one or other of the combatants; in some circumstances a technological advantage becomes crucial.

Many nineteenth-century colonial wars were quite lopsided as European powers had gained a substantial technological advantage over the less developed world. As Hillaire Belloc commented in his contemporary poem on colonial war, 'Whatever happens, we have got the Maxim Gun, and they have not'.[29] Repeating rifles, machine guns and other technological advantages provided European nations with relatively low-cost means to control far larger populations in Africa and other less developed parts of the world in the age of imperialism.

The development of sailing ships able to navigate between continents was another important technological advance, as Kennedy argues:

> There is no doubt that the development of the long-range armed sailing ship heralded a fundamental advance in Europe's place in the world. With these vessels, the naval powers of the West were in a position to control the oceanic trade routes and to overawe all societies vulnerable to the workings of sea power.[30]

For several hundred years this technology was unable to be matched by non-European powers. Quite why is a matter of some conjecture. In explaining the rise of the West, Kennedy refers to advances in arms, maritime mastery, a market system, trade, but what was most different was sustained organization driving innovation; that what 'distinguished the captains, crews and explorers of Europe was that they possessed the ships and the firepower with which to achieve their ambitions, and that they came from a political environment in which competition, risk, and entrepreneurship was prevalent'.[31]

Typically, a technological advance such as the Macedonian spear of Philip and Alexander's army would be quickly copied. But matters of organization were harder to emulate and could threaten internal power structures. For instance, gunpowder and long-distance sea travel were pioneered by China, but these did not lead to lasting change as the Confucian system did not encourage innovation. The conquest by Spanish conquistadors of pre-Columbian civilizations was partly due to better weapons, but was more about ruthless organization against opponents in Mexico and Peru who were incapable of responding when their leadership was removed.

More recent conflicts reduced the technological differential with some exceptions. During the Revolutionary and Napoleonic wars, French naval ships were as good as British ships; the greatest differences were in organization and in the competence of officers and men. The contending parties in the US Civil War and World War I also showed little difference in the quality of their equipment. And in World War II, at least until the invention of the atomic bomb, there was little difference in the quality of equipment even as there became a great disparity in their numbers.

Some initial thought in the design of equipment can reduce casualties and provide an advantage. At the start of World War II, the Japanese maintained a substantial technological advantage in its ships and aircraft. For instance, the Japanese navy's Zero fighter was an impressive aircraft. It was faster, more manoeuvrable and better armed than its American counterparts at the beginning of the war. However, it was surprisingly fragile. Early versions did not have self-sealing fuel tanks, which meant that even a rifle shot could bring down a plane, as fuel would pour out of a holed fuel tank and catch fire. There was no armour protection for pilots as this would have added weight and reduced range and manoeuvrability. By comparison, opposing US planes were slow and appeared less capable. But after learning how to fly against the Zero and quickly designing and building better aircraft, the air war over the Pacific turned against the Japanese. In the early stages of the Battle of Midway the slow US Navy Devastator torpedo planes were shot down with impunity. But later US planes such as the Hellcat and Corsair were more robust, heavier, often able to land riddled with holes and were continually improved. The Zero was little changed and became so uncompetitive it was used as a *kamikaze* plane later in the war.

The Japanese navy appeared to focus more on attack rather than defence, as Parshall and Tully note:

> At its root, the Japanese Navy was wedded to the primacy of the offense. They believed in power projection no less fervently than the American Navy did. But because of their design philosophies, Imperial Naval vessels were notably less damage resistant than those of their opponents. Now after having suffered a shattering attack at the hands of the enemy, these weaknesses were about to be exposed in the most graphic manner imaginable.[32]

At the Battle of Midway, insufficient safeguarding of fuel, bombs and torpedoes on the Japanese flight decks meant that even one bombing strike could doom the entire ship, and that is indeed what appears to have happened for several of their aircraft carriers that day in June 1942.

At the Battle of Midway, the Japanese deployed four aircraft carriers and the US Navy three. All four Japanese carriers were sunk, as was one US carrier, but the US Navy was far better equipped to replace its losses. American aircraft carriers were better organized and designed to absorb damage from enemy bombing than Japanese ones. They incorporated measures such as fuel lines that were emptied and filled with carbon dioxide before battle as well as better damage control management. After Midway the Japanese were to launch only seven more carriers in the whole of World War II, where the Americans 'commissioned more than one hundred fleet, light, and escort carriers by the war's end' and sixteen times the number of major warships as the Japanese.[33]

Even if the quality of ships and aircraft was similar, US production of replacements was far in excess of production in Japan. During 1941, as a wider war had been decided on, Japanese aircraft production was 162 a month. In the United States in the following year, 4,000 a month were ordered to be built, then 10,000 a month in 1943, a rate which the Japanese or Germans could not match.[34] This was a rate of one new aeroplane every five minutes. Nor could the Japanese increase volume much as many parts were still made by hand, whereas planes and even ships were constructed in the US by assembly line, day and night, and on an industrial scale. Harrison argues that the Allies could not produce better weapons but could produce more and do so quicker. As he says, the quantitative superiority of the Allies in weaponry was based on 'standardized products in a limited assortment, interchangeable parts, specialized factories and industrial equipment, an inexorable conveyor belt system of serial manufacture, and deskilled workers who had neither the qualifications nor the discretion to alter designs or specifications'.[35]

From the beginning of the Pacific War US submarines were able to roam far and wide in ways that surface ships obviously could not. The effectiveness of American submarines in the Pacific was quite remarkable. While German efforts in the North Atlantic in both world wars were at times of great concern to the Allies, US submarines in the Pacific were particularly effective and made the Japanese island chain strategy untenable. As Paine argues:

> By war's end Japan's merchant marine had been reduced to one-ninth its pre-Pearl Harbor capacity, and only half the men and supplies sent

from Japan and Manchuria reached the Pacific theatre. These statistics are particularly notable, given the tiny numbers of submariners compared to the other services and specialties. The Japanese empire depended on resources and their transport home. Japanese expeditionary forces scattered throughout the Pacific required supplies delivered by sea. U.S. submariners increasingly prevented this, starving both Japan's expeditionary forces and the home islands.[36]

As early as 1943 Japanese ships were being sunk at a faster rate than new ones could be built.[37] As the US and its allies built capability, the Japanese had no answer to the preponderance of resources ranged against it. As Prange notes, 'A number of Japanese did believe quite sincerely that they enjoyed a heavenly mandate which placed them above such mundane considerations as resources and logistics'.[38] But in the end, the resource disparity was telling as 'in the long run, American strength was bound to prevail, as long as the will to win existed. This the Japanese had assured by hitting Pearl Harbor'.[39]

Engineering

A related capability is that of engineering, in the sense of construction and other support services. The term has an early derivation as 'a designer and constructor of military works', also as a builder of engines of war' (New Shorter Oxford). While engineers and engineering have wider meanings, their contribution to overall capability in times of conflict persists and can provide strategic advantage for one side over another.

The military sense of engineering tends to be more about work on the ground with the rest of the military in construction of bridges, fortifications, airfields and the like. The Roman army was adept at building bridges, roads for military purposes and siege engines. Julius Caesar's engineers built two bridges across the Rhine river into the Germanic lands. While a major achievement – the first time a bridge had been built to cross the Rhine – Caesar simply notes, 'Ten days after the collection of the timber had begun, the work was completed and the army crossed over.'[40] As discussed later (chapter 5), Wellington's construction of the Lines of Torres Vedras during the Peninsular War provided a strategic asset that could not be overcome by a French army under Marshal Masséna in 1810. The Lines comprised three lines of fortresses superbly engineered to enhance the already difficult terrain north of Lisbon forming an impassable barrier to the French forces likely to be committed to Portugal. Even though Wellington was generally outnumbered, the existence of a safe haven meant it would be very hard for him to be defeated.

With greater military mechanization engineers became even more important, ranging from those in charge of the engines from the age of steam, through to railways, telegraphs, telephones and radio. Engineers required more education notably in mathematics; the specialties – civil, mechanical, electrical and electronic – had their antecedents in the military. Drawing on such expertise became a key asset for the armed forces generally.

Of special note are the engineers that went along with the troops, as opposed to those involved in making things in factories at home. An example was the US Construction Battalions, better known as Seabees, that served in the Pacific War. Formed at the start of the war given the obvious need for construction beyond what could be done by civilian contractors, the Seabees became 'a gigantic organization that brought American military industrial power – in the form of cement, tarmac, steel girders, electrical wire, rubber, glass, bulldozers, and lighting equipment – across the 7,000 miles of the Pacific Ocean to the outlying territories of Japan'.[41] The Seabees were all trained as Marines but also had trades and other skills.

The Seabees made a manifest difference to the Pacific War. The Japanese had their own competent construction people but were way behind and often did not have the resources. The record of the Seabees is impressive as Kennedy notes:

> The raw statistics are staggering: in the Pacific alone, these artificers of victory built 111 major airstrips and 441 piers, tanks for the storage of 100 million gallons of gasoline, housing for 1.5 million men and hospitals for 70,000 patients.[42]

Seabees served in Europe and other theatres but it was in the Pacific that their efforts made the most strategic impact. Combining the far greater resources of the US with their ability to construct provided an edge and made a manifest strategic difference given the sheer scale of the Pacific. One of the key tactics of the US, once it had gained local sea and air superiority, was to by-pass fortified places and press on, often by concentrating on a smaller place within aircraft range. They would then build the infrastructure, starting with the airfield that was the key to it all. Port facilities, housing, mess facilities, supplies of all kinds needed to be delivered to men on the ground and were often on remote islands with no infrastructure.

The superior resources of the US in the Pacific included far greater numbers of aircraft and ships than the Japanese as the war progressed. But it also included supplies of concrete, bulldozers and steel and the logistical means of delivering them. And in the Seabees and in the army's engineers the US also had people who could do the work, and do it remarkably quickly.

Human capital

It is a truism that people are any organization's greatest resource. This is no less true of nation-states. Sheer numbers are important, but are not the whole story with other factors such as training, recruitment, promotion systems, medical skills to keeping the human assets healthy with food and equipment, logistics and other supports.

Strategies require people to carry them out as well as people who might devise them. And it is an unfortunate fact of conflict that, to a greater or lesser extent, people are consumable, even expendable. The value placed on the human resource have varied over time and in different cultures.

Along with other disadvantages, the South had a much smaller population than the North during the American Civil War. The total population of the USA in 1860 was 31.4 million. Of these the population of the Southern states was 8.7 million, including 3.9 million slaves that explicitly were not to be included in any Southern army. The border states of Kentucky, Maryland and Missouri had a population of 3.6 million, but their populations were divided and could not be counted on to favour the South. It followed that the North was far better placed to raise its armies and outnumber those of the South. And so it turned out. McPherson argues that somewhere between 850,00 and 900,000 men fought for the South compared to 2.1 million for the North.[43] A numeric advantage such as this was bound to be significant as the war went on, with other things being equal. There is no reason to suppose a qualitative difference between soldiers from the North or the South as they were essentially from the same stock. Add to that the other resource advantages of the North and the outcome of victory perhaps should have followed rather earlier than it did.

Human resources do not need to be immediately in place to be significant for capability. By virtue of a total population resource there can be a much larger potential force available once trained. In 1932, the US army was a mere 120,000 and ranked seventeenth in the world. The US was able to mobilize quickly; its total armed forces were 1.6 million in 1941, increasing to 11.4 million in 1945.[44]

Drawing on an underlying population resource is not necessarily straightforward. Duty, glamour or persuasion can assist in getting recruits as can offering pay and conditions better than in civilian life. But with larger conflicts such staffing sources are insufficient. Conscription had been used for centuries, often with an obligation to serve a noble or a monarch. But the scale of conscription changed during Revolutionary and Napoleonic wars with France being able to field armies of unprecedented size due to conscription. Large wars since then – including both world wars – have often resorted to conscription; some countries – for example, Singapore, Switzerland, Israel, Sweden, Turkey – retain it still.

Even if an army is generally paid, mercenaries form a special class of paid soldiers, in the sense of only fighting for money and not necessarily having any allegiance to the society paying them. Mercenaries have been used for centuries. Many Greek mercenaries were in the Persian army of Darius even in their war against Alexander the Great. During the American Revolution, the British Army supplemented its numbers by recruiting more than 20,000 mercenaries from the German state of Hesse. Their contracts were with the prince of Hesse, who then contracted with Britain. This was common practice – indeed, was one of the key industries of Hesse at the time. But the Hessian role in the conflict was controversial with colonists from the start with a reputation for not taking prisoners and not even fighting for their beliefs.

The use of mercenaries does come with issues. As Machiavelli pointed out:

> Mercenary captains are either excellent soldiers or they are not; if they are, you cannot trust them, since they will always aspire to their own greatness either by oppressing you who are their master, or by oppressing others against your intent; but if the captain is without skill, he usually ruins you.[45]

And, to follow Machiavelli, it is now more generally thought that, for an army to be successful, its people need to have an attachment to their state beyond that of their pay.

Once the human resource has been found, the state has an obligation to look after its people and it is in its interests to have them in good condition to be able to fight on. Military medicine became crucial in keeping the fighters alive and to return them into the ranks. The Crimean War and the US Civil War in the next decade are regarded as turning points in the treatment of wounds and disease in war. In Crimea, four times as many British soldiers died of disease than in battle but, with the work of Florence Nightingale, that war led to nursing being elevated to a profession and to better outcomes for the wounded. As McPherson notes about the Civil War, soldiers may have been right to believe they would be better off outside a hospital than inside, but 'this was owing more to the state of medical knowledge in general than to the particular incompetence of army doctors'.[46] The Union did devote more resources to improve its medical services, but the Confederacy had fewer resources to do as much.

Another human resource difference in practice in the Pacific War was that it was commonplace for Japanese captains and other officers, even admirals, to go down with their ships, taking personal blame for what had happened. American officers typically did not follow this practice but would live to fight another day if they could, thereby retaining valuable expertise. The human resource is valuable and should be conserved as far as possible.

Training

Having a population base is an asset, but in order to be effective, the manpower drawn from it needs to be trained. For the Roman army, a succession of victories occurred not by mere numbers and innate courage, but by skill and training. Vegetius in the fourth century argued that training was the single difference between Rome and its adversaries.

> We see that the Roman people conquered the world by no other means than training in the military arts, discipline in the camp, and practice in warfare. But against all these (peoples) we triumphed by selecting recruits carefully, by teaching them . . . the principles of war,

by toughening them by daily exercise, by teaching them in advance through manoeuvres in the field everything which can happen on the march and in battle, and by punishing severely the lazy. For knowledge of military science fosters courage in battle. No one is afraid to perform what he is confident he has learned well.[47]

Training provided a great advantage for the Romans, particularly against those outside the empire. The idea was 'that military success was based on a series of technical skills that could be learned by both commanders and common soldiers'.[48] Roman soldiers learned to march and survive and were able to carry their packs for long distances; Caesar marched his army from Rome to Spain in a mere 27 days.[49]

The training regime of ordinary soldiers in the US Civil War and the World Wars was much the same as that of the Roman era. Perhaps the training to be a foot soldier was similar as the role itself was similar, but as conflicts became more advanced so too did the training for higher-order roles and where soldiers were required to operate specialized equipment.

The training of naval officers was more thorough, at least from the eighteenth century. In Britain, officers were required to pass examinations in navigation and ship-handling in a more searching process than in the army where nepotism, patronage and purchasing offices lasted longer. Artillery and engineering did require some knowledge of mathematics in navies and armies, but learning to fly a plane was much more complicated.

A substantial part of the cost in running aircraft is in the skills and training of the pilots. An experienced pilot is far more effective than a raw one and therefore likely to last longer. The US Navy in the Pacific saw its pilots as a valuable resource, investing much more in pilot training, better armour protection for the pilot and in finding and saving pilots from downed aircraft. This may have been done for humanitarian and morale reasons but the total cost of pilot training also meant it made economic sense to try to rescue as many fliers as possible.

Equally important was keeping up the supply of new pilots, and in this area too the American capability greatly exceeded the Japanese. As early as the Battle of Midway, the loss of experienced pilots sunk with the four Japanese carriers led to a pilot shortage that was never made up. The overall casualty rate was very high. In the 12 months from mid-1942, land-based Japanese pilots 'suffered an 87 percent casualty rate, and carrier-based aircraft had an astounding 98 percent casualty rate', and though this improved a little later, 'Japan could never replace its lost elite pilots'.[50] Replacements were given less training, but, of course, less experienced pilots were easier to beat in combat further exacerbating pilot shortages. As part of its planning for a lengthy war the US and its allies set in place pilot training programmes of industrial level. Combat pilots were rotated back to become instructors with real experience.

It makes sense to look after the human resource; it makes sense to try to reduce casualties; it makes sense to better use the resources that have been expended in training rather than to continually train new people.

Leadership

As discussed later (chapter 4), will and leadership are crucial for any strategy to be successful. Any organization has a duty to develop, train, socialize and support its leaders and, as a corollary, remove the ineffective from positions where they can do harm. Leadership is also a capability that needs to be found, nurtured and supported. Nowhere is this more pronounced than in military settings where leaders have to somehow get subordinates to, in the end, put themselves in harm's way.

Leaders typically came from the upper echelons of society, from kings and their immediate followers, the medieval knights of yore with their retainers; nobles became knights and knights became leaders. Julius Caesar was from an aristocratic family, as were most of the Roman leaders. Even if he came into leadership roles as part of the great disruption of the French Revolution, Napoleon showed early on that he was a military leader of great ability. Rather than coming from the nobility, Napoleon had risen from an obscure family in a backwater of France, spoke French with a strong Corsican accent, had little money but was simply better than others at the roles.

For some two hundred years from the late seventeenth century, it was normal practice in Britain for military officer ranks to be purchased; meaning, in practice, that only the already wealthy could become officers. Only after the Crimean War did the system of purchasing come to an end, in part due to the career of Lord Cardigan, including the Charge of the Light Brigade. Of course, Lord Cardigan had purchased his military offices and then demonstrated his incompetence. Reforms after

Crimea may have abolished the system of purchasing such roles, but in a heavily class-conscious society it remained the case that high office was largely the preserve of the aristocracy for some time. Aristocratic leaders who had purchased office could be competent, as Arthur Wellesley, the Duke of Wellington, demonstrated, but this may have been more accidental than part of a system that rewarded the capable.

The British Army in World War I is sometimes referred to as 'lions led by donkeys' – the former being the foot soldiers and the latter being incompetent military leaders – said to derive from comments made by German High Command.[51] The saying itself is disputed and in any case had been used before, including in the Crimean War of the 1850s and the Franco-Prussian War of 1870. Applied to World War I the saying does have resonance given the appalling casualty rate and the sheer folly of sending men with rifles to charge entrenched artillery and machine guns. There is something apposite about the slowness of its generals to adapt to changes in technology and their apparent willingness to tolerate the unconscionable casualty lists. Innovation did occur in World War I – the use of aircraft, tanks, better logistics and much else. And even if 'lions led by donkeys' is a caricature there did seem to be callous disregard of the human cost imposed most of all on ordinary soldiers from much lower classes than the highest-ranking officers. Perhaps the training and selection of generals did not lead to those of ability being in charge at that time.

Information and intelligence

Another resource, another capability, is that of intelligence, in the sense of 'knowledge communicated by or obtained from; news; information [specifically] of military value' (*New Shorter Oxford*). The key difference between information and intelligence is that information comprises raw data, facts and observations of all kinds; and intelligence is best seen as the next level higher in that it involves using information for a purpose.

A definition used by the US Central Intelligence Agency is:

> Intelligence is the collecting and processing of that information about foreign countries and their agents which is needed by a government for its foreign policy and for national security, the conduct of non-attributable activities abroad to facilitate the implementation of foreign policy, and the protection of both process and product, as well as

persons and organizations concerned with these, against unauthorized disclosure.[52]

A key point is that for information to become intelligence requires processing: this includes drawing inferences, analyzing raw data, specifically in terms of foreign countries as the CIA notes, but it could have a wider application. Retaining governmental information against disclosure to others should also include countering the activities of foreign agents in the domestic arena although this role is sometimes performed by separate agencies. Intelligence may well include the world of spies and traitors, intelligence services, counter-intelligence, codes and code-breaking, but it is really about turning any useful fact or observation into a product that can be used by policymakers.

Intelligence in these senses has been around since the beginning of history itself, dating back to the Bible and to Ancient Greece, even if often allied to seers, oracles and diviners.[53] The contemporaneous Sun-tzu in China spoke of the need for advance knowledge, as 'If I determine the enemy's dispositions of forces while I have no perceptible form, I can concentrate [my forces while the enemy is fragmented.'[54] Information 'cannot be gained from ghosts and spirits, inferred from phenomena, or projected from the measures of heaven, but must be gained from men for it is the knowledge of the enemy's true situation'.[55] Spies of various kinds are therefore essential and Sun-tzu lists five types of spies as 'a ruler's treasures': 'local spy, internal spy, turned spy [double agent], dead [expendable] spy, and the living spy', adding 'there are no areas in which one does not employ spies'.[56]

Keegan argues there are five stages of intelligence: first, *acquisition* or acquiring information from whatever source, secret or openly available, gathered by people or by electronic or photographic means; *delivery* where the raw intelligence is communicated to a potential user; *acceptance* where the intelligence is believed or not; *interpretation* or the analysis of disparate pieces to make a coherent picture; and *implementation* as the necessary task of convincing decision-makers.[57] However, Keegan adds:

> There is no such thing as the golden secret, the piece of 'pure intelligence', which will resolve all doubt and guide a general or admiral to an infallible solution of his operational problem. Not only is all intelligence less than completely accurate: its value is altered by the unrolling of events.[58]

The most difficult parts in practice are acceptance, interpretation and implementation, where belief or probability of accuracy come into play. Rather than having too little information a bigger problem is making sense of the mountain of information that is available. The raw information needs to be analyzed to make sense of it before it becomes intelligence of value and possible application. There is an inherent gap between information and its interpretation, between data and intelligence.

Prior to the German invasion of the Soviet Union in June 1941, the Soviets had received very good intelligence from a variety of sources, from the US, from Britain, from Russian diplomats as well as Soviet soldiers on the front line that the Germans were preparing for attack. Over the year prior to the invasion more than a hundred unequivocal warnings were passed on to Stalin as to what Hitler was planning.

The Soviet spy Richard Sorge, based in Japan, was one source providing the exact date of the attack.[59] This was an instance of that one vital piece of pure intelligence of legend, but the problem was it was not believed. The interpretation of the data was flawed – it seems mostly by Stalin himself –even as his generals wanted to act on the intelligence received. As Kotkin relates:

> Now, after half a year of contradictory secret reports about a possible German invasion of the Soviet Union, intelligence warnings of an imminent titanic war were coming from everywhere . . . Almost all of it was hearsay, rather than purloined documents. The reports were contradictory, contaminated with obviously false information, and often delivered with scepticism. In London, the Soviet ambassador to the United Kingdom wrote in his report that he considered a German attack 'unlikely' despite having received information to the contrary from British intercepts of secret German military communications. In Berlin, however, the Soviet ambassador to Germany, after months of equivocation, finally averred that Germany's actions signalled an imminent invasion. But Stalin evidently concluded that his envoy in Berlin had been fed disinformation and remarked that he was 'not such a smart fellow'.[60]

To be fair to the position that Stalin was in, all kinds of information came in from all sorts of sources. Some reports were contradictory; some were fabricated by the Germans to disguise their actual intention; some were believed to be disinformation from Britain designed to lead the Soviet Union into war. Stalin did not want to provoke Hitler and reasoned that the Germans understood that it would be suicidal for them to attack the Soviet Union in the east before defeating the United Kingdom in the west. Stalin would conclude that 'the colossal build-up of German forces on his doorstep was not a sign of imminent attack but rather Hitler attempting to blackmail him into giving up territory and making other concessions without a fight'.[61]

As the intelligence about German invasion became even more compelling, Soviet generals came to believe there was a problem to be countered. But Stalin was obdurate and despite a last-minute warning to its armies Soviet forces were quite unprepared. As Kotkin argues:

> When Stalin damned his intelligence as contaminated by disinformation, therefore, he was right. But the despot had no idea which parts were disinformation and which might be accurate intelligence. He labeled as 'disinformation' whatever he chose not to believe.[62]

The real task of intelligence may well be 'to tell the truth to powerful decision makers, whether they like it or not'[63] But it becomes difficult to do this with someone like Stalin who could and did punish those who tried to put their own views forward against what was deemed permissible.

The collection of information has its dangers. Despite being disparaged and disregarded by Stalin, the Soviet spy Richard Sorge in Japan found astonishing information of great accuracy. Not only were the dates of German invasion of Russia reported to Moscow ,as noted earlier, but Sorge also reported that Japan would not invade the Soviet Union in Asia. As addition, as Hotta argued:

> Sorge was happy that Japan's acrimonious relationship with the United States at least made it certain that Japan would not attack the Soviet Union. He had accomplished his mission in the best way possible. 'If the United States does not make any compromise by mid-October, Japan will attack the United States, and then Malaya, Singapore and Sumatra as well,' he said in an authoritative message he had dispatched to Moscow earlier that day. The Soviet Union was no longer an enemy in Japanese strategic thinking. After eight years, Sorge felt his mission

was officially over. He decided he would ask Moscow if he could return to the Soviet Union or even to Germany.

At this point Sorge was arrested by Japanese authorities and never seen again.

The Japanese attack on the US Pacific Fleet at Pearl Harbor should be considered an intelligence failure for the US. This was 'the classic case of a nation actually having all the key intelligence indicators of an impending attack, but failing to recognize them or act upon the warning'.[64] Some indications had been received about Pearl Harbor as a possible target but were not passed on clearly to those on the ground. US radar installed on Oahu picked up a large number of aircraft approaching on the morning of 7 December 1941. This was potentially useful information but was not interpreted correctly or communicated to others. The inexperienced radar operators reported this to a junior officer, who surmised it must be a flight of US planes that were expected and not the far larger number of Japanese planes headed for Pearl Harbor.

Even though the US was able to read the Japanese diplomatic code, it could not do so completely and was insufficiently organized to make sense of it as 'the key question was whether the decoded information could be used, in time, and at the right place'.[65] What was missing in Washington at the time was 'a national intelligence assessment and briefing staff with access to all available intelligence from every source'.[66] Warnings were not passed on to Hawaii. One clear warning was sent over the commercial wires, was late and only arrived as the battle was going on. The army and the navy did not coordinate their intelligence; even on the ground in Hawaii the two services had little contact. Hughes-Wilson argues:

> The brutal fact remains that, by any professional and objective measure, the USA had ample and timely intelligence of a Japanese surprise attack somewhere in the Pacific and probably on Pearl Harbor from a wide variety of indicators and sources . . . Pearl Harbor stands as an awful warning of the ultimate intelligence 'cock-up' perpetrated by a badly organized and uncoordinated group of parochial intelligence providers who had the tools but didn't know how to do the job properly. In the final analysis they failed to disseminate the vital intelligence to the people who needed to know.[67]

Kennedy argues that 'one thing that emerges from the study of intelligence in the 1939–45 war, frankly, is the preponderance of intelligence failures',[68] and mentions a number including Pearl Harbor, and the Soviets over the German invasion. One exception, though, is the great success at decoding Japanese signals about Midway.

Within a few months after Pearl Harbor the collection and dissemination of intelligence by the Americans had improved vastly. From radio traffic, from other sources and from decoding intercepts, it had been evident for a while that a big Japanese offensive was being planned, but the question of where was contested within the US military. Some believed it would be a raid on San Francisco, others a further attack on New Guinea or the Solomons. Admiral Nimitz, the Pacific commander-in-chief was persuaded it was going to be Midway by his intelligence officers, but others in Washington did not agree.

By May 1942, even as the Battle of the Coral Sea was happening, a clever plan was worked out to find out what the Japanese target was. It was already known that American possessions were designated by the Japanese with a two-letter code and much of the intercepted radio traffic referred to a place designated 'AF', but there was still a question as to what 'AF' stood for.

Midway was still connected to Hawaii by an old undersea cable, so, over that secure link, Midway was told to send a message to say that the desalination plant had broken and to do so via radio in the clear. When this false radio message was sent, and duly picked up by the Japanese, subsequent intercepts showed that AF was short of water as its desalinator was broken. With AF then confirmed as meaning Midway, other intelligence intercepts were able to use the 'astonishing amount of top-secret information' the Japanese sent out by radio, and a 'remarkably complete estimate' of the Midway operation was able to be put together.[69] The Japanese invasion force even carried new desalination equipment as it would be needed once they took Midway.

Possessing such good intelligence was crucial for the battle that followed. After the Battle of the Coral Sea where it had been damaged, the US aircraft carrier *Yorktown* was repaired in three days instead of the weeks and months a full repair would warrant. The reason for this hurry was the intelligence assessment that the Midway battle was imminent. The direction of the attack was accurately estimated, as was its date. Instead of a trap to lure the US navy, accurate advance knowledge was able to reverse the trap, which now became one for the Japanese.

The Battle of Midway is a great example of how superior intelligence can affect the overall outcome. As Hughes-Wilson notes, 'Midway changed the balance of power in the Pacific overnight. Intelligence had changed the course of world history.'[70] This is not an overstatement. The loss of four of the six aircraft carriers that had carried out the attack on Pearl Harbor to one American carrier meant that Japan lost its clear naval superiority in what was a disaster for Japan. With extra aircraft carriers on their way to the Pacific, the US Navy would maintain its naval air superiority until the end of the war. The supply of accurate intelligence and the wise use of it meant that the US ships were in the right place at the right time to sink those four carriers.

If Midway is an example of intelligence being accurate and well used to great effect, the same cannot be said about intelligence assessments of Iraqi capability prior to the second Gulf War. At a press conference in February 2002, US Defense Secretary Donald Rumsfeld was asked a question about weapons of mass destruction and the invasion of Iraq. His response was:

> Reports that say that something hasn't happened are always interesting to me, because as we know, there are known knowns; there are things we know we know. We also know there are known unknowns; that is to say we know there are some things we do not know. But there are also unknown unknowns — the ones we don't know we don't know. And if one looks throughout the history of our country and other free countries, it is the latter category that tend to be the difficult ones.[71]

Mr Rumsfeld's answer does encapsulate the difficulty of gaining intelligence and working from it, even if it does divert into the somewhat metaphysical. The intelligence that Iraq possessed weapons of mass destruction was simply wrong; it had no such capability. As it turned out, Iraq was invaded anyway and the weapons of mass destruction were not there.

Conclusion

Capability is about gaining, maintaining and deploying resources and doing it better than a possible adversary. The examples used here are just a few of the great variety possible for inclusion. The availability of finance, suitable equipment, well-trained and well-led human resources is fundamental, with these elements generally able to be added up and compared. Some capabilities are able to be measured reasonably precisely; others require substantial judgement.

Intelligence is also essential but is different in kind from the other kinds of capability. Hughes-Wilson argues capabilities are relatively easy to measure, that 'Anyone can count ships, tanks or aeroplanes – but determining an adversary's true plans or intentions is fiendishly difficult to measure or quantify.'[72] This is a good point. Trying to work out what a potential or actual opponent is aiming to do is the ultimate aim of intelligence, but it is not easy to do. Trying to discern intention is one reason that intelligence often fails even as it is universally regarded as essential. It would have been of little consolation to Richard Sorge that he was correct but was not believed. Analysis of information and inferring from it seems to be a general weakness.

Even if possessing superior resources does not automatically mean a win for its holder, the probability of success is certainly greater. Having superiority in one kind of resource can overcome a weakness in other kinds. During the Napoleonic War Britain was outnumbered in human resources, but was able to gain greater financial strength and to use that to maintain a superior navy and help fund European powers willing to fight against France.

Capability in its various dimensions is certainly essential for strategy. Any strategy requires resources and those resources need to be available at the right place and time. But capability alone does not make for success in strategy; the other facets are required as well.

Notes

1   Chas W. Freeman Jr., *Arts of Power: Statecraft and Diplomacy* (Washington, DC: United States Institute of Peace Press, 1997), p. 18.

2   Ibid., pp. 18–19.

3   Ibid., p. 19.

4   Ibid., pp. 19–20.

5   Ibid., p. 20.

6   Michael E. Porter, *Competitive Strategy* (New York: The Free Press, 1980), p. 63.

7   Ibid., p. 47.

8   Sun-tzu, *The Art of War*, in Ralph D. Sawyer (ed. and transl.), *The Seven Military Classics of Ancient China* (New York: Basic Books, 2007), p. 157.

9   Paul Kennedy, *The Rise and Fall of the Great Powers* (London: Unwin Hyman, 1988), p. 332.

10 Carl von Clausewitz, *On War*, edited by Anatol Rapoport (Harmondsworth: Penguin, 1968), p. 174.

11 James M. McPherson, *Battle Cry of Freedom* (New York, Ballantine, 1988), p. 318.

12 Ibid.

13 Richard Holmes and Martin Evans (eds), *Battlefield: Decisive Conflicts in History* (Oxford: Oxford University Press), p. 294.

14 Kennedy, *The Rise and Fall*, p. 332.

15 Ibid.

16 Paul Kennedy, *Engineers of Victory* (London: Allen Lane, 2013), p. 350.

17 Martin van Creveld, *Supplying War: Logistics from Wallenstein to Patton* (Cambridge: Cambridge University Press, 1977), p. 1.

18 Roger Knight, *Britain against Napoleon: The Organization of Victory 1793–1815* (London: Penguin, 2013), p. 392.

19 Kennedy, *The Rise and Fall*, p. 129.

20 Knight, *Britain against Napoleon*, p. 400.

21 Ibid., p. 401.

22 Ibid., p. 392.

23 Ibid., p. 466.

24 van Creveld, *Supplying War*, p. 1.

25 Anthony W. Gray, 'Joint logistics in the Pacific Theater', in Alan Gropman (ed.), *The Big 'L': American Logistics in World War II* (Washington, DC: National Defense University Press, 1997), p. 293.

26 Mark Harrison, 'The Economics of World War II: An Overview', in Mark Harrison (ed.), *The Economics of World War II: Six Great Powers in International Comparison* (Cambridge: Cambridge University Press, 1998), p. 2.

27 S.C.M. Paine, *The Wars for Asia, 1911–1949* (Cambridge: Cambridge University Press, 2012), p. 193.

28 Kennedy, *Engineers of Victory*, p. 250.

29 Hillaire Belloc and Basil Temple Blackwood, *The Modern Traveller* (London: Edward Arnold, 1898).

30 Kennedy, *The Rise and Fall*, p. 26.

31 Ibid., p. 28.

32 Jonathan B. Parshall and Anthony P. Tully, *Shattered Sword: The Untold Story of the Battle of Midway* (Washington, DC: Potomac Books, 2005), p. 248.

33 Victor Davis Hanson, *Carnage and Culture* (New York: Anchor Books, 2001), p. 341.

34 Craig L. Symonds, *The Battle of Midway* (New York: Oxford University Press, 2011), p. 38.

35 Harrison, 'The Economics of World War II'.

36 Paine, *The Wars for Asia*, pp. 195–6.

37 D. Clayton James, 'American and Japanese Strategies in the Pacific War', in Peter Paret (ed.), *Makers of Modern Strategy: From Machiavelli to the Nuclear Age* (Princeton, NJ: Princeton University Press, 1986), p. 717.

38 Gordon W. Prange (with Donald M. Goldstein and Katherine V. Dillon), *Pearl Harbor: The Verdict of History* (Harmondsworth: Penguin, 1986), p. 503.

39 Prange, *Pearl Harbor*, p. 546.

40 Caesar, *The Conquest of Gaul* (London: Penguin, 1982), p. 96.

41 Kennedy, *Engineers of Victory*, p. 328.

42 Ibid., p. 330.

43 McPherson, *Battle Cry of Freedom*, p. 485.

44 See Mark Harrison, 'The Economics of World War II', p. 14.

45 Peter Bondanella and Mark Musa (ed. and transl.), *The Portable Machiavelli* (Harmondsworth: Penguin, 1979), p. 42.

46 James M. McPherson, *Battle Cry of Freedom*, pp. 306–7.

47 Brian Campbell, *The Roman Army: A Source Book 31 BC–AD 337* (London: Routledge, 2006).

48 Michael M. Sage, *The Republican Roman Empire: A Sourcebook* (London: Routledge, 2013), p. 229.

49 Jonathan P. Roth, *The Logistics of the Roman Army at War (264 BC–AD 235)* (Leiden: Brill, 1999), p. 296.

50 Paine, *The Wars for Asia*, p. 194.

51 Alan Clark, *The Donkeys* (London: Pimlico, 1991).

52 US Central Intelligence Agency, 'A definition of intelligence'. Centre for the Study of Intelligence, *Studies Archive Indexes*, 2, 4, 2008.

53 Christopher Andrew, *The Secret World: A History of Intelligence* (London: Penguin, 2018).

54 Sun-tzu, *The Art of War* (Sawyer edn), p. 167.

55   Ibid., p. 185.

56   Ibid.

57   John Keegan, *Intelligence in War* (London: Pimlico, 2004), pp. 3–4.

58   Ibid., p. 4.

59   Alan Bullock, *Hitler and Stalin: Parallel Lives* (New York: Vintage Books, 1991), p. 712.

60   Stephen Kotkin, 'When Stalin faced Hitler: Who fooled whom?' *Foreign Affairs,* 96, 6, 2017.

61   Ibid.

62   Ibid.

63   John Hughes-Wilson, *On Intelligence* (London: Constable, 2016), p. 50.

64   Ibid., p. 245.

65   Paul Kennedy, *Pacific Onslaught: 7th Dec. 1941/7th Feb. 1943* (New York: RosettaBooks, 2014).

66   Hughes-Wilson, *On Intelligence*, p. 269.

67   Ibid., pp. 269–70.

68   Paul Kennedy, *Engineers of Victory* (London: Allen Lane, 2013), p. 358.

69   E.B. Potter, *Nimitz* (Annapolis, MD: Naval Institute Press, 1976), p. 81.

70   Hughes-Wilson, *On Intelligence*, p. 156.

71   *New York Times*, 25 March 2014.

72   Hughes-Wilson, *On Intelligence*, p. 56.

4

WILL

Introduction

The third facet of strategy is will – more accurately, will and leadership. There are times and situations in which all the other facets of strategy in place but a decision-maker does not wish to take action, does not wish to move. At base, will is about persons, about personality – that is, the roles and behaviours of decision-makers. It does include leadership in that someone has to be able to make that final decision, but it is rather more than that. There are instances where a person, a group or even a country does have the purpose and the capability to pursue an action but lacks the drive or desire to make that next step into action. Even if having a purpose implies will, a decision-maker still may not commit to action, or may simply let others do so instead.

A classic example of lack of will can be seen in the inaction of General George McClellan, the leading Union general during the early part of the US Civil War. Despite amassing a great excess of resource capability, McClellan was simply unable to move, unable to take the resources made available and deploy them. This reluctance appears to have been a personal characteristic rather than an institutional one. His failure to act became an increasing source of frustration to President Abraham Lincoln and even some of McClellan's subordinates. By contrast, later Union generals, notably Ulysses S. Grant and William Tecumseh Sherman, were both able and willing to prosecute the war fully, to move ahead. Only then did the superior resources of the Union start to be decisive.

Leadership is an integral part of will; indeed, leadership could be considered the visible manifestation of will. A determined leader can drive will in some circumstances, to take an organization further than it may have been able to go before. Leadership of people may not easy given the personalities, positive and negative, both of the leader and the led. But an absence of leadership is much worse in terms of outcome as it makes effective action harder to achieve. Will and leadership are clearly related; without will, action will not happen; without leadership that will may be misdirected, inefficient and ineffective. Both will and leadership are about people; trying to get them to do something, trying to corral them; trying to enthuse them to do something together.

The human element embodied in will is another reason that strategy is necessarily more of an art than a science. The foibles and weaknesses of individuals; the mistakes, the hubris and the miscalculations are all part of personality and interactions among people. This leads to the crucial roles of individuals and groups in contributing to strategy either positively or negatively.

Will is only one of the five facets of strategy, but an important one. To reiterate, the five facets of the PCWTT model work together. Will is needed to take action, to go beyond capability and purpose to actually do something. Terrain and tactics may impose constraints or opportunities but the reality is that someone, somewhere, needs to make the decision to act and to commit.

Too much reliance on will, or an overly inflated perception of one's own will compared to that of an adversary, is fraught with danger. Will by itself is unlikely to be able to overcome defects in any of the other four facets, an important point to be looked at later. At best, high levels of will can only partly overcome any weakness in capability, tactics and terrain, and assuming that will by itself can prevail even in a wildly unrealistic purpose is to risk failure.

The meaning of will

Will is defined as 'the faculty by which a person decides on and initiates action; (also willpower)[mass noun] control deliberately exerted to do something or to restrain one's own impulses; a deliberate or fixed desire or intention; the thing that one desires or ordains' (*New Shorter Oxford*). As the definition notes, will is related to action or prospective action or intention for action. Related to 'will' is 'willing', an adjective meaning 'ready, eager, or prepared to do something' or 'given or done readily'. Being willing or displaying willingness both imply an intention to take action, and that action results from its exercise.

In the PCWTT model, will forms a bridge between preparedness – purpose and capability – and action – terrain and tactics. Being willing to act is separate from being able to act. Even if a clear purpose exists or should exist there is a leap, a hurdle, in agreeing to take action and in following through. For instance, France and Britain did not act when German forces occupied the demilitarized Rhineland in 1936, in clear violation of the Treaty of Versailles and the Treaty of Locarno. At that time the French army was far more capable than the German army and a treaty violation did offer a clear purpose to move. Britain could have assisted, but in a mood of appeasement did nothing. A show of force would likely have met with German capitulation, but choosing to do nothing emboldened Hitler to make further demands, leading, seemingly inexorably in hindsight, to World War II in Europe. But the political and economic situation in both France and Britain was fraught and the sheer will to do something to counter Germany was not there at that moment.

Will is needed by leaders and by states, its absence means irresolution and prevarication. Clausewitz argues that war is about will, that 'War . . . is an act of violence intended to compel our opponent to fulfil our will.'[1] He adds later, 'to defeat the enemy we must proportion our efforts to his powers of resistance', and, in turn, 'this is expressed by the product of two factors which cannot be separated, namely, *the sum of available means* and *the strength of the Will*'. The first of these can be measured as it depends on numbers and on resources or capability. But 'the strength of volition is more difficult to determine, and can only be estimated to a certain extent by the strength of the motives'.[2] Willingness may be a societal trait, as in Japan before World War II; more democratic regimes usually seek public support.

Motives, motivations or reasons for getting into conflict vary and cannot be taken for granted. Many Americans were unwilling to fight in the Vietnam War; many Italians, though patriotic, did not support Mussolini.

An interesting usage of 'willing' is that of US defense secretary Donald Rumsfeld in 2003 in a speech at a US airbase in Italy. Referring to a proposed invasion of Iraq, Mr Rumsfeld said:

> We have every week a growing number of countries who have volunteered to participate in a coalition of the willing, if it proves to be necessary; a number of countries that have indicated that they're not able to participate in a coalition of the willing unless there's a second resolution in the U.N., and that number is a reasonable number; and then a third group that says they would like to participate in a post-Saddam Hussein Iraq reconstruction effort.[3]

The novelty here is that of terminology, the use of words (without getting into a discussion of the Iraq war). Rumsfeld was not talking about possible allies who were able or capable but about those who were willing to move, prepared to take action. 'Coalition of the willing' is an evocative phrase. A potential ally may have capability, but being able to contemplate the commitment of resources is something else altogether. Capability and will are separable; someone could be capable but still not wish to take action.

McClellan, Grant and Sherman

It was noted earlier (chapter 3) that during the American Civil War the North far outweighed the South using the usual measures of capability. But the war seemed to drag on as the North found it difficult to translate its capability into decisive action. To President Lincoln it became increasingly apparent that a major part of the problem was the lack of will evident in his commander General George McClellan. Despite Union forces vastly outnumbering the opposing army, McClellan somehow believed they were outnumbered. This appeared to be a sheer lack of will, a lack of enterprise, and a refusal to contemplate risk, even low risk.

McClellan was personally courageous and excelled at administration and preparation for battle, but he found it difficult to contemplate acting without being perfectly prepared. And almost by definition for McClellan, such a state of readiness was never reached and was never able to be reached. He kept demanding more resources, overestimated the strength of the enemy's army and was slow in responding to events. His men thought him wonderful – they were far better fed, housed, and uniformed than soldiers from the South. But despite their disadvantages, soldiers from the South appeared to out-fight the unionists. There was no good reason for this other than a lack of effective leadership.

McClellan was great at organizing and training his people and perhaps he did not want to risk them in battle. But avoiding conflict was also risky; avoiding battle even when McLellan retained a great advantage in numbers meant that the war dragged on. Quite simply, he appeared to lack will, as McPherson argues:

> Military success could be achieved only by taking risks; McClellan seemed to shrink from the prospect. He lacked the mental and moral courage required of great generals – the will to act, and to confront the terrible moment of truth on the battlefield . . . McClellan excelled at preparation, but it was never quite complete. The army was perpetually *almost* ready to move – but the enemy was always larger and better prepared.[4]

In January 1862, President Lincoln met with generals Franklin and McDowell, two of the McClellan's subordinates after having called at McClellan's house where the unwell general had not wished to meet with him. He told them that

> he wished their opinion on how to commence operations with the Army of the Potomac – soon. The president told them that if something was not done, 'the bottom would be out of the entire affair'. He suggested that if General McClellan did not want to use the army, he 'would like to *borrow* it, provided he could see how it could be made to do something.' After some discussion, in which both generals confessed ignorance of the army's actual condition, Lincoln said he wished them to consult with one another, get more information, and meet with him again the following evening.[5]

It beggars belief that any American general would refuse to see his president, but this was one of a piece with McClellan who seemed to consider himself to be a higher being than any mere political leader.

McClellan was politically compromised as well, even if this may not have directly affected his leadership of the army. He was privately scathing of Republicans in the administration, including Lincoln, and later, in 1864, ran against him in the presidential election as a Democrat and lost. He was lukewarm about ending slavery and lacked understanding of the political pressures on Lincoln or the ends of the war. As Sears argues:

> McClellan's chief failing – his persistent unwillingness to make common cause with the civilians charged with managing the war – virtually nullified his accomplishments. By resolutely refusing to share with Lincoln either his knowledge or his confidence, by dismissing as mere clamor the concerns of public opinion and the political realities of the time, he squandered nearly all the trust and support that earlier had been his without question.[6]

While a good point, there is more involved than that. It seems that, although competent enough, McClellan lacked self-awareness, lacked humility and was psychologically unprepared for the role. The self-importance, the unwillingness to move, the consistent overestimation of the strength of the opposition and the exaggerated fear of incurring casualties – odd in a general – point to some kind of personal inadequacy. McClellan 'lacked the mental and moral courage to act; he did not have the quality possessed by Lee and Grant and Jackson of willingness to risk defeat as the only way to gain victory'.[7]

It may be a truism that the higher the role, the more personality becomes crucial to success or failure. Later in the Civil War, Union generals Grant and Sherman were not really charismatic in the glowing sense, but they knew who they were and were willing to act. Compared to McClellan, Grant and Sherman are less complicated, at least at first glance. Both had been to West Point like McClellan, but unlike him both had known personal hardship before the Civil War. The Union possessed much more in terms of material resources, as discussed earlier, but the South appeared to have better generals – Robert E. Lee, Stonewall Jackson, for instance – or did have until Grant and Sherman emerged.

As leaders Grant and Sherman worked to win and to do so as quickly as possible. They did so not as rivals as might normally be the case, but as friends; neither belittled the other, they were mutually supportive. As Sherman once said, 'Grant stood by me when I was crazy, and I stood by him when he was drunk; and now, sir, we stand by each other always.'[8]

After Grant moved to the Army of the Potomac, he and Sherman were in different theatres of the war, with Grant in a higher role. They remained supportive of each other. Sherman's plan to march through Georgia with only limited logistical support was initially not favoured in Washington, and Grant asked for a short delay at the request of President Lincoln. When Sherman's plan was finally agreed, due to Grant's support of it, the result showed the South to be a hollow shell. Sherman's march to the sea likely shortened the war.

Grant credited Sherman with the plan, writing later, 'the question of who devised the plan of march from Atlanta to Savannah is easily answered: it was clearly Sherman, and to him belongs the credit of its brilliant execution'.[9] Perhaps McClellan had not wished to be responsible for the lengthy casualty lists that would have resulted from risking the army, but by not moving, the war was arguably prolonged and with far greater overall casualty numbers. Grant and Sherman wanted the task done and as expeditiously as possible. They wanted it to be over.

Grant was criticized at the time for incurring too many casualties, but not acting, not trying, not being willing – like McClellan – was more costly. Action may pose risks, but so too does inaction. As part of a political contest, Lincoln could not afford inaction or failure because this would empower his political opponents in Washington. The superior resources of the Union were only effective if he had generals who could carry out the overall strategy and had the will to move. In Grant and Sherman and others – Sheridan, Thomas, Meade – Lincoln found generals with the will to persist.

National will

Even if will and leadership mostly refer to individuals, there may be something called national will, and its presence or absence may make a difference in a conflict. Long before the Vietnam War was over, significant numbers of Americans and in other societies regarded the war as unachievable and wanted their country out. As Kubiak argues,

Some attribute the U.S. loss in Vietnam to artificial political limits placed on the employment of the military or to the military choosing the wrong strategy against a weaker enemy. The bigger truth is that the decision to leave Vietnam as a loser was a policy decision made not of military necessity, nor dictated by circumstances in the international environment, but because the U.S. had simply lost its political will to persevere.[10]

The US had the *capability* to keep going in terms of resources of all kinds; it had undoubted control of the air and sea terrains, a much bigger population, a much bigger economy, but for domestic political considerations it held back from fully committing all its forces. In addition, its military capability and undoubted technological advantage were ineffective in the jungles of Vietnam. But all this counted for nought as domestic opponents of the war in the US gained increasing support for ending a war that seemed pointless anyway. And a loss of political will followed with regard to prosecuting the war in Vietnam. Oddly, perhaps, there are quite strong parallels between the Vietnamese fight for unification and independence and the US fight for independence against Britain two centuries earlier. In both cases a smaller, less well-equipped force prevailed against a much larger, better-armed force from across the sea assisted by the terrain, clearer purpose and will.

On the other hand, World War II has been seen by many in the US and its allies as 'the last good war'; the last one where the nation as a whole was united and where the moral imperatives underlying it were clear and unambiguous. The Japanese attack on Pearl Harbor and the German occupation of much of Europe certainly clarified what the vast proportion of the American population wanted to do. If there is a national will, this was an exemplar.

In Europe, the notion of national will was resorted to by both Hitler and Mussolini, and the fall of France in 1940 is often regarded as a failure of national will. The stories are rather more complicated than that – indeed, there are real questions as to whether the will of individuals can be usefully aggregated to the nation as a whole, except perhaps in quite exceptional circumstances.

As in Germany and Italy, the 1930s in France were years of political and economic instability. From mid-1932 to the outbreak of war in 1939, there were 19 governments in France and 'the populace loathed the politicians; the politicians loathed each other'.[11] Unemployment was high and industrial production low, with many of the disaffected joining up with extremists either of the far right – neo-fascists – or the far left and communists. There may have been some sympathy for fascist views within higher ranks of the French army and there certainly was quite open contempt for politicians particularly for those of the left.

If will is a personal attribute, and leadership another related one attached to persons, it is hard to establish national will as an aggregation or a collectivity of individual views and attitudes. In the same vein, seeing the loss of France as a national failure of resolve or will is too sweeping. The failure of France to oppose the German occupation of the Rhineland in 1936 was an opportunity lost, but only in hindsight. At the time, France was simply too weak, in both its politics and its economics.

Certainly, how the German army used its forces in May 1940 – concentrating on weak points during the invasion, masterful use of time and space – combined with the apparent ineptitude of the French political and military leaders led to capitulation. The nation's elite capitulated while the ordinary soldiers were fighting on, and when France still had more military resources than Germany. But the invasion and occupation were never a total defeat; France's armies had been outmaneuvered.

It is an overstatement to say that France was defeated in 1940 as the result of having lost its will. Clausewitz argues that 'if War is an act of violence to compel the enemy to fulfil our will, then in every case all depends on our overthrowing the enemy, that is, disarming him and on that alone'.[12] He adds that there are then three objects to this disarming: 'the military power, the country and the will of the enemy'. The military power must be effectively destroyed, the country must be conquered, and then Clausewitz adds a quite profound comment:

> But even when both these things are done, still the War, that is, the hostile feeling and action of hostile agencies, cannot be considered as at an end as long as the will of the enemy is not subdued also; that is, its Government and its Allies must be forced into signing a peace, or the people into submission; for while we are in full occupation of the country, the War may break out afresh, either in the interior or through assistance given by Allies.[13]

As shown by the many Free French fighters, by the active resistance by some and passive sullenness by many others, France was not conquered. Indeed, for Germany to hold a country the size of France meant garrisoning troops all over the country. French resources were indeed exploited, including by sending forced labour to Germany, while its location was handy for airfields and U-boat bases in the fight against Britain and the United States. But France was not going to be incorporated into Germany any more than it could have been in 1870 or in 1914. If there is such a thing as national will, the French did not give up theirs during their resentment at four years' occupation.

Too much focus on national will and too much focus on a leader can lead to national and international tragedy. The idea that national will not only exists but is personified in a single, great and glorious leader can be seen in the rise of Fascism in Europe in the 1920s and 1930s. As Perry argues:

> Fascists exalted the leader – who according to the Fascist view, intuitively grasped what was best for the nation – and called for rule by an elite of dedicated party members. The leader and the party would relieve the individual of the need to make decisions. Convinced that the liberal stress of individual freedom promoted national divisiveness, Fascists pressed for monolithic unity: one leader one party, one ideology, and one national will.[14]

Italy and Germany between the wars were divided societies, with left and right in often violent conflict in with what appeared to be a failure of democracy. Despite rigorous attempts to get rid of opponents after seizing power there was opposition to both Hitler and Mussolini from within their own societies. Such movements may not have been large, but they certainly existed. The Nazi Party became the largest party in the Reichstag before dissolving it, but it did not win a majority of the votes or seats in the German elections of 1932 and 1933. Mussolini's fascists dominated Italy, but had also captured power against the will of many in that society. As Shirer argues: 'The Italian people, at heart, had never, like the Germans, embraced fascism. They had merely suffered it, knowing it was a passing phase.'[15]

Despite claiming that their power expressed itself as national will acclaimed by the populace, seizing power 'by brutally illegal means' created internal enemies, 'greatly exacerbating the mood of fear, social tension and uncertainty which gripped the country immediately after the First World War, none of which made for a promising basis for successful or lasting government'.[16]

It is a myth that Mussolini made the Italian trains run on time,[17] but the idea that a leader can get more done by assuming dictatorial powers does persist. The invocation of national will is at best propaganda used to motivate the susceptible, rather than anything more substantive.

Ideology

Ideology can be an important motivator, a way of uniting a society into following a course of action, but is not without its limits. Societies and the people within them, including its military, have their beliefs, both individual and collective, and an appeal to those beliefs can provide motivation. Some may believe in their country, their *patrie*, or the ideas that underpin institutions of governance. Wars have been fought for religion, territory and much else. As an instance, even before the 1519 expedition to Mexico led by Cortés, the mainland of America 'represented a temptation to all Spaniards in Cuba; the desire for glory, the desire for gold and the desire to bring pagans to the true God'.[18] Add to that the capture of resources from territory and trade and we have a reasonable summation of the key reasons for many conflicts.

An ideological motivation strong enough to provide a willingness to fight for principles of any kind is rather deeper. Societies where support for government is tested in some way through elections, or even a Napoleon-like plebiscite, can claim a stronger attachment to their rulers than those that cannot. Thompson and Thompson argue that when an extreme political organization assumes governmental power without majority support through the ballot box, it must of necessity focus its attention (and resources) on the dual problems of the overt opposition and the uncommitted if it is to survive and consolidate its position and power.[19] As they continue:

> In such circumstances, one may conveniently divide the attitudes of a society to such a regime into five typical categories: (i) the already committed; (ii) the uncommitted sympathizers; (iii) the politically indifferent or ignorant (in general, the majority of the populace); (iv)

the hostile or disaffected but politically unorganized; and (v) the politically organized and active opposition.[20]

Repression of dissidents may work for a time, but most often cannot be sustained, although Germany and Italy tried. But repression and fear do not create national will. If the gold standard of national will is that of the United States after Pearl Harbor, these other societies did not get to that level and were to some extent captured and made hostage by their leaders.

Leadership

Discussion of will inevitably leads to discussion of leadership. The exercise of will requires, in the final analysis, a decision-maker – or decision-makers – in order to make a commitment. At base, a choice needs to be made as to whether to proceed with a particular strategy, whether to act or to not act. It is inevitable that accounts of past events tend to focus on individuals in a leadership position who are or have been faced with making such decisions.

As an instance, consider the final timing of the invasion of Europe in June 1944. With uncertainty over the weather, a decision had to be made to go ahead with the D-Day landings on 5 June as originally planned, wait until the next day, or defer until an unspecified date later, perhaps even the next month. In the event, the decision was to go for 6 June. Ultimately that decision was made by the Allied Supreme Commander in Europe, US General Dwight D.Eisenhower. Even for an exercise as large and complex as D-Day, someone had to make the final call as to whether to proceed or not, and that was Eisenhower. This was leadership in action – the buck had to stop somewhere. To allow for the possibility of failure Eisenhower had prepared a communique accepting his personal responsibility for such a failure. Of course, the landings succeeded and the communiqué was not needed, but the point is that a single person accepted this responsibility as a part of being a leader.

Leadership is a somewhat elusive concept. Even if the acquisition, retention and exercise of individual leaders may be overly emphasized in historical accounts, it cannot be denied that there are real examples of leadership – , for instance, Julius Caesar and Napoleon Bonaparte – where the role and actions of a particular individual were crucial to what followed. But the kind of leadership where everyone sees a particular individual as a 'born leader' detracts from other kinds of leadership that may be more effective.

The view of the leader as a person possessing extraordinary authority through personal charisma was outlined best by German sociologist Max Weber. Charismatic leadership is where there is a single 'glowing' individual who attracts others who wish to follow. Weber argued that charismatic authority was one of the three types of authority, along with traditional authority – that of a tribal chief – and rational/legal authority – formal organization through bureaucracy and hierarchy. Charismatic authority involves the personal qualities of an individual who is then able to lead others by the exercise of those attributes. Some individuals are regarded as 'leaders', others as 'followers', with both qualities being innate. As Weber described it:

> There is the authority of the extraordinary and personal 'gift of grace' (charisma), the absolutely personal devotion and personal confidence in revelation, heroism, or other qualities of individual leadership. This is 'charismatic'domination, as exercised by the prophet or – in the field of politics – by the elected war lord, the plebiscitarian ruler, the great demagogue, or the political party leader.[21]

Usually, as in the cases of Caesar and Napoleon, they are simply better than everyone else, more competent at, in particular, the difficult art of personal politics. It follows that leadership in this sense is not an attribute that is inherent in many people, just in those lucky few possessing innate qualities that make them leaders in contrast to the mass of followers. But this is an unsatisfactory explanation of leadership in general or even a leadership to which everyone aspires. But sometimes this dominance, being seen as 'the smartest person in the room', is problematic.

A charismatic view of leadership can describe some people in leadership roles but not that many – oddly, perhaps, given the apparent yearning for such a person in many societies. Historical examples might include Caesar, Napoleon, Hitler, Gandhi, Churchill, Thatcher and Mandela, but the true charismatic, in the sense of the glowing personality that everyone wants to follow, seems to be quite rare. Perhaps many leaders see themselves in this way, but it is an external standard, and one that is not often met.

Weber recognized that charismatic authority can exist and that leadership can be based on charisma. But he sees it as obsolete, belonging to an earlier, pre-modern age. Even more than the traditional authority of a tribal chief, charismatic authority is essentially non-rational and cannot last. The charismatic leader leads and the followers merely follow where the leader takes them, whatever the destination might be. If success is not found, the authority of the charismatic leader falls away. The bureaucratic system was set up precisely to avoid charismatic authority and replace any kind of personal authority with impersonal rules. To Weber, charismatic authority is temporary and less effective than the rationality to be found in bureaucracy.

A leader is someone who gets results and this may be able to be achieved without the obvious exercise of charismatic qualities. Leadership can be found at all levels inside organizations and not merely at the top. This kind of leadership is not to be disparaged; indeed, a leader in this sense may well be just as effective as, or even more than, the glowing, charismatic leader. US Civil War general Ulysses S. Grant was by no means charismatic, and his friend and colleague William Tecumseh Sherman would likely have scoffed at the very notion. But they were effective and got results. Their opponent Confederate general Robert E. Lee was described as charismatic but lost. In World War II, General Douglas Macarthur was widely regarded as charismatic, but he made mistakes and ultimately failed in Korea, essentially by seeing himself as more important than his own president.[22]

A leader needs to work well with others. Eisenhower managed to persuade, and prevail over, very strong – often wilful – leaders, ranging from his own subordinate General George S. Patton, British general Bernard Montgomery, Soviet general Marshal Zhukov as well as political leaders including Roosevelt and Churchill. To work with such leaders and get an agreed outcome takes quite remarkable skill, but not through the kinds of attributes associated with the charismatic leadership model. Eisenhower was a planner, a facilitator, a consensus builder and used to working with others. He was not seen as charismatic at that time or later, but he was still a very effective leader. A leader may attain high levels of emotional intelligence and also have skills and passions that can influence subordinates but not be someone who is innately charismatic in the full sense.

The idea of the leader who has all the wisdom for a group – the leader-as-dictator, the leader whom everyone fears and to whom everyone defers regardless of their own opinions – does seem unrealistic. In 1965, a few years after his two terms as US president, Eisenhower wrote an article setting out what he thought were the main characteristics of leadership, reflecting on the people he had worked with. These qualities were described by him as: selfless dedication, courage and conviction, fortitude of spirit, humility, thorough homework, power of persuasion, heart and mind, and finally, leadership at every level. On the first point Eisenhower argued that

> Perhaps the greatest of these qualities is single-minded and selfless dedication to the task at hand. Any leader worth his salt must of course possess a certain amount of ego, a justifiable pride in his own accomplishments. But if he is a truly great leader, the cause must predominate over self.[23]

Leadership should be about achieving a result, with the cause being greater than the self; for the charismatic leader, self is likely to be much more important than the cause. As well as a statement of his own kind of leadership, Eisenhower sets out a more realistic view of leadership. Personality is involved in all the characteristics he mentions, but humility does not fit a charismatic model, nor does power of persuasion, which contrasts with direction and authority. Selfless dedication does not fit in a charismatic model where it is the self and selfishness of the charismatic leader that drives their every action.

Someone in a leadership position may be able to gain the commitment of others based on their authority level, but they are also more likely to be effective if they bring some aspects of personality to that process. Clausewitz argues for steadfastness, for maintaining one's balance in spite of 'powerful feelings', and adds: 'Even with the violence of emotion, judgment and principle must still function like a ship's compass, which records the slightest variations however rough the sea.'[24]

The last item on Eisenhower's list was leadership 'at every level', meaning that leadership is needed at all levels in any organization. This is related to some of the other points, such as humility, but is also antithetical to the strict charismatic view. Leadership cannot be reserved by the one glowing leader at the top but needs to be distributed to all levels, as Eisenhower added:

> Any man [sic] who does his work well, who is justifiably self-confident and not unduly disturbed by the jeers of the cynics and the shirkers, any man who stays true to decent motives and is considerate of others

is, in essence, a leader. Whether or not he is ever singled out for prominence, he is bound to achieve great inner satisfaction in turning out
superior work.[25]

Perhaps the best effect of good leadership is to empower others to become
leaders of their own, no matter their level, no matter their personal attributes. Will is linked to leadership, but leadership is too important to be left
to the charismatic leader alone.

Seeking and taking advice

The charismatic leader is assumed to determine decisions and policies; and
there is an implicit assumption that they do so themselves without advice
from others, unless such advice aligns with the preconceived views of the
charismatic leader. Such a process is unlikely to succeed in the longer term
and is one of the reasons that the charismatic leader ultimately fails. Weber
argues that charismatic authority is inevitably transformed into rational-legal
authority as charisma fails. Even if some in society may wish for a dictator to
cut through impediments and established process, the downside can be that
the sole leader makes mistakes. No one is that good; no one is that smart.

   This failing can be seen in the sorry history of absolute monarchy, especially with those European rulers who claimed divine right – a legitimacy
derived from God. Frederick the Great, who ruled Prussia for half the eighteenth century, may have been seen as an enlightened despot who achieved
much, but there were many others who did not. A single source of authority –
a dictator or a monarch – is likely to be inefficient in terms of administration
compared to a system of delegated authority based on law and process.

   Napoleon Bonaparte was another charismatic leader and, like Caesar,
was simply more able than anyone else. But he, too, suffered in the end
by being unable to set up a system of administration that could persist
without his direct intervention, without micromanagement. He chose his
staff according to their talents of 'intelligence, energy, industry and obedi-
ence' and this 'worked for a while until he too, the classic victim of hubris,
destroyed himself through overextension'.[26] As Knight argues:

   While Napoleon had the advantages of continuity and speed of decision, he eventually lost a sense of reality. By about 1810, his ministers

were telling him only what he wanted to hear. Just at the moment when the British government administration was jolted out of old ways, by getting up-to-date and complete information to parliament so that estimates and policy could be fully formulated and understood, Napoleon disappeared behind a cloud of illusion, ordering ships to be built by men whom he had sent to the army, to be paid for by an income that was disappearing as his control over his vassal states loosened and the Continental System disintegrated.[27]

The great flaw of Napoleon was in not setting up a robust system of administration; in leaving too much to himself, mistakes were made making his eventual defeat inevitable. He was 'undoubtedly a genius in battle', but he 'lacked political subtlety'.[28] Napoleon was a charismatic leader, more able than his marshals, more able than most of his opponents. But he was too far ahead of his subordinates in some ways. A system to follow up efficiently was not instituted; devolved authority was threatening to the regime and led to repression. All of this meant that Napoleon was required to do everything. But one person cannot run a state for long, no matter how able. The most remarkable thing is that he lasted so long, not that he was finally defeated.

A more realistic kind of leadership is where the leader maintains the role of making a final decision but comes to that point by seeking out, evaluating and accepting advice from subordinates who feel free enough to be able to state their own views without fear of retribution. As Allied Supreme Commander in Europe, General Eisenhower gained results more by consensus and diplomacy than by single-mindedly making a decision and forcing this on subordinates. In making his decision about the D-Day timing he facilitated open discussions with officers from the various military arms, other officials, the meteorologists, political leaders. Importantly, all were free to say what they thought, and views did diverge.

Similarly, the Cuban missile crisis and its decisions only came after intense discussion over the 13 days[29] of the crisis between President Kennedy and his high-level advisers, many of whom had differing views. The Executive Committee of the National Security Council was set up to include Kennedy and 14 other officials, including his brother Robert, then attorney general. These men (all were men) despite coming from different parts of the armed forces, from the White House, the intelligence community, the State

Department and so on operated as individuals without their staff rather than as representatives of their own agency, and all points of view were encouraged. To be sure, like Eisenhower, Kennedy was in the position of making the final call, but in neither case was there a unilateral decision that everyone else had to simply follow regardless of what they thought. By contrast, Hitler – usually seen as charismatic – often made decisions against the professional advice of his generals, to the country's detriment. Dissent was unwelcome, and even unhealthy for those who spoke up.

A leader, any leader, needs some level of humility in order to be able to accept advice, to make a final decision based on the views of others. That committee of 15 assisted in Kennedy making a call on the Cuban Missile Crisis; he was the leader, but leaders need both help and a willingness to accept it. No one authoritarian leader is so far above everyone else as to be capable of deciding everything.

Leadership and motivation

Any leader needs followers, leading to an obvious question: how should subordinates be motivated to carry out what the leader wants. Any workplace finds this difficult enough, but keeping military personnel going in times of real peril is obviously more difficult, especially on those occasions when their own lives may be at risk. Leaders may persuade their followers or threaten them with consequences if they do not obey. A leader may be authoritarian, a leader may be inclusive, a leader may be aloof. There are no fixed and certain rules, no single menu that always works.

A classic question explored by Machiavelli is whether a leader should aim to be loved or aim to be feared. A leader – a prince – needs to be judicious and balance several things:

> A prince must be cautious in believing and in acting, nor should he be afraid of his own shadow; and he should proceed in such a manner, tempered by prudence and humanity, so that too much trust may not render him imprudent nor so much distrust render him intolerable. From this arises an argument: whether it is better to be loved than to be feared, or the contrary. I reply that one should like to be both one and the other; but since it is difficult to join them together, it is much safer to be feared than to be loved when one of the two must be lacking.[30]

Machiavelli seems to admire the cruelty of Cesare Borgia, advocate treachery, and argue that in the real world leaders need to be half beast, possessing the fox's guile and the lion's brutality – or does he? One story he relates is that of Ramirro de Orco who, following instructions from his duke, Cesare Borgia, pacified the Romagna but did so too severely and was then himself punished by his leader:

> He [the Duke] decided that if he wanted to make it [the province] peaceful and obedient to the ruler's law, it would be necessary to give it good government. Therefore, he put Messer Ramirro de Orco, a cruel and able man, in command there and gave him complete authority. This man, in little time, made the province peaceful and united, and in doing so made for himself a great reputation. Afterward, the Duke decided that such excessive authority was no longer required, for he was afraid that it might become despised . . . And because he realized that the rigorous measures of the past had generated a certain amount of hatred, he wanted to show, in order to purge men's minds and to win them to his side completely, that if any form of cruelty had arisen it did not originate from his but from the harsh nature of his minister. And having come upon the opportunity to do this, one morning at Cesena he had Messer Ramirro placed on the piazza in two pieces with a block of wood and a bloody sword beside him. The ferocity of such a spectacle left those people satisfied and amazed at the same time.[31]

Apparently Ramirro de Orco had gone too far and was adversely affecting the reputation of his leader. 'No one knows the reason for his death,' Machiavelli wrote to his superiors, 'except that it has suited the Prince, who shows he can create and destroy men as he pleases.'[32] It may have been better to be feared, as Cesare was, than loved, but it was important not to be despised or hated:

> The prince should nonetheless make himself feared in such a mode that if he does not acquire love, he escapes hatred, because being feared and not being hated can go together very well. This he will always do if he abstains from the property of his citizens and his subjects, and from their women . . . But above all, he must abstain from the property of others, because men forget the death of a father more quickly than the loss of a patrimony.[33]

A prince who worries only about keeping his power is better for the common good than a prince who seeks to be virtuous. Without ruling out the possibility that a prince may be both loved and feared, Machiavelli argues it is safer to be feared rather than loved if a choice must be made. But leadership that is solely about fear is unlikely to be effective in the longer run.

Burning the boats

An oft-repeated story, albeit with details varying, is the one where a commander takes away any prospect of retreat of his forces by burning the ships or destroying a bridge. The belief is that with their backs to the wall, the soldiers will fight harder and therefore carry the day, or so the theory goes. One such myth is that Julius Caesar burnt his ships during the invasion of Britain. In actuality, on both expeditions to Britain, a number of his ships were damaged by bad weather while at anchor.[34] In any case Caesar's expeditions were really summer raids rather than conquest; that came a hundred years later under the emperor Claudius.

As a motivational tool, burning the boats may or may not be effective. Resentment or mutiny could well follow and in strategic terms the idea is even more problematic. For all the celebrated instances, it is more likely that retreating and surviving in good order is better than making a stand with no possibility of exit.

In October 1776, George Washington destroyed the King's Bridge leading north from Manhattan Island to the mainland, but did so after the remnants of his army had crossed. He could have fought a last-ditch battle with a broken bridge behind him but retreated instead, almost certainly the best strategy in the circumstances. In running away, Washington followed the strategic imperative of keeping his army in existence; he retreated further into New York state, then New Jersey and Pennsylvania for the winter, surviving and eventually prevailing. A last stand at King's Bridge or anywhere else could have led to the loss of his army and the end of the American Revolution.

The conquest of Mexico by Hernan Cortés in 1519 is another story where the mythology is greater than the likelihood. One of the things that Cortés has entered mythology for is disabling his ships before setting off into the interior of Mexico on an expedition that led to conquering the Aztec empire. The story is usually that Cortés burnt his ships after landing on the Mexican coast near Vera Cruz so that the men would not be tempted to return to Cuba and would therefore fight harder. There are two aspects to look at here: first, whether or not – and how – the ships were destroyed, and second, the purpose of the act, which does not seem to be as straight-forward as simply motivating his men.

On the first point, it does appear that the ships were indeed destroyed. In the second of his letters to King Charles V in 1520 Cortés observed 'that he found the means to run the ships on the shore under the pretext that they were no longer fit to sail'.[35] Luecke states that the ships were scuttled.[36] Bernal Diaz, one of the conquistadors, says the ships were destroyed, adding later that they were scuttled. In the most comprehensive account, Thomas writes that Cortés 'proceeded with an action which took even his friends by surprise' in that he 'ordered the masters of none of the twelve ships which were anchored off Villa Rica to sail their ships on to the sands'.[37] Cortés did order his ships to be run ashore – the practical difference between this and scuttling is not large – but not to be burnt, as the myth usually requires. As Thomas notes:

> The action was, as all who observed the thing agree, and as Cortés himself wrote, a grounding, not a burning. The famous usage – 'the burning of boats' – with which the world is proverbially familiar, began to appear in the second half of the sixteenth century.[38]

Burning the boats – on this occasion at least – appears to be without foundation.

The second question is quite why the ships were run ashore. Such an act is usually seen as motivational, to make the soldiers fight harder. Dixit and Nalebuff argue that burning ships goes back at least to William the Conqueror in 1066 'making an unconditional commitment to fight rather than retreat', then add:

> Cortés followed the same strategy in his conquest of Mexico. Upon his arrival in Cempoella, Mexico, he gave orders that led to all but one of his ships being burnt or disabled. Although his soldiers were vastly outnumbered, they had no other choice but to fight and win.[39]

They add that burning the ships advantaged Cortés in two ways: first, his soldiers would be united and would have to no choice but to fight to the end; and second, this act would greatly impress the opposition. Similarly, Luecke argues:

> Cortés ordered that the compasses and gear of the remaining ships be brought ashore; then he had them all scuttled! There would be no turning back for anyone. Cortés understood what Sun-tzu had postulated long before – an army that lacked an escape route would fight 'with the courage of despair.' The outcome for the army would be either victory or death.[40]

Other than the point about burning rather than scuttling, these accounts are similar in pointing to motivation of the troops and making wider claims for such a tactic.

The real story may be more prosaic. Cortés did not want anyone taking a ship and returning to Havana, but this was because his expedition had rather dubious legal grounds. Rather than solely aiming to motivate his people, the scuttling was more likely about safeguarding his ownership of the venture that was under threat under threat from possible prosecution and execution for mutiny.

Cortés had been licensed for his expedition by Diego Velásquez, the governor of Cuba, who was an investor in it along with Cortés. It was a big undertaking with some twenty ships and around six hundred men. Even before departing Cuba, Velásquez attempted to recall him, but Cortés sailed anyway, leaving some legal ambiguity around his position. Some of his men were loyal to the governor of Cuba and tried to get back to Cuba in an ill-starred mutiny just before the destruction of the ships. Rather than trying to fortify valour, it was more to prevent the Cuban governor asserting his rights to the venture. Rather than being an exemplar of a great leader motivating his men, it should be seen as a result of the mutual distrust between Cortés and his men.

An account by Bernal Diaz del Castillo, one of the conquistadors who was there, sets it out clearly. Rather than landing on the beach and destroying the ships immediately, as the myth has it, it is clear from Diaz that Cortés and his men had been in Vera Cruz or nearby for three months before heading off into the hinterland. In the meantime the town of Vera Cruz had been established and a fortress built. There had even been interactions with emissaries from Moctezuma. Diaz discusses the destruction of the ships, saying it came up in discussions with Cortés immediately following an abortive attempt at escape when mutineers had tried to capture a ship and sail it to Cuba:

> And as the conversation went on from one point to another, we who were his friends advised him (though many were of the opposite opinion) not to leave a single ship in port, but to destroy them all immediately, in order to leave no cause of trouble behind. For when we marched inland others of our people might rebel like the last.[41]

Besides, as Diaz adds, the hundred or so sailors 'would be better employed fighting and keeping watch than lying in port', and some turned out to be 'very good soldiers'; after this a party was sent to the harbour to bring ashore 'all anchors, cables, sails, and other things that might be useful, and then destroy the ships'.[42]

Diaz claims 'the ships were destroyed with our full knowledge and not . . . in secret', as others had argued, and that some days later Cortés made a 'honeyed and eloquent' speech that 'as we had no ships in which to return to Cuba . . . we must rely on our own good swords and stout hearts'.[43] In other words, the ships were indeed destroyed and Cortés later made a 'honeyed and eloquent' speech, but it appears that the motivational aspect was an afterthought, a rationalization, with the main motivation Cortés' own self-preservation from Velásquez the governor of Cuba.

There was a real threat to Cortés from Cuba. Other ships had been sent from Cuba by Velásquez, and later a large expedition was sent with orders to arrest and execute Cortés. Both Cortés and Velásquez tried to enlist the support of the Crown in Spain. Cortés bypassed Cuba by sending gold to the king, who subsequently took his side. There were other attempts at mutiny, with further executions of conspirators; the conquistadors could not be regarded as united behind their great leader.

Diaz does not seem to have regarded the destruction of the ships as a particularly big deal. There were some more practical issues. Leaving ships at anchor at Vera Cruz would have required a detachment of guards to watch them, and the ships themselves would have become worthless quickly anyway as the hot sun would open up their seams. Given that shipworms in tropical waters typically meant that ships were worn out in six months or so, there would have been reason to believe that they were indeed already worn out or would be by the time an expedition returned. More important than the ships was the equipment and tools that had been saved and the expertise to build ships. Sailors of that era were adept at cutting down local trees and constructing ships. For the later battle for Tenochtitlan, the Spanish sailors with Cortés constructed several sizeable ships for warfare on the lake.

There is no doubt that Cortés used the destruction of the ships by either scuttling or running aground – or both – as a motivation for his soldiers, but it seems unlikely that was the main motivation. Reynolds argues:

> Cortés did not actually burn his ships, as is popularly believed. Making what really happened more vivid and grandiose, the myth has become lodged in the common heritage of our historical beliefs and linguistic experience. Cortés did not burn his ships, although it is true that he destroyed them.[44]

The motivational aspect of destroying the ships certainly existed but was only incidental. Burning bridges or burning ships may appear vivid and grandiose and apparently glorious, but it is removed from reality. Using such a tactic purely to motivate is not likely to work, or does so only rarely.

Leadership and hubris

Weber argued that charisma exists and could be a form of authority, but also that charismatic authority most often fails. The Greek word 'hubris' is ascribed to a person who behaves in a presumptuous or arrogant manner – originally towards the gods – and this leads to failure and even nemesis. By any measure Julius Caesar was charismatic; clearly too he invited failure by going too far and was assassinated in the Senate, perhaps as a classic example of hubris in action.

Julius Caesar is often seen as an exemplar of will and the relationship of leadership with will. As Grant argues:

> Caesar lived at a faster tempo than the people who had to contend with him, and this gave him an enormous advantage, offering the widest scope to that capacity for the unexpected, unpredictable action which his friends found such an irresistibly attractive feature of his talents . . . In most of what he did . . . clear vision of this kind was Caesar's out-standing characteristic: the product of exceptional brain-power guided by a will of steel.[45]

There was also a certain ruthlessness. As a young man, according to Suetonius, Caesar was kidnapped by pirates on a voyage to Rhodes:

> They kept him prisoner for nearly forty days, to his intense annoyance . . . As soon as the stipulated fifty talents arrived . . . and the pirates duly set him ashore, he raised a fleet and went after them. He had often smilingly sworn, while still in their power, that he would soon capture and crucify them; and this is exactly what he did.[46]

Caesar started his career when still young, as a member of one of the aristocratic families of Rome. But even with that advantage his rapid progress within the Roman system was extraordinary. Even a short summary shows quite remarkable achievements − the wars in Spain and the east, the conquest of Gaul, the first visit to Britain, the builder of the first bridge across the Rhine, the civil war against Pompey, one of the Triumvirate, consul, dictator and much else.

The history of Roman conquest generally involved either surrender or annihilation; by definition, to be conquered meant dead warriors and enslaved women and children, with the pillage of all they owned. It was only during the civil war, when Caesar did not apply this normal standard to fellow Romans, that his clemency was considered remarkable. His harshness towards the Gauls when they refused to accept their conquest would increase over time.

Caesar appears to have been an outstanding soldier and leader of others. According to Suetonius, he was personally brave, a skilled swordsman, with powers of endurance, always led his army 'more often on foot than in the saddle, went bareheaded in sun and rain, and could travel long distances at incredible speed in a gig, taking very little luggage'.[47] Gathering information and intelligence and being very well prepared are understandable enough, but Caesar seems to have gone further in this regard. As Suetonius later argued:

> It is a disputable point which was the more remarkable when he went to war: his caution or his daring. He never exposed his army to ambushes, but made careful reconnaissances; and refrained from crossing over into Britain until he had collected reliable information about the harbours there, the best course to steer, and the navigational risks. On the other hand, when news reached him that his camp in Germany was being besieged, he disguised himself as a Gaul and

picked his way through the enemy outposts to take command on the spot.[48]

The Germans had the larger army and the fighting prowess of the Germanic tribesmen was renowned. But they did not possess the iron discipline of the Roman army. Caesar felt sufficiently confident to meet them in battle.

Caesar was always well informed. On learning that the Germans believed in a prophecy that they should lose the battle if they fought before the new moon, Caesar forced a battle upon them immediately. The Germans were defeated and large numbers of them were slaughtered trying to escape the field of battle. It is notable, particularly in the conquest of Gaul, just how curious Caesar was about his opponents – much of what is now known about the Druids in Britain or the various tribes in Gaul and Germany comes from Caesar's writings.

Throughout Caesar's career, one point is crystal clear. The overall purpose was all about politics in Rome itself. This was a very personal but brutal, systematic and deadly game. He was a political player and the military campaigns and everything else need to be seen as furthering his interests in the governance of Rome and the politics at home.

It was at home too that Caesar ultimately fell, having miscalculated the antipathy of his colleagues arising from his disregard for some of the old traditions. Some thought that being appointed dictator for life was not enough and that Caesar wanted to be king. A month after being appointed dictator Caesar was assassinated. Even if hubris is a Greek word, it applied to Caesar's situation. He appeared to believe that he was better than his contemporaries; a better soldier, a better leader, a better politician. He was most likely correct in his estimation, but even if his assassination was an act carried out by inferiors it still happened.

Caesar was aware of threats against him. He had been warned by the prophet Spurinna against venturing out that fateful day – 'beware the Ides of March', as Shakespeare wrote – but had apparently decided on confrontation with his opponents. Suetonius relates what happened next:

> Despite consistently unfavourable omens, he entered the House, deriding Spurinna as a false prophet. 'The Ides of March have come', he said. 'Yes, they have come,' replied Spurinna, 'but they have not yet gone.' As soon as Caesar took his seat the conspirators crowded around him as if to pay their respects.[49]

What followed was 23 dagger thrusts from a large band of conspirators, and Caesar was soon dead.

Caesar had said that if anything happened to him, Rome would enjoy no peace.[50] So it turned out. If the conspirators were acting against autocracy or anyone setting themselves above others, they most certainly failed as the as the outcome was just that: a series of emperors, starting with Caesar's grand-nephew and heir Octavian, who took the title of Caesar Augustus.

There are many lessons from Caesar in terms of leadership – and personal leadership at that. In many of his actions and his writings he seems frighteningly modern. By any standard he had a profound impact on the world, notably that part deriving from Europe and the Mediterranean. His reform of the calendar lasted some 1,600 years before minor change, with one of the months named after him still. The very name Caesar became synonymous with leader in the words kaiser and tsar. His writings, notably on Gaul, still resonate. He was a great writer, even if rather self-obsessed, although that trait is typical of the charismatic leader. As Stevenson argues:

> From a personal perspective there seem to be qualities to admire and to despise in the evidence relating to Julius Caesar. He was a fine public speaker, a man of influence over both men and women, a driven character, a self-assured man, an outstanding intellectual, and a mightily successful military figure, though perhaps not an outstanding strategist. If some of this is admirable, certainly there are other considerations. He was ultimately responsible for death and mayhem in the Mediterranean world on a huge scale, and his motivation was very largely selfish, propelled by concern for his *dignitas*, or personal standing, in Roman society. Furthermore, while he may have gained power personally, he only increased the insecurity and depression of his world, becoming a figure of repression, and managing to provoke assassination.[51]

Caesar was popular with his troops and with the lower ranks of Roman society, who were horrified that their leaders in the Senate would take it on themselves to assassinate their leader. Caesar was something of a populist, to use a later term, and subverted some customs and institutions in a populist way. As Stevenson argues:

> He was hardly a model leader for present world tensions. His way was a way of violence, death and repression that did nothing to provide

security for the inhabitants of Rome's empire. In fact, it condemned all of them to ongoing civil and foreign war.[52]

Other leaders, including Mussolini and Franco, have been declared 'Caesarists' on the grounds of charismatic authority, military prowess, an appeal to popular authority directly rather than through institutional means, as well as claiming some of the great Caesar's aura. But whether or not Caesar was a Caesarist in this sense is debatable. He was a politician firmly in the Roman tradition and pushed convention as far as possible. He may have wished to be a monarch but probably did not. He was better than everyone else at almost everything. He knew this and so did they. But at the end he went too far and simply miscalculated; leadership descended to hubris.

Psychological advantage

The very reputation of a leader can be a useful asset even without conflict taking place. Alexander's reputation was such that on appearing outside the gates of an adversary he could declare that if the city surrendered everyone would be spared, but if opposed everyone would be slaughtered. In most instances this was a successful approach, gaining capitulation without battle.

A story from The Three Kingdoms and known to generations of Chinese schoolchildren is what has been called 'the open door' or 'the ruse of the empty city', involving the great Zhuge Liang, the strategist for Liu Bei of the Shu kingdom. Pursued by the much larger army of Marshal Sima Yi, Zhuge Liang – also known as 'Sleeping Dragon'[53] and Kongming – accompanied by a small party of soldiers took refuge within the walls of a small town. Surprisingly, he ordered the gates of the town to be opened and was within relaxing, playing his lute amid clouds of incense. Sima Yi saw this, declared it must be a trap and departed with his army. As Minford translates this story, Zhuge's men ask why this has happened:

'The Marshal has always known me for a cautious man,' Zhuge began. 'He knows I never take risks. He was bound to suspect an ambush. That is why he decided to retreat . . . I wasn't gambling. I simply had no other option . . . ' His officers were dumbfounded at their commander's inscrutable genius.[54]

The most important point, though, is in what follows. The original novel adds: 'His explanation made, Kongming clapped his hands and laughed aloud. "But were I Sima Yi, I would not have gone back!" he said.'[55]

In other words, Zhuge Liang is saying that if it been him he would not have been fooled. Zhuge's reputation, moral authority and leadership enhance his situation. Not only is the great strategist showing his superiority in strategy, his opponent implicitly accepts this as well. There is no battle that day, but strategic mastery belongs to the weaker party.

The regard of ordinary soldiers and their belief in their leaders can affect the result of a conflict, other aspects being equal. According to Wellington, Napoleon's presence on the battlefield was 'worth several divisions, not only because of his tactical skills, but because his very presence inspired men to do their utmost'.[56]

Limitations of will

Will by itself will not overcome deficiencies in the other four facets of strategy. If purpose is unclear or if a purpose, while clear enough, is so far out of touch with reality as to be unachievable, the greatest amount of will in the world will not overcome reality and resource capability. An example of this is the Japanese attack on the United States in December 1941 described earlier as a failure of purpose (chapter 2). The overwhelming view in their military and even in the wider society was that superior Japanese will could prevail against any opposition. Japanese leaders appeared to believe that they could overcome anything due to their superior will. This was a belief more firmly held than a mere supposition; it was an unquestioning belief in cultural and racial superiority. But as they found, even very high levels of will and morale can only partially compensate for lower capability.

Prior to the war beginning, there was substantial information in Japan about the military and industrial capability of the United States. The resource gap was understood but was also ignored, and the pursuit of glory through battle became the only option able to be considered by its militarist leaders. As Prange argues, 'the Japanese had something which no amount of training could instil – a consuming belief in their mission and in themselves'.[37] In the event, though, this belief was one of their greatest weaknesses.

Japanese soldiers were renowned for their devotion to their emperor, their fanatical resistance, even to the extent of mass suicides rather than surrender. As Hanson argues:

> Religious fervour, Bushido, hara-kiri, going down with the ship, and the kamikazes lent the Japanese a sense of arrogance in victory – and fanaticism and fatalism in defeat. But such practices often had negative ramifications in the mundane practice of war itself . . . Brilliant admirals are still needed after their ships blow up. Seasoned pilots are more valuable as instructors than as suicide bombers.[58]

Warrior spirit is certainly an asset, but sheer will, sheer belief in righteousness and moral superiority, cannot overcome huge disparity in resources. Japanese fighters were fierce and believed in their cause fanatically, but will or psychological force is limited, notably in machine-age warfare.

Gompert et al. argue that decision-makers are especially prone to blunder into war when:

> information is ignored, filtered, misconstrued, or manipulated to fit predispositions; excessive reliance is placed on intuition and experience; a rigid but wrong strategic concept or vision prevails; contingencies are not considered; enemy will or capabilities are underestimated; operational difficulty or duration is underestimated; dissent and debate are stifled.[59]

Japanese strategy in World War II illustrates many of these points very well. Looking at the first few: information was indeed ignored and manipulated and any dissent from the prevailing view was not tolerated; there was too much reliance on intuition; a rigid but wrong strategy was in place; and contingencies were not adequately considered. But it is the other three where the most egregious errors were made.

It is quite apparent that 'enemy will and capabilities' were underestimated by the Japanese. As Paine notes, 'Like the Germans, the Japanese dismissed the fighting ability and willpower of others', and both countries also 'grossly underestimated US productive capacity' and what this would mean for a longer war.[60] As Wohlstetter argues of the Japanese:

> Most unreal was their assumption that the United States, with ten times the military potential and a reputation for waging war until

unconditional victory, would after a short struggle simply accept the annihilation of a considerable part of its air and naval forces and the whole of its power in the Far East.[61]

It is unbelievable to imagine that the United States would merely accept the new order and make a deal as had happened with the Japanese war with Russia forty years before. This was but one of many blunders leading up to the Pacific War.

There was a belief that the US will would not be able to resist the far superior Japanese will and culture, but this was nothing less than folly of enormous proportions. As Tuchman notes:

> Japan seems never to have considered that the effect of an attack on Pearl Harbor might be not to crush morale but to unite the nation for combat. This curious vacuum of understanding came from what might be called cultural ignorance, a frequent component of folly.[62]

The biggest folly of all was to assume that Japanese fighters could overcome any resistance, any amount of resources ranged against them, merely by using their superior will. In a technological age this was naïve in the extreme. American capabilities were underestimated by the Japanese, especially how quickly the US could rearm, ramp up production of ships and planes, and mobilize its population. If ships or planes are similar in capability, then the side with more of them has a great advantage. The side with better training of sailors, officers and pilots has an advantage too. In all of these facets, the US quickly became superior.

Operational difficulty and duration were also underestimated. While there was some understanding earlier that Japan could not win a long war, there was little thought about how to avoid getting into a protracted conflict. Finally, debate and dissent were indeed stifled, by both a militarist government that stifled any kind of adverse commentary and a cultural unwillingness to go against groupthink and the absence of leadership. Paine refers to 'the bankruptcy of Japanese leadership in virtually every sphere from the late 1930s until the end of the war and the utter dedication with which Japanese citizens carried out a ruinous strategy'.[63] By any measure Japanese soldiers, sailors and pilots demonstrated their will time after time in World War II. But it was all quixotic; using will alone against the machines and production of the US was bound to end in failure, unless the US failed in its own will. It was a colossal blunder to not only assume that

Japanese will could carry all before it but also compound their problem by disparaging the will of their opponents.

Conclusion

Will is indeed important in strategy; important enough to be one of the pantheon of five facets of strategy discussed here. Will, at base, is about people, their motivations and the ways in which they can be persuaded to contribute to a course of action. Leadership can be seen as the manifestation of will. The case studies show that will is a consideration in many instances, but also that there are instances where over-reliance on will or over-reliance on leadership leads to disaster.

There are many kinds of leadership, one of which is that of the charismatic leader. Despite the attention paid to individual leaders of wars, charismatic leadership generally fails. In the wider political system, for much of the twentieth century and into the twenty-first, charismatic leadership has been associated with disorder rather than order.

Another lesson about will is that strong, indomitable will cannot overcome everything, despite what might be imagined. If all else is equal perhaps the greater will can prevail, but if all else is not equal, there is a limit beyond which superior will simply does not work. The Japanese in World War II appeared to believe that their implacable will could overcome any odds, that the righteous path of glory and the emperor could prevail even when they knew that their enemies enjoyed far greater resources. They also greatly underestimated the will of the United States, notably after their ill-considered venture at Pearl Harbor. Although there are countless examples of Japanese bravery, of suicide missions willingly entered into, there was no way these could substitute for US capability made real by an economy and population many times the size of Japan's. It was a grave misjudgment of the respective wills of the participants; a misjudgment that cost millions of lives.

Notes

1   Carl von Clausewitz, *On War*, edited by Anatol Rapoport (Harmondsworth: Penguin, 1968), p. 101.
2   Ibid., pp. 104–5.

3   Donald Rumsfeld, US Secretary of Defense, speech to US troops at Aviano Air Base Italy, 8 February 2003.

4   James M. McPherson, *Battle Cry of Freedom* (New York: Ballantine, 1988), p. 165.

5   John C. Waugh, *Lincoln and McClellan: The Troubled Partnership between a President and His General* (New York: St Martin's Press, 2010), ch. 8.

6   Stephen W. Sears, *George B. McClellan: The Young Napoleon* (New York: Tickner & Fields, 1988), p. 166.

7   James M. McPherson, 'How the North Nearly Lost', *New York Review of Books*, October 12, 1989.

8   Kevin Dougherty, *The Vicksburg Campaign: Strategy, Battles and Key Figures* (Jefferson NC: McFarland, 2015), p. 18.

9   Ulysses S. Grant, *Personal Memoirs of U.S. Grant* (Cambridge, MA: Da Capo Press, 2001), p. 500.

10 Jeffrey J. Kubiak, *War Narratives and the American National Will* (New York: Palgrave Macmillan, 2014), p. 148.

11 Alastair Horne, *To Lose a Battle: France 1940* (London: Penguin, 1990), p. 101.

12 Clausewitz, *On War*, p. 123.

13 Ibid.

14 Marvin Perry, *Western Civilization A Brief History, Volume II, From the 1400s*, 10th edn (Boston: Wadsworth, 2013), p. 461.

15 William L. Shirer, *Rise and Fall of the Third Reich: A History of Nazi Germany* (New York: Simon & Schuster, 1990), p. 997.

16 Doug Thompson and Aron Thompson, *State Control in Fascist Italy: Culture and Conformity, 1925–43* (Manchester: Manchester University Press, 1991), p. 62.

17 *The Economist*, 3 November 2018.

18 Hugh Thomas, *Rivers of Gold; The Rise of the Spanish Empire* (London: Weidenfeld & Nicholson, 2003), p. 421.

19 Thompson and Thompson, *State Control*, p. 62.

20 Ibid., p. 63.

21 H.H. Gerth and C. Wright Mills (eds), *From Max Weber: Essays in Sociology* (London: Routledge, 1970), p. 79.

22 See William Manchester, *American Caesar* (New York: Dell, 1979).

23 Dwight D. Eisenhower, 'What Is Leadership?', *Reader's Digest*, June 1965, pp. 49–54.

24 Carl von Clausewitz, *On War*, edited by Michael Howard and Peter Paret (Princeton: Princeton University Press, 1976), p. 107.

25 Eisenhower, 'What is Leadership?', pp. 49–54.

26 Barbara Tuchman, *The March of Folly: From Troy to Vietnam* (New York: Alfred A. Knopf, 1984).

27 Roger Knight, *Britain against Napoleon: The Organization of Victory 1793–1815* (London: Penguin, 2013), p. 464.

28 Lawrence Freedman, *Strategy: A History* (Oxford: Oxford University Press, 2013), p. 93.

29 Robert F. Kennedy, *Thirteen Days* (New York: W.W. Norton, 1969).

30 Peter Bondanella and Mark Musa (ed. and transl.), *The Portable Machiavelli* (Harmondsworth: Penguin, 1979), p. 131.

31 Ibid., pp. 99–100.

32 Ross King, *Machiavelli: Philosopher of Power* (New York: Harper Perennial, 2009), pp. 52–3.

33 Bondanella and Musa, *The Portable Machiavelli*, p. 132.

34 Caesar, *The Conquest of Gaul* (London: Penguin, 1982).

35 Winston A. Reynolds, 'The Burning Ships of Hernan Cortes', *Hispania*, 42, 3 (September, 1959), p. 318.

36 Richard Luecke, *Scuttle Your Ships Before Advancing* (New York: Oxford University Press, 1994), p. 33.

37 Hugh Thomas, *The Conquest of Mexico* (London: Pimlico, 1994), p. 222.

38 Ibid., p. 223.

39 Avinash Dixit and Barry J. Nalebuff, *Thinking Strategically: The Competitive Edge in Business, Politics and Everyday Life* (New York: W.W. Norton, 1991), p. 153.

40 Luecke, *Scuttle Your Ships*, p. 33.

41 Bernal Diaz, *The Conquest of New Spain*, edited with an introduction by J.M. Cohen (London: Penguin, 1963), p. 130.

42 Ibid., p. 130.

43 Ibid., p. 131.

44 Winston A. Reynolds, 'The Burning Ships of Hernan Cortes', p. 317.

45 Michael Grant, *The Twelve Caesars* (New York: Scribner, 1975), p. 31.

46 Suetonius, *The Twelve Caesars* (London: Penguin, 1979), p. 2.

47 Ibid., p. 29.

48 Ibid., p. 29.

49 Ibid., p. 40.

50 Ibid., p. 43.

51 Tom Stevenson, *Julius Caesar and the Transformation of the Roman Republic* (London: Routledge, 2015), p. 12.

52 Ibid., p. 12.

53 John Minford, 'Introduction' to Sun Tzu, *The Art of War* (New York: Penguin, 2009), pp. xii–xv.

54 Ibid., p. xv.

55 Luo Guonzhong, *The Three Kingdoms*, vol. 4 (Beijing: Foreign Languages Press), pp. 1738–9.

56 Gunther E. Rothenberg, *The Art of Warfare in the Age of Napoleon* (Bloomington: Indiana University Press, 1980), p. 136.

57 Gordon W. Prange (with Donald M. Goldstein and Katherine V. Dillon), *Pearl Harbor: The Verdict of History* (Harmondsworth: Penguin, 1986), p. 482.

58 Victor Davis Hanson, *Carnage and Culture* (New York: Anchor Books, 2001), p. 367.

59 David C. Gompert, Hans Binnendijk and Bonny Lin, *Blinders, Blunders, and Wars: What America and China Can Learn* (Santa Monica, CA: Rand Corp, 2014).

60 S.C.M. Paine, *The Wars for Asia, 1911–1949* (Cambridge: Cambridge University Press, 2012), p. 191.

61 Roberta Wohlstetter, *Pearl Harbor: Warning and Decision* (Stanford: Stanford University Press, 1962), p. 355.

62 Barbara W. Tuchman, *The March of Folly: From Troy to Vietnam* (London: Abacus, 1985), p. 37.

63 Paine, *The Wars for Asia*, p. 184.

5

TERRAIN

Introduction

The fourth facet of strategy is terrain, used here as an overarching term for strategic constraints and opportunities that are imposed by physical or natural settings broadly defined. The limitations imposed by terrain may be more salient in some circumstances than others, but there will always be some limits imposed from the outside. Business strategy often uses 'the environment' to account for external factors, but this term is too broad and, in the end, too nebulous. The environment includes any factor outside the strategy, whether it is natural or constructed, directly relevant or only indirectly relevant. Terrain is argued to be a better term for present purposes. The terrain is about the arena, the sphere of influence, the prevailing conditions affecting a contest but without being a direct party to it.

In virtually all strategic situations there will be physical or geographical features – mountains, rivers, weather, seasons, night and day – or other external features that affect the contest but cannot be directly influenced by human action. They can be used by parties involved to their advantage but if neglected can result in disadvantage. Terrain can be considered as those fixed environmental assets and liabilities in a physical or natural sense and not necessarily confined to earth, but including air, space, sea and land. Even the weather is an external influence that can be used to advantage or be a disadvantage to be overcome.

It is easy to find instances where terrain was not only important but crucial in a conflict. Napoleon's march on Russia in 1812 and the German attack on the Soviet Union in 1941 were profoundly, and similarly, affected by weather leading to muddy roads and then to the snows of winter. Britain's geography was favourable to its development as a maritime power; Germany and Russia were constrained by theirs in the same sphere of terrain. Terrain is not usually a determinant of outcome by itself – rather, it is an external factor that can be used strategically or a recognized constraint that needs to be taken into consideration.

Terrain has many aspects affecting strategy and tactics. The physical constraints of geography can mean costs but also benefits if used well. The weather cannot be controlled but can be utilised. A river or lake can be a barrier, but it also can be an asset in providing a highway for transport. A forest can be considered impassable, but it also can provide an opportunity if the perception of impassability allows an attacker to find a way through the forest catching the other side unawares, as occurred in the Ardennes in the German invasion of France in May 1940.

However, terrain only rarely provides an impediment that is final. It is more often the case that terrain provides a challenge that could be overcome by greater capability. For example, the Lines of Torres Vedras in Portugal constructed by Wellington in the Peninsular War were not impassable in the abstract but *practically* impassable given the strength of the French army facing it and their lack of heavy siege equipment. A much greater force could have forced its way through.

One relatively minor point of demarcation here is that fortifications are seen as part of terrain. They could be considered matters of capability in that they are assets available for use by armed forces and constructed and paid for by government. Terrain and capability are related; however, it is argued here that fortifications should be considered as a matter of terrain in that they are often forms of enhanced terrain or alterations to a terrain. It is not coincidental that fortresses are often sited at or near the top of a hill or on a defensible part of a river. There are instances where it becomes difficult to separate a fortress from its terrain – for example, the Lines of Torres Vedras were not exactly a set of fortresses. Rather, the British and Portuguese constructed strongpoints to enhance the already difficult terrain to advantage. The sea should also be seen as a terrain – and as a venue for conflict between nations, an important one.

The meaning of terrain

Terrain is defined as 'a stretch of land, especially with regard to its physical features' (*New Shorter Oxford Dictionary*). Its usage dates from the early eighteenth century: its derivation is from French, from a popular Latin variant of *terrenumin* and *terra* meaning earth. It is argued here that despite this derivation terrain may be used more widely and even encompass the sea. The point is natural features that are outside the immediate control of a party or parties. Other terms that are sometimes used, such as 'battle space' and 'human terrain system', also convey a wider sense of terrain.

Terrain has always been a concern of military leaders. Alexander used rivers to advantage; Caesar studied the terrain more than was usual at the time, and Napoleon and Wellington were masters of terrain in their own ways, although they did not face each other directly until near the end of the two-decade war between Britain and France.

Seeking the high ground is a time-honoured response to situations of peril. For literally millennia, defenders used higher parts of the terrain. Advantages of higher ground for defence include: being able to see further for an approaching enemy; the superior range offered to any ballistic weapon; and the mechanical advantage of gravity, including that an attacker trying to move uphill has to move more slowly and will be more fatigued. A disadvantage is that supplies need to be carried up, too, but for many situations the advantages outweigh this. As the Roman writer Vegetius notes:

> When you are about to join battle you first seek help from the place; it is generally held to be more useful, the higher the ground occupied. For weapons fall with greater velocity from above on those standing below, and soldiers on higher ground force back with greater impetus those opposing them. But the soldier who struggles up a slope has a twofold contest, with the ground and the enemy.[1]

In addition, the terrain can be modified. By digging, natural advantages can be enhanced; an essential part of the equipment carried by Roman soldiers was a short but effective shovel. Walls, redoubts, fortresses, castles are all modifications of terrain, often, but not always, built to take advantage of the natural conformation of the land.

A leader must take account of the terrain in making plans. As Sun-tzu notes, 'One who does not know the topography of mountains and forests, ravines and defiles, wetlands and marshes cannot manoeuver the army, one who does not employ local guides will not secure advantages of terrain.'[2] In another passage he argues:

> When in difficult country, do not encamp. In country where high roads intersect, join hands with your allies. Do not linger in danger-ously isolated positions. In hemmed-in situations, you must resort to stratagem. In desperate position, you must fight.

Sun-tzu refers to nine terrains: 'dispersible terrain, light terrain, conten-tious terrain, traversable terrain, focal terrain, heavy terrain, entrapping terrain, encircled terrain and fatal terrain'.[3]

A recent US Army field manual is remarkably similar to Sun-tzu's but with more detail. It refers to:

> dominant terrain; broken terrain; open, rolling terrain; obstacles, ave-nues of approach, observation and fields of fire, cover and conceal-ment, obstacles, minefields/wire, roadblocks, antitank ditches, deep rivers or streams, urban areas, swamps, cover and concealment, cover protects you from enemy fire, bunkers, fighting positions, concealment that protects you from enemy observation, dense vegetation, man-made camouflage.[4]

In the attack, the correct use of terrain 'increases fire effect and diminishes losses', while in defence:

> the nature of the terrain is a major factor influencing the commander when deciding upon position defense or a mobile defense. When the terrain restricts the ability of an attacking enemy to maneuver and pro-vides natural lines of resistance, a position defense may be desirable and

of course, terrain that facilitates maneuver by defending forces will favor a mobile type of defense. In selecting the key areas for defense, the commander depends largely upon a terrain study.[5]

The constraints of terrain mostly affect tactics, although due consideration of the terrain involved in any venture should be a fundamental part of overall strategy. Different aspects may be emphasized at different times. Planning for a campaign must consider natural obstacles such as mountains, rivers, forests or swamps. Some can be overcome by deploying superior resources, but any obstacle needs to be taken into consideration in the planning process.

For some cases, terrain will be about logistics and getting material where it is needed at the right time and place given natural constraints. A clear demarcation between terrain and capability is sometimes difficult, although this merely reinforces the general point that the five facets of the PCWTT model are interdependent. As an instance, transport and other infrastructure – railroads, roads, communication links, waterways – may be about capability combined with terrain, rather than exclusively one or the other.

There are other terrains that may influence strategy. If the definition is to be parts of the natural world that can affect a conflict, the environments of the air and space can be added. The air has been a contested domain at least since World War I and space since the first satellite Sputnik was launched by the Soviet Union in 1957. In December 2019, the United States Space Force was created as a new branch of the military; its missions include 'Space Superiority and Space Domain Awareness (military, civil, and commercial)'.[6] The domain of space is another terrain.

In addition, the term 'battlespace' has gained some currency. This includes such matters as terrain and weather, but also other factors in the environment of an operational area, friendly and adversary forces and even intelligence and cyber capability.[7] This is yet another way of conceptualizing wider matters of terrain, although it does include matters of capability as used here.

Weather, climate and time

The weather, climate and time are classic instances of external factors that can be used but are beyond direct control. Taking advantage of these can be a choice in some instances – attacking at sunrise or in a snowstorm – but the conditions cannot be altered by human agency. Washington's army was able to escape from Brooklyn into Manhattan in 1776 with the assistance of heavy fog over the East River. Mist and approaching darkness affected the Battle of Jutland in 1916, making it difficult for the British to achieve an overwhelming victory free of risk. And in the ensuing darkness the German fleet was able to escape and return to harbour.

For several hundred years, sailing ships were reliant on the weather as without wind their ships could not move. And wind in the wrong direction posed problems in battles of single ships against each other or even entire fleet conflicts. Although ships could to some extent sail in the direction the wind was coming from, they could not sail directly into it and had to tack one way and then the other. A ship upwind of an adversary possessed the 'weather gage' and could choose whether to engage or not. Storms were an occupational hazard, with many ships lost that way – for instance, immediately after the Battle of Trafalgar in 1805.

The Japanese surprise attack on Pearl Harbor in December 1941 came early on a Sunday morning – a normal day of rest for a peacetime US navy. And the Japanese force had sailed across the little-travelled northern Pacific deliberately using its notoriously bad weather to advantage to avoid detection. Even worse weather further north in the Aleutians greatly affected the conflict between Japanese and American forces from June 1942 to August 1943. Both sides fought the appalling weather as much as they fought each other.

A classic stratagem involving weather is outlined in *The Three Kingdoms*. Zhuge Liang – the strategist for the Shu kingdom – was tasked with the seemingly impossible task of sourcing 100,000 arrows for the impending naval battle on the Yangtze River against the forces of Cao Cao from the Wei kingdom. He promised it would be done in three days. At night on the third day, under cover of a thick fog, Zhuge Liang sent 20 ships with skeleton crews covered only in hay bales towards the anchored enemy fleet, making a noise and beating drums. The opposing fleet did not dare sail out into the fog but shot arrows into Zhuge Liang's ships as they sailed past. Upon returning to their base the arrows were collected from the hay bales, and with five or six thousand arrows collected by each ship the task was completed. Upon being asked how he knew there would be a fog, Zhuge Liang replied:

> One cannot be a leader without knowing the workings of heaven and the ways of earth. One must understand the secret gates and the

interdependence of the elements, the mysteries of tactics and the value of forces. It is but an ordinary talent. I calculated three days ago that there would be a fog today, and so I set the limit at three days.

Zhuge Liang's observation of the weather thus assisted in preparation for battle against great odds. Even if it was only a small victory, and probably apocryphal, it does show that a commander's knowledge of weather can be of tactical and strategic benefit. He not only predicted the weather three days out but also foresaw that the response of the Wu fleet commander would be to tether his ships together to ride out the storm and an unwillingness to engage.

Weather and climate are distinguished from each other by time period, with weather observations over a shorter time and climate more about longer-term averages. European wars tended to start in spring, persist through summer and then wind down in autumn, with the contenders then mutually retreating to winter quarters. But if strategy is to be about winning or losing then the old leisurely ways needed to be discarded.

The terrain of New York harbour greatly assisted Britain as it was the overwhelming maritime power and contributed to the American debacle discussed earlier (chapter 2). After this, though, George Washington, the American commander, decided he would have to follow a broad strategy of maintaining the army as a force in being rather than getting into battles where the army and the war itself could be lost. And in this enterprise, Washington was able to utilize the terrain of the countryside and wilderness to avoid risk. But staying away from risk was always predicated on striking back if an opportunity presented itself. And opportunities to counter-attack did present themselves in the winter.

On Christmas Day 1776, Washington crossed the Delaware River into New Jersey and attacked Trenton early next morning in 'a fierce storm that mixed hail, rain, and snow',[8] catching its Hessian mercenary defenders off guard. Washington's men suffered no dead and only three wounded and took more than nine hundred prisoners in what was 'Washington's first significant battlefield victory of the war'.[9] This attack used weather, climate and time to advantage. The weather was dreadful, with ice floes on the Delaware River, and so cold that two American soldiers froze to death. By late December, the climate in that part of North America should have meant that the participants would be in winter quarters for several months, snowed in as would have been normal in Europe.

Indeed, the British commander General William Howe had decided almost two weeks earlier, on 13 December, that the army would retire to winter quarters as the weather had turned much colder. Howe had settled himself into comfortable quarters in New York for the winter with some of his troops in smaller towns nearby. As McCullough argues:

> It was commonly understood that eighteenth-century professional armies and their gentlemen commanders did not subject themselves to the miseries of winter campaigns, unless there were overriding reasons to the contrary. Considering all he had achieved in the year's campaign and knowing the helpless state of the rebel army, Howe saw no cause to continue the fight or to remain a day longer than necessary in a punishing American winter in a place like Trenton.[10]

The date and the time were significant, with the attack at Trenton taking place early in the morning on the day after Christmas. Hessian troops were likely still celebrating Christmas, little guessing that Washington would use the bad weather to attack. This was a small battle, but one that had strategic consequences as it helped the French decide to become involved in the war.

The Allied landings in Normandy in World War II were greatly assisted by not only fair weather but also better weather forecasting. In early June 1944, better weather forecasts assisted the Allied landings in Normandy on D-Day 1944 and disadvantaged the German preparation to oppose them:

> Allied weather stations were reporting a ridge of high pressure that would reach the beaches of Normandy on June 6th. The weather wouldn't be ideal, but it would be good enough to proceed. Eisenhower gave the order to reschedule the invasion. The German meteorologists had also foreseen the storms, but they'd missed the significance of the brief glimpse of calm. They were so confident that an Allied attack was impossible that Field Marshal Erwin Rommel, the commander of the Normandy defences, decided to take a few days' leave for his wife's birthday. He'd even bought her a new pair of shoes in Paris for the occasion. Years later, when Eisenhower was asked why D Day had been a success, he reportedly said, "Because we had better meteorologists than the Germans."
>
> (*The New Yorker*, 24 June 2019)

Of course, the Allied planners did not know until much later that German meteorologists had miscalculated. The latter were operating under a relative handicap in any case, as Allied meteorologists had access to far better data from further into the Atlantic where the weather came from. The landings would still have occurred sometime, but perhaps with higher Allied casualties if the invasion force had waited. Bad weather cannot be created at will, nor can good. But a good commander can take account of the weather and use it to advantage.

Conformation of the land

The Revolutionary War provides some more general lessons in the use of terrain and the constraints and opportunities imposed by geography. The British colonies were still huddled on the east coast of the North American continent, reliant on the sea for trade and commerce. The British navy was then the world's pre-eminent maritime power overwhelming the Americans in that sphere. But this was not enough. Even the mighty British navy could not impose a full blockade on hundreds of ports over some three thousand miles of Atlantic coastline.[11]

Key ports could be targeted, such as Boston in the early stages, but the topography of the Boston area was not a conducive terrain for the British. They had limited use of the surrounding countryside and were essentially besieged. In what became known as the Battle of Bunker Hill in June 1775, British soldiers advanced uphill and against fortifications, and while they won on the day, their casualties were much higher than those of the defenders, who were able to retreat. In March 1776, George Washington deployed artillery on the top of Dorchester Heights, another hill overlooking Boston Harbour. The presence of Washington's artillery with its hastily constructed fortifications on the top of the hill drove the British to leave Boston altogether and fall back on Halifax rather than incur the casualties that would be required to take the position. This use of the terrain by Washington was highly effective.

The British were expected to return from Halifax and did so in greater numbers. As the British commanded the sea they could choose to land anywhere on the coast. The expectation was that they would aim for New York, and so it turned out. However, New York was uniquely vulnerable to naval attack, as Fischer argues:

> In the late eighteenth century, New York was open and largely unfortified, like most towns in the British colonies. Its prosperity

grew from the free flow of commerce and its location provided easy access by water from every side: the Hudson River from the north and west, Long Island Sound from the east, the Atlantic Ocean from the south. For many years the seaport towns of British America had not needed fortifications, because they were secure behind the wooden walls of the Royal Navy. Now their old protector had become the enemy and every approach to New York was an avenue for a seaborne invader.[12]

Defending New York from the British proved beyond the capability of Washington's army and, following a set of lost battles on Long Island and on Manhattan, the remnants of Washington's army fled further into northern New York state and subsequently into New Jersey and Pennsylvania for the winter.

As noted earlier (chapter 2), Washington then made a remarkable but understandable decision. He would remain a force in being and keep retreating instead of making a stand at a set-piece battle where a loss would mean the end of the army and the end of the war.

Once Washington had decided on this Fabian campaign of retreating to Pennsylvania and New Jersey, avoiding battle unless an opportunity presented itself, the terrain of the United States became significant. Washington could always if necessary go further inland, even into the wilderness. The British had nowhere near enough soldiers to retain the territory they held, let alone follow Washington further into the interior and set up garrisons along the way. Even though the Royal Navy controlled the seas and key ports, it could not use its superiority in that terrain to impose its will on the land or on Washington's army. As shown by the attack on Trenton and later Princeton, Washington did not settle for total retreat but would keep running and look for occasions where a blow could be struck at little risk to his own forces.

As would be seen later in the Revolutionary and Napoleonic wars there is a limit to what a maritime power can do to defeat a land-based power. Despite the British retaining overwhelming maritime power on the American coasts there was little they could do about the ability of Washington's army to retreat into the hinterland. The British could only win if the Americans allowed their army to be totally defeated, but the terrain and Washington's masterful use of it, as well as support from much of the civilian population, meant this was most unlikely to happen.

Enhancing the terrain

Another example of the enhancement of terrain is that of Wellington in Portugal during the Napoleonic Wars. Rightly celebrated as a great British general, Arthur Wellesley – later, 1st Duke of Wellington – showed himself to be a true master of terrain.

The long period of conflict with Britain since the French Revolution had by 1808 settled into a contest of land versus sea, with neither able to defeat the other. British victories at sea, including the definitive Battle of Trafalgar in 1805, may have been heartening but did little to defeat Napoleon on land. A succession of coalitions against Napoleon – using British subsidy – rose and fell, but without great effect. The two kinds of terrain had little contact.

To defeat Napoleon would require British soldiers on the ground in Europe working with allies. Many in Spain and Portugal chafed against French rule, and the placing of Napoleon's brother Joseph on the Spanish throne did not go well with the ordinary populace. Despite a series of French victories on the Iberian Peninsula, a British army could conceivably work with the Spanish and Portuguese to push Napoleon out of the Peninsular.

An expeditionary force under Sir John Moore sent to assist the Spanish was forced to retreat in some disarray to its ships and return to Britain after the Battle of Corunna in January 1809. Three months later a new expedition was sent to Lisbon under the command of Arthur Wellesley – not yet Duke of Wellington – with 30,000 soldiers. But with the French forces in the Iberian Peninsula totalling more than 200,000 soldiers, Wellington was always going to be at a numerical disadvantage and would have to work with Spain and with Portugal, Britain's traditional ally on the Continent. The Peninsular campaign is complicated and does not need much elaboration here; the significant point for now is Wellington's masterly use of terrain for strategic purposes.

Presumably to avoid the same fate as Sir John Moore's forces, Wellington established Lisbon as a base that could be defended even if pushed back by the French in Portugal or Spain. With British naval protection of the Tagus River to the east of Lisbon and of the sea to the south and west the Portuguese capital could only be captured by an army arriving from the north. The terrain north of Lisbon is difficult country for an army to pass through anyway, so, by careful survey and construction of well-sited earthworks, the natural advantage for the defenders was enhanced.

Together with his Portuguese allies, Wellington and his engineer Colonel Richard Fletcher built the Lines of Torres Vedras in the hills north of Lisbon. They were built, in secret, over the course of only one year. This did not mean building a fifty-kilometre wall from the Tagus River to the sea. It meant, rather, supplementing already difficult terrain with well-placed forts and strongpoints that were designed and built to be virtually impregnable, or at least to require a very large force willing to accept many casualties.

After winning the Battle of Buçaco on 27 September 1810 Wellington withdrew in good order south towards Lisbon, taking up the positions already prepared at Torres Vedras. Having apparently beaten Wellington and believing that the path to Lisbon was open to them, the French, under Marshal Masséna, were confident they had won. With their numerical superiority they thought there was no impediment to them driving the British out of the Peninsular altogether and enjoying the booty of Lisbon. But Masséna had not taken the Lines of Torres Vedras into account; he did not even know of their existence.

After trying at the Battle of Sobral to force his army through the Lines, Masséna decided it could not be done without reinforcements of men and heavy guns. These were not forthcoming. The supply lines into France were long and difficult and subject to attack from Spanish and Portuguese partisans. Supply columns were attacked, isolated soldiers and encampments were effectively under siege from the population, especially outside the cities and towns. It is significant that the term 'guerrilla' – 'little war' in Spanish – was first used during this conflict. Large numbers of French troops were required to protect French assets, reducing the effective numbers available for regular army work.

Camped in front of the Lines of Torres Vedras, Masséna faced another reality in the use of terrain; the countryside had been deliberately denuded of provisions that the French could use. The inhabitants had been brought behind the lines into Lisbon with their provisions. Anything that could not be carried was destroyed to prevent its usage by a French army accustomed to living off the land. Using a scorched-earth policy in the countryside was controversial and did cause civilian casualties, but it was done with the full cooperation of the Portuguese authorities. Facing the possibility of starvation Masséna withdrew, as Roberts notes:

> By January 1811 . . . Masséna's army at Santarém outside the Lines was starving, deserting and marauding. Masséna stayed until the retreat could not be put off any longer, and on the night of March 5, erecting scarecrows stuffed with straw to resemble sentries, he left Santarém.[13]

The fortress that Lisbon had become required considerable resources to maintain the army personnel and the civilian population that had left the countryside. But as the Royal Navy was in complete control of that terrain Lisbon could be supplied by sea. Wellington understood that British command of the sea gave him an enormous advantage, saying, 'If anyone wishes to know the history of this war, I will tell them that it is our maritime superiority gives me the power of maintaining my army while the enemy are unable to do so'.[14] As Knight notes, over the six years from 1808 there were 'nearly 13,500 individual ship voyages from England' to the Peninsular carrying supplies to support the campaign.[15]

By retreating behind the Lines of Torres Vedras – conceding territory stripped of resources – Wellington showed his command of strategy. He was in a position where he could not lose other than through Napoleon sending substantial French reinforcements, but given demands from other theatres these were highly unlikely to arrive. So long as the government in London kept the supplies coming, the Peninsular campaign could keep going and would eventually prevail. If forced back by a larger French army, Wellington could always fall back to the prepared positions at Torres Vedras. And with secure supply lines from Lisbon, Wellington could start pushing the French out of Portugal and Spain, even into France.

Wellington is celebrated as a great general and a great tactician, in the Peninsular War, into France, then at Waterloo. But he also deserves plaudits for appreciating the totality of his situation in the Peninsular; his grasp of the overall strategy. So long as the army kept itself in being and was not risked recklessly; so long as Wellington maintained political support in Lisbon and London; so long as the British navy kept command of the sea, it was hard to see how Wellington could be defeated. Even though he was outnumbered in the Peninsular War, often greatly outnumbered, the resources ranged against his forces and those of his allies needed to be much greater to make a difference. Wellington had the foresight to establish Lisbon as a virtually impregnable fortress, protected by the Lines of Torres Vedras, just in case it might be needed. To add to this, the engineering skill in building the Lines, along with managing to build them in secret and quickly, meant there was a bolt hole to which he could make a tactical retreat. In turn, the Peninsular campaign contributed in part to the downfall of Napoleon.

There are several aspects of terrain in this case: first, using the geography itself as a natural fortification; second, enhancing this terrain with well-placed redoubts; third, removing any food and other resources from the countryside; and fourth, using the sea and British command of it for supplies and to prevent the Tagus being used as an alternate route to Lisbon. Wellington used terrain to advantage. There was no great battle of Torres Vedras. Wellington's strategy did not require that in order to eventually win. Wellington operated in the Peninsula with a marked disadvantage in numbers of soldiers but used his assets in concert with advantageous terrain to such skilful extent that he eventually prevailed.

Walls and fortresses

Terrain could be regarded as being fixed, involving permanent features in the natural environment that are beyond human agency. And moving beyond the strictly natural through digging or constructing an artificial terrain could be seen as creating capability and not about terrain at all. Walls or fortresses could be regarded as fixed assets, as capability, but are better seen here as aspects of terrain. Terrain can be created. There is little conceptual difference between a soldier using the protection of a rise in the land, a hilltop or a ravine and digging into the ground or gathering rocks together to construct protection.

Walls, or their fortress variants, have several possible uses: they can keep intruders out; they can buy time; they can be used to keep the disaffected inside. A wall may mark a border between nations or nation-states, the boundaries of a city, an ideological line between religious or ethnic groups. Walls to keep people out include Hadrian's Wall across northern England, the Israeli border wall, the US border with Mexico, some of which is walled and all is patrolled. Walls to keep people in include the Berlin Wall between West Berlin and East Berlin from 1961 to 1989 and also between the then East Germany and its neighbours.

The Great Wall of China – in reality a set of several walls – is most often seen as being built to guard against outsiders, safeguarding the fertile farming areas of central and southern China. However, Lovell argues that the northern walls are remote from farmable land, adding,

> the position of these walls gives the sense that they were designed not to defend China but to occupy foreign territory, to drive the nomadic inhabitants out of their land and to facilitate the setting up of military posts that would police the movement of people across these areas.[16]

The Great Wall is thus seen as an extension of imperial power rather than purely defensive. Seen in this light, the Great Wall can be seen as a way of extending territory, as well as pointing to the wealth and majesty of the empire.

Defensive fortifications provide sanctuary and a safe place. A fortress provides shelter from the elements in relative comfort as well as protection from conflict and stores to feed those inside. Any besieging force must contend with weather and with maintaining supplies. Little wonder then that Sun-tzu would argue:

> The worst policy of all is to besiege walled cities. The rule is, not to besiege walled cities if it can possibly be avoided. The preparation of mantlets, movable shelters, and various implements of war, will take up three whole months; and the piling up of mounds over against the walls will take three months more. The general, unable to control his irritation, will launch his men to the assault like swarming ants, with the result that one-third of his men are slain, while the town still remains untaken. Such are the disastrous effects of a siege. Therefore, the skilful leader subdues the enemy's troops without any fighting; he captures their cities without laying siege to them.

But there are also disadvantages to having walls and fortresses and advantages for an outside force. A fortress is in a fixed location and an attacker can move to it. Defenders have to monitor the entire length of a wall, while an attacker can concentrate on a section or a weak point. Medieval fortresses included ramparts and passageways so that the defenders could hurry to a point under attack while remaining under shelter. But once a wall was breached, the advantage passed to the attacker.

The walled city or the medieval castle can be seen as a valid response to the technology of bows and arrows or of projectiles thrown by catapult. As early as Machiavelli's time the invading French army was able to batter down medieval-style fortresses with their vertical walls without too much difficulty. Firing cannonballs at the base of a fortress wall would eventually cause it to collapse on itself, creating a breach.

New fortress designs in response to cannon incorporated sloping walls so that cannonballs would bounce off and provided for protection of the wall by making the approach more difficult. One new design, much lower and flatter, was of 'a polygon, usually regular, with bastions projecting from each angle, in such a manner as to subject the attacker to an effective crossfire'. There were three main divisions: 'a thick low rampart, with parapet; a broad ditch; and an outer rampart, the glacis, which sloped gently down to the level of the surrounding countryside'.[17] But even these could be overcome. Indeed, any fortress could be taken eventually given enough time and adequate equipment and soldiers. At times a siege could be broken by another army, or by a besieging force giving up and leaving. But there are instances, too, of the best-designed, manned and stocked fortress being taken. Any wall is permeable, even the Great Wall, and any fortress can be reduced to ruin.

In the American Civil War it became a rule of thumb that 'attacking forces must have a numerical superiority of at least three to one to succeed in carrying trenches defended by alert troops'.[18] Sending troops against fortifications was very wasteful of lives, as McPherson argues: 'The tactical predominance of the defense helps explain why the Civil War was so long and bloody. The rifle and trench ruled Civil War battlefields as thoroughly as the machine-gun and trench ruled those of World War I.'[19]

The use of rifles in the US Civil War meant much greater accuracy than the older muskets had permitted and also assisted the defence when dug into the terrain. However, World War I generals did not take sufficient heed of what had been learned fifty years earlier in America and persisted with bayonet charges against dug-in soldiers equipped with machine guns.

The French fortress builder Vauban, largely responsible for the building of a line of forts on France's eastern border in the latter part of the seventeenth century, did not totally rely on forts. Toward the close of his career, the great engineer came to lay more emphasis on armies and less on fortification, stating that 'the true defence of a country is its army, not its fortifications'.[20]

A fortress mentality

A fortress or a wall does provide for protection or even safety but can conceivably become a trap for its defenders, leading to static and defensive thinking. A fortress may create a fortress mentality, a psychological state where being fixed in one place leads to a preference for stasis rather than movement.

Wellington's army at Torres Vedras was not stuck behind the lines. It was quite mobile, with half of his army manning the various fortresses and the other half able to move along a prepared road to anywhere that needed reinforcement or to leave the lines and attack if an opportunity presented itself. The fortress was not as a static instrument, it was being used as a part of a wider strategy.

Vauban too never thought that fortresses were solely for defence; he was careful to stress their importance as a base for offensive operations against the enemy. A fortified frontier should be close to the enemy at all the points of entry into the kingdom and at the same time facilitate an attack upon the enemy. A string of forts was built around France's borders, concentrated on the north and east. Fortified places should be situated to command the means of communication within one's own territory and to provide access to enemy soil by controlling important roads or bridgeheads. They should be large enough to hold not only the supplies necessary for their defence but also the stores required to support and sustain an offensive based upon them.

The best-known recent instance of walls or fortresses as the basis for national strategy is that of the Maginot Line, built in the 1930s along France's eastern border with Germany and from Switzerland north to Belgium. Rather than being something completely new, this line was an enhancement of policy; border towns such as Strasbourg, Metz and Nancy had some centuries of experience of forts, including some designed by Vauban.

The Maginot Line was unfinished at the outbreak of World War II. Continuing towards the coast would have meant building above a high water table and, besides, under the mutual defence treaty with Belgium, that country would become the forward defence for France. But in 1936 the Belgian government cancelled the treaty and declared its neutrality. The French army could not base itself in Belgium, but its plan was to advance into Belgium north of the Maginot Line if attacked by Germany.

On 10 May 1940 the Germans moved into Belgium and the Netherlands in a Blitzkreig attack without warning. Assuming this was the main attack, French and British forces duly advanced into Belgium. But within a few days the main German force advanced rapidly through the Ardennes forest – previously thought impassable – and crossed into France near Sedan, just past the northern end of the Maginot Line and through the rear of the Allied armies that had advanced into Belgium. German forces then advanced rapidly towards the English Channel, cutting off the French and British armies that had advanced into Belgium. By the beginning of June, British and some French forces withdrew to Dunkirk and were taken back to Britain by a flotilla of ships and small boats. By 14 June Paris had fallen, and a week later an armistice was signed with Germany.

The suddenness of the German victory and the capitulation of France led to the questioning of French strategy, in particular its reliance on the Maginot Line. There are three key aspects: first, the ineffectiveness of the Line itself as a barrier; second, that the existence of the Line as a key part of French strategy unduly restricted its army's freedom to manoeuvre; and third, that the Maginot Line engendered a fortress mentality in France, a psychological condition causing low morale and indecision.

On the first point, it must be said that the Maginot Line was hardly directly tested as the initial attacks by the German army simply bypassed it, as can occur with any wall. Where there was actual contact with German forces the Maginot Line and its soldiers held up well. Whether or not the expenditure in construction was justifiable compared to investment in better aircraft or tanks and other mobile forces is a valid question but really only one for hindsight.

The second point on constraining action elsewhere does have some validity. The idea of the Line was to free up French forces to manoeuvre in the space from its end into Belgium. Jackson argues that 'The Maginot Line had never been conceived as a sort of Great Wall of China sealing France off from the outside world', adding: 'Its purpose was to free manpower for offensive operations elsewhere – especially important given France's demographic inferiority to Germany – and to protect the forces of manoeuvre'.[21] The German line facing the Maginot Line was only lightly defended as it was assumed, and correctly, that the French would not leave their fortresses. Even if the German forces in that region were inferior in number, this did not matter greatly unless there was some chance that the French would sally forth from their defensive line. One problem of a fortress is that everyone knows where it is; an army of manoeuvre has freedom to move.

The third and more controversial point is whether basing strategy around the Maginot Line led to a 'fortress mentality', some kind of moral and morale failing for the nation that would derive from relying on such a static strategy. The British general Alan Brooke, on visiting in December 1939, wrote in his diary that 'the Line reminded me of a battleship built on land, a masterpiece in its way . . . And yet! It gives me but little feeling of security.'[22] And on another visit two months later, General Brooke noted,

> the most dangerous aspect is the psychological one; a sense of false security is engendered, a feeling of sitting behind an impregnable iron fence; and should the fence perchance be broken; the French fighting spirit might well be brought crumbling with it.[23]

He bemoaned the 'millions of money stuck in the ground for a purely static defence'.[24] Taking his two diary entries together, General Brooke appreciated the impressive engineering achievement, but worried about how the Maginot Line might be used and the effects on those relying on it.

Economic circumstances reduced the spending on more mobile armies that had been planned and demographic trends led to the belief that France could not keep up with Germany in military numbers. Even if the intention had been to use the Maginot Line as a supplement to mobile armies, perhaps it became the main strategy rather than its adjunct. As Horne argues:

> Rapidly the Maginot Line came to be not just a component of strategy, but a way of life. Feeling secure behind it, like the lotus-eating mandarins of Cathay behind their Great Wall, the French Army allowed itself to atrophy, to lapse into desuetude. A massive combination of factors – complacency, lassitude, deficiencies of manpower and finance – conspired to rust the superb weapon which the world had so admired.[25]

And yet, this is somewhat unfair. The problems that arise from being static in a fortress are evident when it comes to the fall of France in 1940, but insufficient to be a total explanation. There are obvious issues resulting from the fortresses being bypassed as the Germans advanced, but bypass is an endemic problem for all fortresses.

Rather than the cause of the French defeat being the Maginot Line by itself, there were other contributing factors. The German attack came as a surprise even after eight months of war. The massing of German forces across the border should have been better monitored, as should the possibility of armour being able to get through the Ardennes forests. Moving the French and British armies into Belgium as the German attack occurred was probably a mistake as it then left a gap and enabled the army sent to Belgium to be cut off. The generals in charge made many mistakes, such that although French armour and aeroplanes were both numerous and of good quality they were not well deployed. In addition, political will – or support for and from politicians – was weak due to something of a breakdown in the political system over the previous decade. Rather than a psychological explanation it would be more pertinent to look at the failures of the political system. Combined with well-prepared mobile armies the Maginot Line may have been able to serve its purpose, but the French and British armies were simply out-manoeuvred.

Is a wall or fortress good strategy? In some circumstances, being behind a wall, behind fortifications, is good strategy. In World War I casualties were far greater when armies were on the attack and opposed to entrenched artillery and machine guns. In the Peninsular War, the lines at Torres Vedras proved crucial for the eventual success of Wellington and of Britain and its allies. Even though the Lines were hardly used, they still provided a safe haven to which Wellington's army – usually inferior in numbers – could retreat at any time it chose.

But walls and fortresses have limitations. A wall can lead to complacency and to psychological effects on those behind the wall. Strategy can become too static and too obvious to an adversary. There are temporary advantages only. During the Pacific War the Japanese built up Rabaul in New Guinea and the island of Truk in Micronesia as fortresses. Instead of attacking them directly, American forces reduced their capability to deploy aircraft and then left them to wither until the end of the war. Any wall can be overcome or bypassed, every line has an ending, every fortress can be taken. A wall or a fortress may be the appropriate response in some circumstances,

but in general the cost in building and staffing and the reduction of flexibility provide severe strategic limitations.

The sea as terrain

Although the word terrain derives from earth or land, the sea is also a kind
of terrain; another field, another locus of potential or actual conflict and a
space where strategic contests take place. It is argued here that terrain on
land is one kind, the sea is another. For present purposes, it is apparent that
strategy on, in and around the sea is often quite different from that of the
land. The sea is often seen as such a different setting that it requires its own
strategic thinking involving the concept of sea power.

A relatively neutral definition is that of Till, who argues that sea power
'consists of influence exerted by a mixture of military (mainly naval but with
associated air and land) and non-military forces'.[26] Till adds that 'maritime
strategy will be taken to refer to the methods by which countries attempt to
maintain or increase their sea power and how they try to use it to achieve
desired objectives in peace and war'.[27] These linked definitions encapsulate
the narrow sense of sea power as essentially naval power and the wider concept of maritime capability including that of trade and commerce.

There are advantages of naval power in grand strategy. It is mobile, flex-
ible and substantial force can be just over the horizon. It is easier to hide
than on land as the sea seems boundless. Naval ships from the sixteenth
century onwards were able to carry large guns that would be difficult to
move very far on land. Expertise in naval shipping led to commercial links.
While commerce can exist without force, the possession of naval force
enables political power to be exerted to support trade. For centuries, the
transport of large quantities of goods has been more cost-effective by sea
than by land, and the carriage of such goods assists commerce bringing
prosperity to maritime countries. Small states located in geographically
advantageous places – Venice, Portugal, the Netherlands, Holland, Britain –
became more important than their populations warrant through using
their maritime prowess commercially. Other countries, such as Russia,
Germany, and China, were constrained by limited access to the sea or lack
of interest in it. Still others – France, Spain, the United States – were continental but also maritime; at times their land-based issues dominated, at
other times their maritime interests were pre-eminent.

However, for defence purposes, naval power does have some disadvantages compared to a large land-based army. Humans live on land and venture onto the sea; doing so requires territory or at least a base. The sea is an unforgiving and sometimes dangerous terrain and the building and operation of ocean-going ships has always required considerable expertise. The age of sail necessitated large crews, especially when ships were used for war, and sailors require more training than soldiers. Ships were always costly to build and to maintain. Navies are expensive.

Some societies and some geographies have enjoyed more maritime advantages than others. Ancient Athens was a sea power, while Sparta was mainly land-based. The Romans were famous for their armies but were also a sea power. The Spanish, Portuguese, French and British empires relied on their ships; these were a sophisticated technology that the lands they conquered did not possess.

In the present era, some societies – the United States, Britain and key allies such as Japan – are still essentially sea powers, while Russia and China, notably, are essentially land powers. As Paine argues:

> The United States has emulated the British maritime strategy of keeping the seas open to trade so that the home economy can produce uninterrupted by warfare, of relying on its oceanic moat to insulate itself from foreign threats, and of fighting wars far from home, at times and places of its choosing. Land powers possess no such strategic flexibility: fighting often occurs on home territory, which disrupts the economy, while a maritime enemy can cut off their overseas markets and an attacking neighbor can choose the time and place of hostilities. Maritime powers, such as the United States, primarily influence the littoral – the places where they can most easily project military, diplomatic, and economic influence. Continental powers such as China and Russia influence events deep inland along their land borders.[28]

It could be argued that there is an ongoing conflict between the two – the land and the sea – but neither is able to fully conquer the other. This contest may date back to the times of Athens and Sparta. The Napoleonic Wars illustrated that the result can be a stalemate; Napoleon was peerless on land and Britain on the sea. Decisive victories or losses were possible – Salamis,

Trafalgar, the Nile – but rare. Trafalgar was decisive in the defeat of French sea power, but it still took a further ten years to defeat Napoleon. The sea cannot really conquer the land; conquest requires boots on the ground.

Mahan and the British wars with France

The key theorist of sea power is Alfred Thayer Mahan, a US Navy officer who taught at the US War College in the late nineteenth century. His books argued that mastery of the seas made nations victorious in war and prosperous in peace and that it was command of the sea that led to European empires dominating the world.[29] As he argued, 'Naval strategy has indeed for its end to found, support, and increase, as well in peace as in war, the sea power of a country.'[30] Sea power was about more than naval forces – the enhancement of commerce was integral to it. Much of Mahan's work was centred round the long conflicts between Britain and France in the eighteenth century, up to the end of the Napoleonic Wars in 1815, an era in which France controlled the land with its armies and Britain controlled the sea with its navy. From his lengthy case study broader conclusions would be drawn.

To Mahan, Britain was one of the nations advantaged in terms of sea power through such factors as geography, ports and access to the interior, extent of territory, population, character of the people and character of the government and national institutions. The first of these is when a nation is 'neither forced to defend itself by land nor induced to seek extension of its territory by way of the land' and can direct itself to the sea and thereby gain 'an advantage as compared with a people one of whose boundaries is continental'.[31] Mahan refers here to Britain with its favourable geographic position compared to much of Europe, and France in particular. Britain's long-standing strategy policy was to support its navy and spend much less on the army. On the other hand, the French 'with rare exceptions, subordinated the action of the navy to other military considerations, grudged the money spent upon it, and therefore sought to economize their fleet by assuming a defensive position'.[32] While understandable given France's long land borders, it was usually the case that Britain's navy was larger and more competent.

Napoleon did not seem to understand the importance of the sea and the navy; that aspect of grand strategy 'was always one of Napoleon's weaknesses; in all his long list of victories, none was at sea'.[33] The Peninsular War was enabled by British naval supremacy, and French commerce was constantly disrupted along its coasts. Napoleon brought in the Continental System as a kind of autarky to reduce British economic power by denying it access to trade with the continent of Europe. In fact, Britain and its colonies thrived, while France and its European allies became poorer.

Mahan's theory of sea power included sea-borne commerce, and in this aspect Britain undoubtedly benefitted from its maritime superiority in the Napoleonic Wars. For Mahan,

> The first and most obvious light in which the sea presents itself from the political and social point of view is that of a great highway; or better, perhaps, of a wide common, over which men may pass in all directions, but on which some well-worn paths show that controlling reasons have led them to choose certain lines of travel rather than others. These lines of travel are called trade routes; and the reasons which have determined them are to be sought in the history of the world. Notwithstanding all the familiar and unfamiliar dangers of the sea, both travel and traffic by water have always been easier and cheaper than by land.[34]

Sea power was able to establish superiority in maritime commerce as well. Mahan referred to

> That overbearing power on the sea which drives the enemy's flag from the sea or allows it to appear only as a fugitive; and which by controlling the great common, closes the highway by which commerce moves to and from the enemy's shores.[35]

Maintaining maritime supremacy led to the control of communications. Britain was able to capture enemy shipping and colonies in the Napoleonic Wars for its economic benefit as the strongest maritime nation.

Mahan argued that naval power was founded on battleships and on seeking out decisive fleet engagements. This part of Mahan, though widely believed at the time, does not really stand up when tested. There were very few fleet actions following Mahan, and fewer that were really decisive. The whole notion of two great fleets firing their big guns against each other in a battle to decide the fate of nations was almost obsolete by the end of World War I. Battleships became irrelevant after Taranto in 1940 and Pearl Harbor a year later.

There may have been something in the idea of fleet battles when individual ships were of parity as in the Napoleonic Wars. The line-of-battle ships of each navy were of similar size with similar numbers of guns also of similar size. Ships were so similar that when captured they would be readily absorbed into the other side's navy. These constraints had been driven by centuries of technological development in carpentry, sails and casting of guns to the very limits of that technology. In such conditions, the sheer numbers on each side did matter. But when one side had a technological advantage and ships were not matched, numbers became less relevant.

The Battle of Jutland in World War I was one of the last occasions when two great fleets sallied forth. But a decisive battle did not occur that day and this part of Mahan was no longer relevant (see chapter 6). Britain started and ended the day superior at sea and kept that position for the remainder of the war. As command of the air became more important, battleships became obsolete and aircraft carriers were the new capital ships. Sea power too became somewhat less important. More to the point was sea power combined with air and land power, as shown by World War II. As Freedman argues:

> While Mahan was a great booster for naval power and gained countless admirers among American and British naval circles for doing so, his lasting theoretical contributions were limited. As with others who believed that history offers timeless principles, he was unable to accommodate into his basic framework the massive changes in naval power resulting from the new technologies exemplified by steam power.[36]

Even if there were some logical and practical flaws in Mahan, his ideas did gain advocates before and after World War I.

Mahan and policy

There were clear policy implications derived from Mahan's arguments. He argued that the United States needed a great navy as a mark of national greatness, one designed to fight an enemy in fleet engagements to win control of the sea, not for commerce raiding or protection. The United States needed to maintain naval strength during peacetime. It needed to build a fleet of capital ships, and with steamships powered by coal there was a need for colonies as locations for coaling stations. Mahan advocated building a canal through the Isthmus of Panama, considering it a necessity for the United States given its frontage on two oceans. The United States was not as quick to accept Mahan's teachings as other countries, although President Theodore Roosevelt would use them as the foundation of his naval policy in the early 1900s. And after 1900 the United States would become and remain one of the world's leading naval powers.

In Europe, Mahan was seen as validating the naval and colonial policies of Britain, France, Germany and Japan. Colonies were needed for coaling stations around the world, and a strong navy was seen as a requirement of imperial commerce. Mahan's writings clearly influenced Germany's rapid build-up of its navy prior to World War I, with the naval arms race in Europe between Germany and Britain one of the contributing factors to the commencement of that war. Kaiser Wilhelm was a 'keen nautical hobbyist and an avid reader of Mahan'; he became 'obsessed with the need for ships, to the point where he began to see virtually every international crisis as a lesson in the primacy of naval power'.[37] In the event, German battleship building posed no real threat to Britain; no matter how many battleships Germany built, in the period immediately before 1914 Britain was easily able to build more. Clark argues that 'the naval scares that periodically swept through the British press and political circles were real enough, but they were driven in large part by campaigns launched by the navalists to fend off demands for funding from the cash-starved British army'.[38]

Continental statesmen, with their big armies, never seemed to understand that the navy was for Britain a matter of its very existence. Without the navy, Massie argues, Britain 'was instantly vulnerable'; without the navy, 'Britain itself, a small island state, dependent on imported food, possessing an insignificant army, could be in immediate peril of starvation or invasion.'[39] On the other hand, 'with control of the seas, all was reversed':

> While Britain maintained naval supremacy, no Continental power, no matter how large or well-trained its army, could touch the British homeland. With naval supremacy, Britain acquired diplomatic freedom; British statesmen and diplomats could afford to stand back and

regard with detachment the rivalries and hatreds which consumed the youth and treasures of Continental powers facing each other across land frontiers.[40]

If this dependence on its navy was little understood across the Channel, the point was that without its navy, Britain would be an irrelevance. It would face an existential threat; therefore no continental power would ever be allowed to threaten its naval position in Europe. Even if the experts were little bothered, the German building programme did turn public opinion in Britain against Germany and helped drive the British to seek allies in Europe in the pre-war period.

Mahan's arguments for the pre-eminence of sea power were not unchallenged. Although sea power helps to explain the rise and prominence of smaller nations such as Portugal and Britain, it does not explain the rise of continental powers such as Germany and Russia, or the continued prominence of China, which until recently showed little interest in the sea.

In 1904, the British geographer Halford Mackinder published a critique of Mahan arguing that more important than maritime power was control of what he called the 'World Island'. the vast continent of Europe and Asia. Mackinder's dictum was 'Who rules East Europe commands the Heartland; Who rules the Heartland commands the World-Island; Who rules the World-Island commands the World.' Russia and Central Asia form the pivot of history (heartland): inaccessible by sea, armies can retreat into vast territory. Transoceanic shipping from the fifteenth century tipped the balance toward sea power; initially by Spain and Portugal, then the Netherlands and Britain. Mackinder argued too that the cost advantage for maritime freight could change with the building of railways and that railroads might shift power away from the maritime powers. A hundred years later this has not really happened, although things may change with China's Belt and Road initiative.

In 1911, Julian Corbett published a book countering some of Mahan's precepts. He argued that the decisive fleet engagement by battleships was only one aspect of maritime power and that the sea needed to be looked at as a different environment from the land. He argued, first, that 'you cannot conquer sea because it is not susceptible of ownership, at least outside territorial waters', and second, that 'you cannot subsist your armed force upon it as you can upon enemy's territory'.[41] This meant that

> Command of the sea . . . means nothing but the control of maritime communications, whether for commercial or military purposes. The object of naval warfare is the control of communications, and not, as in land warfare, the conquest of territory. The difference is fundamental.[42]

To Corbett, 'if the object and end of naval warfare is the control of communications it must carry with it the right to forbid, if we can, the passage of both public and private property upon the sea'.[43] This leads to disruption of commerce and blockade as viable tactics for nations and navies to use in a conflict.

Britain's geographical position did provide great advantage, as set out by Mahan, and disadvantage to those countries that had to escape into the open sea through the North Sea or the Channel. The classic British strategy in a European conflict was to institute a blockade – for example, the close blockade of ports such as Toulon and Brest in the wars against France. Germany's geography also made it vulnerable to British naval blockade, and this was instituted as soon as war broke out in World War I and II. In both there was a more distant blockade of the North Sea and the English Channel rather than a close blockade of ports. Blockades were especially effective in reducing German commerce with the rest of the world; denying it imports while its surface raiders and merchant ships were swept from the seas. Blockade is rather a blunt instrument and, in World War I in particular, led to real starvation in Germany, but in both wars was also slowly but inexorably effective.

For the weaker maritime powers, resort to commerce prevention – as argued by Corbett – was a viable strategy, allied with a preponderance of land forces. Britain's reliance on trade was also a source of vulnerability and for a time in both world wars German submarines came close to closing Britain's Atlantic trade, regardless of the relative strength of battle fleets.

That the sea is a terrain is undoubted; that it affects strategy is also without doubt. But strategy about the sea is different from strategy on land.

Conclusion

Terrain is an important part of strategy, sufficient to be one of the five facets of strategy. There are many instances where matters of terrain can affect a strategic outcome, and any strategist needs to take cognisance of the terrain in which conflict is to take place. The point really is that terrain of all kinds needs to be taken into consideration when devising strategy. Terrain is regarded as important by theorists, including Sun-tzu, Clausewitz and Mahan.

Terrain is considered quite broadly here to include external aspects of other kinds as well as the various conformations of the earthly terrain where the word derives. The sea is a terrain, as are the air, the weather, tides and climate. These are all external influences from the natural environment on strategy; natural influences that should be understood but cannot necessarily be directly controlled. A wall or fortification is taken here to be part of terrain as they are a modification of it rather than something entirely new. The Lines of Torres Vedras constructed by Arthur Wellesley, later the Duke of Wellington, were clever enhancements of already difficult terrain.

Terrain could conceivably include other factors, as indicated by the term 'battlespace', but the separation between capability and terrain used here includes within terrain those factors which occur naturally and are beyond human agency, and within capability, those factors within the broader environment that are created by human hands and minds. Thus, intelligence, cyberspace or the strength of adversaries are matters of capability.

The strategist may not be able to directly control aspects of terrain but can still use them to advantage or devise tactical responses to counteract them if disadvantageous. A disadvantageous terrain can be overcome but the costs are greater; fighting is more difficult uphill than downhill.

Notes

1   Vegetius, 'Epitome of Military Science', in Brian Campbell (ed.), *Greek and Roman Military Writers: Selected Readings* (Abingdon: Routledge, 2004), p. 86.

2   Sun-tzu, *The Art of War*, in Ralph D. Sawyer (edited and translated), *The Seven Military Classics of Ancient China* (New York: Basic Books, 2007) p. 183.

3   Ibid., p. 178.

4   United States, Department of the Army, *Terrain Intelligence*, Field Manual 30–10, 1967, p. 45.

5   Ibid.

6   United States, Department of the Air Force, *Comprehensive Plan for the Organizational Structure of the U.S. Space Force*. February 2020.

7   United States, Department of Defence, *Defence Dictionary of Military and Associated Terms*.

8   Alan Taylor, *American Revolutions: A Continental History, 1750–1804* (New York: W.W. Norton, 2016), p. 171.

9   Ibid., p. 171.

10 David McCullough, *1776* (New York, Simon & Schuster, 2005), p. 267.

11 David Hackett Fischer, *Washington's Crossing* (Oxford University Press, 2006), p. 75.

12 Ibid., p. 81.

13 Andrew Roberts, *Napoleon the Great* (London: Penguin, 2014), p. 546.

14 Martin Robson, *History of the Royal Navy, A: The Napoleonic Wars* (London: I.B. Taurus, 2014), p. 178.

15 Roger Knight, *Britain against Napoleon: The Organization of Victory 1793–1815* (London: Penguin, 2013), p. 425.

16 Julia Lovell, *The Great Wall: China against the World* (London: Picador, 2009), p. 43.

17 Henry Guerlac, 'Vauban: The Impact of Science on War', in Peter Paret, Gordon A. Craig and Felix Gilbert (eds), *Makers of Modern Strategy from Machiavelli to the Nuclear Age* (Princeton: Princeton University Press, 2010), p. 69.

18 James M. McPherson, *Battle Cry of Freedom* (New York: Ballantine, 1988), pp. 476–7.

19 Ibid.

20 Guerlac, 'Vauban: The Impact of Science', p. 90.

21 Julian Jackson, *The Fall of France: The Nazi Invasion of 1940* (Oxford: Oxford University Press, 2003), p. 27.

22 Field Marshal Lord Alanbrooke, *War Diaries, 1939–1945* (Berkeley: University of California Press, 2001), p. 26.

23 Ibid., p. 37.

24 Ibid.

25 Alister Horne, *To Lose a Battle: France 1940* (London: Penguin, 1990), pp. 75–6.

26 Geoffrey Till, *Maritime Strategy and the Nuclear Age*, 2nd edn (Basingstoke: Macmillan, 1984), p. 14.

27 Ibid.

28 S.C.M. Paine, *The Wars for Asia, 1911–1949* (Cambridge: Cambridge University Press, 2012), p. 7.

29 Alfred Thayer Mahan, *The Influence of Sea Power upon History, 1660–1783* (Boston: Little, Brown, 1890) and Alfred Thayer Mahan, *The Influence of Sea Power upon the French Revolution and Empire, 1793–1812* (Boston: Little, Brown, 1894).

30 Mahan, *The Influence of Sea Power upon History*, p. 19.

31 Ibid., p. 25.

32 Ibid., p. 5.

33 Andrew Roberts, *Napoleon the Great* (London: Penguin, 2014), p. 57.

34 Mahan, *The Influence of Sea Power upon History*, p. 22.

35 Ibid., p. 121.

36 Lawrence Freedman, *Strategy: A History* (Oxford: Oxford University Press, 2013), p. 117.

37 Christopher Clark, *The Sleepwalkers: How Europe Went to War in 1914* (New York: Harper, 2014), p. 134.

38 Ibid., p. 150.

39 Robert K. Massie, *Dreadnought: Britain, Germany, and the Coming of the Great War* (New York, Ballantine, 1991), p. xxii.

40 Ibid.

41 Julian S. Corbett, *Principles of Maritime Strategy* (Mineola, NY: Dover, 2004) (orig. 1911), p. 89.

42 Ibid., p. 90.

43 Ibid., p. 91.

6

TACTICS

Introduction

The last facet of the PCWTT model of strategy is that of tactics. These are the more operational aspects of strategy; those subsidiary actions that aim to further the purpose of a particular strategy. The difference between them is that strategy is about how to fulfil the overall, longer-term purpose that has been set out and tactics are about the day-to-day, lower-level actions. Of course, tactical decisions should contribute to the overall strategy and not be counter-productive. Tactics should be seen as those actions that are followed to contribute to, and further, the agreed strategic purpose.

As an instance, Sherman's march to the sea through Georgia during the American Civil War was a bold strategy for which the tactics that followed were quite seamless with the strategy. The overarching purpose – to bring the Civil War to an end as soon as possible – was clear enough to Sherman's superiors, President Lincoln and General Grant. In order to help achieve this, the march through Georgia could be seen as a stand-alone strategy, but it makes more sense to see is as a brilliant exercise of tactics with strategic consequences.

The five facets of strategy work together. Any misalignment between them means that achieving the strategy becomes more difficult, or in some instances completely unachievable. A misalignment between purpose and tactics may be more damaging than a misalignment of any other two of the five facets. If purpose and tactics are well aligned it can even become difficult to tell them apart, but tactics that divert from purpose are wasteful and may be counter-productive.

Tactics definition

A tactic is defined by the *Shorter Oxford* as 'a tactical ploy, action or manoeuvre; an instance of military tactics'. Tactics, as a plural, then becomes 'the art of deploying military, air, or naval forces in order of battle, and of planning and executing military manoeuvres in actual contact with an enemy' or 'the plans and procedure adopted to carry out a scheme or achieve an end. Also a skilful device or devices.' To Clausewitz, tactics are 'the theory of the use of military forces in combat' and strategy is 'the theory of the use of combats for the object of the war'.[1] The Clausewitz formulation is quite definitive and points clearly to the difference in level between the two but also their interdependence.

Freeman argues that strategy is concerned with long-term advance and 'must be applied through tactics', adding:

> Tactics are the detailed plans and means by which strategy advances in the short term. Tactical actions pursue gains or defend interests in particular circumstances. The sum of tactical gains may constitute strategic advance, but the results of disparate tactics uninspired by a strategic design do not add up to a strategy. To allow tactics to define or drive strategy is opportunism. This risks the achievement of short-term gain at the expense of longer-term overextension, exhaustion, and vulnerability to reversal.[2]

As Freeman argues, disparate tactics do not necessarily advance an overall strategy and to engage in tactical actions that are opportunistic leads to problems, including a waste of resources. Tactics need to be allied with strategy, indeed to all aspects of the PCWTT model.

Sun-tzu is a master of tactics, too, with stratagems and tricks on offer for particular situations – indeed, much of The Art of War is tactical rather than truly strategic.

A classic, if elaborate and fictional, instance of deception in tactics involves the Shu strategist Zhuge Liang, as described in The Three Kingdoms. Pursued by a much larger army, part of Cao Cao's army led by Cao Hong and Cao Ren, Zhuge Liang instructed his officers to break into three groups. Guan Yu's thousand troops were to proceed to the upper parts of the nearby White River with bags to fill with sand and earth to dam the river. Zhang Fei, another officer, was directed with his troops to the Boling Ferry, where the current from the river slows. Zhao Yun, another officer, was told to divide his three thousand troops into four parties, one for each gate of Xinye, a nearby city. House roofs in the city were to be piled high with combustibles in order to set fire to the city when the army of the enemy entered it for shelter. When a strong breeze sprung up the next evening, fire arrows were to be shot into the city from all sides. The east gate was to be left open for an ambush. As evening approached, two other officers lured the enemy army on a wild goose chase towards the city. When Cao Ren and Cao Hong arrived they ordered an attack on the city but found it deserted:

> The soldiers were fatigued with marching and hungry as well, so they lost no time in scattering among the houses and setting about preparing food in the deserted kitchens. The leaders took up their quarters in the state residence to rest. After the first watch the wind began to blow. Soon after the gate guards reported that a fire had started. 'The careless men have let sparks fly about,' said Cao Ren.

There were other reports of like nature and Cao Ren realized that the fires breaking out in all quarters were not due to accident. So he gave orders to evacuate the city. Soon the whole city seemed on fire, and a red glow hung in the sky.

> Officers and troops dashing through the smoke and fire in utter confusion sought some way of escape, and hearing that the east gate was free, they made for that quarter. Out they rushed pell-mell, many being trodden down and trampled to death. Those who got through took the road to the east. But presently there was a shouting behind them, and Zhao Yun's company came up and attacked. Then Cao Cao's troops scattered, each fleeing for his life. No stand was made. A

little later Mi Fang and Liu Feng came to take another toll. The fleeing Cao Ren then had very few followers, and those left him were scorched and burned. They directed their way to the White River, joyfully remembering that the river was shallow and fordable. And they went down into the stream and drank their fill, humans shouting and horses neighing. Meantime Guan Yu, higher up its course, had dammed the river with sandbags so that its waters were collected in a lake. Toward evening he had seen the red glow of the burning city and began to look out for his signal. About the fourth watch, he heard downstream the sounds of soldiers and horse and at once ordered the breaking of the dam. The water rushed down in a torrent and overwhelmed the men just then in the bed of the river. Many were swept away and drowned. Those who escaped made their way to where the stream ran gently and got away.

This was a rather elaborate tactical plan, one that relied on the enemy doing just what was expected. The fire inside the empty city drove the enemy out through the one gate leading towards the river. Many drowned in the water, many others were attacked as they tried to cross the river at the ford. So from an initial position of weakness, Zhuge Liang contrived a great victory for the Shu through clever tactics, at little cost to his own side. While these events are likely apocryphal, the tactics are timeless. The aim is often to strike at a point of disadvantage, to achieve a localised superiority and to use a small victory as part of a larger campaign or strategy. As Sun-tzu argued:

> If they are rested, force them to exert themselves. If they are united, cause them to be separated. Attack where they are unprepared. Go forth where they will not expect it. These are the ways military strategists are victorious. They cannot be spoken of in advance.[3]

Tactics of this kind are stratagems, even trickery, but certainly have their place; for Sun-tzu, warfare is the 'Way of deception'.[4] In some instances, however, deception is not necessary.

Sherman's march to the sea

Another instance of innovative tactics supporting strategy and furthering the overall purpose is Sherman's march to the sea in the US Civil War.

Having reached and taken Atlanta by conventional means for that war – advancing with railway support and conventional logistics – Union general William Tecumseh Sherman was faced with deciding quite what to do next. Instead of either holding Atlanta or going back to earlier positions, Sherman proposed abandoning Atlanta, leaving much of his logistical support behind and heading to Savanah 480 kilometres away. When his army arrived at the sea Union ships could resupply, but until then much of the provisions needed would be found by commandeering them from the local population.

The overall strategy for the Union to win the Civil War was to isolate the South through naval blockade, to cut its links to the Mississippi from the west and use the North's superior resources to prevail in Virginia against Confederate general Robert E. Lee. While that contest was going quite well, at least since Union general Ulysses S. Grant had taken charge, casualties were high, and this caused some political cost to Lincoln and the Republicans. What Sherman proposed would, if successful, strike into the heart of the South and show its overall strategy to be unsustainable. Sherman's plan may have been common sense, but still someone had to devise it and bring it into being. While it might have appeared risky, it was a risk worth taking to further the intended overall purpose. In the event, the march through Georgia and the Carolinas did shorten the war and most likely saved many lives on both sides.

Both General Grant – the overall commander – and President Lincoln had reservations about Sherman's plan but eventually agreed to it. And the operation succeeded brilliantly: it began in Atlanta on 3 November 1864 and Savannah surrendered on 21 December. Advancing in two columns but close enough for mutual reinforcement if necessary, Sherman's troops shook off sporadic opposition and cut a swathe through the countryside of Georgia. His men took produce from farms, tore up railroad tracks and, in general, made the populace pay in a part of the South where the war on the ground had not been experienced in such a direct way. Buildings were burnt, though not by order, slaves freed and Georgia made 'to howl', as Sherman had promised.

Tactically, the novelty was not only taking a large force of 60,000 into enemy territory without support but also bringing some of the economic consequences of the conflict to the civilian population. Sherman was not the first to do this. It was a timeless tactic, used, for instance, by Fabius against Hannibal in his invasion of Italy. A scorched earth policy was used by the Russians to counter Napoleon's advance to Moscow in 1812, and by Wellington and the Portuguese government in their effective evacuation of the local population to Lisbon during the Peninsular War.

Sherman made no apology for his uncompromising approach. He just wanted the war to be over. Referring to the forced evacuation of Atlanta, he said: 'If the people raise a howl against my barbarity and cruelty, I will answer that war is war and not popularity-seeking. If they want peace they and their relatives must stop war.'[5] And replying to the mayor and aldermen of Atlanta who had protested about civilians being homeless in the winter, Sherman said:

> You cannot qualify war in harsher terms than I will. War is cruelty and you cannot refine it . . . You might as well appeal against the thunder-storm as against these terrible hardships of war . . . We don't want your Negroes, or your houses, or your land, or anything you have, but we do want and will have first obedience to the laws of the United States . . . if it involves the destruction of your improvements, we cannot help it . . . But, my dear sirs, when peace does come, you may call on me for any thing. Then I will share with you the last cracker, and watch with you to shield your homes and families against danger from every quarter.[6]

The march through Georgia involved brilliant tactics combined seamlessly with overall strategy and helped bring the Civil War to an end.

With the main Confederate army under Robert E. Lee stalled facing Grant in Virginia, the Confederacy's other armies were ineffective. The resource disparity of men and supplies compared to the North was now becoming critical and the Confederacy was shown to be unable to defend its heartland. And then, having arrived at Savannah, Sherman turned north to run through the Carolinas as he had run through Georgia. After that, with Sherman approaching rapidly from the south and with Grant's army much greater than his anyway, Lee's position under siege in Virginia was increasingly untenable.

With little actual conflict and only light casualties on both sides, Sherman's march achieved all it set out to do. Rather than defeat a Southern army, he demonstrated that the South was a hollow shell, too weak to even show up at this stage of the war. As Freedman argues:

The important point about Sherman's strategy is that it worked. Taking Atlanta raised morale in the North and helped secure President Lincoln's re-election in 1864. The devastation caused by his troops moved the Confederacy, as its military position became increasingly hopeless, from defiance to surrender.[7]

Setting off without a secure line of communication was an innovation in a war heavily dependent on seizing and maintaining railway lines to provide logistical support. Living off the land was not new and had been a hallmark of Napoleon's armies, six decades earlier. What was effectively a scorched earth policy was not novel, but bringing the realities of war home to the civilian population was a forerunner of the wars that were to follow in the next century. Sherman later said, 'War is Hell'[8], and in this he was surely right. But for him and for Grant there was a job to do and it had best be done quickly or even greater suffering would result.

Tactical lessons

By the time of World War I, Britain's long period of supremacy at sea, of more than a century since the Battle of Trafalgar, had been achieved by hard work and technological superiority combined with clear strategy. But the Battle of Jutland during World War I showed the dangers, at least for some of the participants, and even the nation as a whole, in relying on tactics that had been successful but were now outdated. In brief, looking at three cases – the Nile, Trafalgar and Jutland – shows the need to draw on the real tactical lessons of the past, not the superficial ones.

Mahan had argued that 'From time to time the superstructure of tactics has to be altered or wholly torn down; but the whole foundations of strategy so far remain; as though laid upon rock.'[9] Britain's naval strategy during World War I was essentially the same as that of the Napoleonic Wars and even earlier. This included such elements as: maintaining superiority in number of ships; parity, at least, in armaments; highly trained and effective personnel; maintenance of trade; and the blockade of continental exits through the English Channel and the North Sea. Following from Mahan, then, the change from sail to steam in battleships did not change British *strategy*, as this was laid on rock as it were, but the *tactics* needed to change. As it turned out, the wrong lessons were drawn from the century before.

The Nile and Trafalgar

In May 1798, a French invasion fleet carrying Napoleon Bonaparte – not yet consul, let alone emperor – sailed from Toulon with its destination unknown. British admiral Horatio Nelson was tasked with finding the fleet, and eventually located it three months later anchored in Aboukir Bay near Alexandria in Egypt. Napoleon and his army of some 30,000 had disembarked and were in Cairo 250 kilometres away.

Even though it was late in the day Nelson ordered his 14 line-of-battle ships to attack immediately. The French fleet under Admiral de Brueys was seemingly well positioned; anchored in a line at the edge of the shallows with its guns facing outward. French tactics assumed an attacker would sail along the outside of the French line, engaging ship to ship, as this would be the normal, predictable response. Nelson allowed his captains to go through the French line and even sail along the shallow side, having decided that it was likely that there would be sufficient room for ships to pass without running aground. As the French guns and gun crews were facing outward, their ships were even more vulnerable on the shallow side. The French fleet was destroyed with all but two of their line-of-battle ships sunk or captured and their flagship Orient exploding.

Strategically, the British navy became dominant in the Mediterranean and would keep that position until the end of the war. Nelson was hailed as a great hero for his innovative tactics and charging straight at the enemy. Napoleon and his army were stranded in Egypt for a time, unable to return to France, and an attempt to use the army to fight their way to Constantinople and back to France overland failed at the siege of Acre in 1799. Napoleon and some of his senior staff were able to get back to France but not his army, with the remnants eventually capitulating.

Another, even more substantial victory further reinforced Britain's maritime dominance. In 1805, seven years after the Battle of the Nile, Nelson and his fleet comprehensively defeated a French and Spanish fleet near Cadiz in the Battle of Trafalgar. Napoleon's overall strategy was for Admiral Villeneuve to gather the French and Spanish ships from the ports where they had been blockaded, gain a numerical advantage and enough of a command of the English Channel to enable an army to embark on ships in Boulogne and other Channel ports and invade Britain.

At Trafalgar, Nelson was technically outnumbered but handled his fleet brilliantly. Instead of staying in a line as traditional tactics would expect, Nelson formed two columns and broke through the French line. This caused disarray and led to the French and Spanish fleets being comprehensively defeated, with 22 ships of the line destroyed out of 33 compared to none of the British fleet of 27. As Roberts argues:

> Displaying what later become known as 'the Nelson touch' of inspired leadership, the British admiral split his fleet into two squadrons that attacked at a ninety-degree angle to the Combined Fleet's line and thereby cut the enemy into three groups of ships, before destroying them piecemeal . . . The battle led to British naval dominance for over a century.[10]

Britain was saved and an invasion by Napoleon became unrealistic, if indeed it had ever been possible. For the next ten years of war the primacy of the British navy was hardly challenged. Trafalgar established once and for all that the British navy had maritime supremacy in Europe, a position, as Roberts notes, it would keep it for more than the following century.

Nelson was the great hero of the hour. This was the man who saved Britain from invasion, the man who destroyed Napoleon's ambitions, and the man who was tragically cut down by a French musket at the height of Trafalgar. Nelson is rightly celebrated – think of Nelson's Column in Trafalgar Square in London – but his legend became bigger than reality, a travesty of itself, and almost ended in disaster for Britain 110 years later in the Battle of Jutland. The lessons of Nelson had been misconstrued. It was not the tactical innovation of breaking the line or the dash and glory of Nelson that won Trafalgar, it was a cool appreciation of strategy and relative capability.

Jutland

The beginning of the twentieth century saw a naval arms race between Britain and Germany based on the number and capability of battleships that each could build. This led to a worsening of relations and partly contributed to World War I breaking out. The arms race had been clearly won by the British; it could build more ships than Germany, indeed, Germany had given up challenging in this sphere well before the war.

This was an era when there was rough parity in terms of ship capability. German ships were good but there were fewer of them. The respective battleship classes were comparable; both the German and British fleets included battleships and battlecruisers. Battlecruisers carried large guns and were fast but were less well armoured than battleships. In this era, the weight of ships, the amount of armour, their armament and their speed were related; the more armour and the bigger guns the greater the weight and reduction in speed, Relying on speed would mean less armour and greater vulnerability. Bigger guns meant weight too, but allowed for longer-range firing. It was a difficult equation.

Britain's overall naval strategy at the beginning of World War I was as far as possible to: keep the German High Seas Fleet in harbour; shut down German maritime commerce; safeguard communications with France; and keep sea lanes open for trade with the rest of the world. Blockade was the time-honoured strategy for Britain in European conflicts and was immediately followed in World War I. Using its geographic position and naval supremacy to blockade the Channel, the British also shut off any exit to the North Sea by moving its Grand Fleet to its wartime anchorage at Scapa Flow north of Scotland.

When the war broke out, Germany had a very good battle fleet but could not match the numbers in the British Grand Fleet. In order to be able to break the British blockade the German navy needed to reduce the number of British battleships until there could be a fleet engagement on more or less equal terms. The German plan at Jutland was to lure out part of the British fleet by sending out its battlecruisers under Admiral Hipper, but with the High Seas Fleet under Admiral Scheer following behind to deliver a decisive blow, along with submarines stationed along the way. The hope was that by isolating a part of the British fleet it could be overwhelmed and the overall disparity in number of battleships thereby reduced. Success was possible, if unlikely.

Unbeknownst to the German fleet, the Admiralty was able to read its encrypted radio signals. From this source, the overall commander of the British Grand Fleet, Admiral John Jellicoe, knew the general plan and prepared to sail with the British Grand Fleet from Scapa Flow. Further south at Rosyth the battlecruiser fleet under Admiral David Beatty sailed out to meet the German battlecruisers, unaware that the main German fleet was following.

As would be expected a century after Nelson, any British admiral would aim directly at any opposing fleet and try to gain a Nelson-like overwhelming victory. Accordingly, Beatty headed straight for the German battlecruisers. His force included his six battlecruisers and four *Queen Elizabeth*-class battleships that had been seconded to his command. These were far more capable than earlier models – new battleships that had managed to combine armour, big guns and speed. In his hurry to attack Beatty did not effectively deploy these new battleships – a signalling error was later blamed – and impetuously headed to battle without them. This error was compounded in the headlong rush to engage. The British battlecruisers carried larger guns with greater range than their German counterparts and were faster. It would have been possible by holding back to stay out of range of the German battlecruisers but have them within range of the British guns and maintain that advantage by superior speed. And the four *Queen Elizabeth*-class battleships were equipped with even larger guns with even greater range and were faster again. Well deployed they could have used their superior speed and greater range to destroy the German fleet. Instead, Beatty headed straight at the German battlecruisers, providing them with the opportunity to fire at him.

Quite quickly two of Beatty's battlecruisers were sunk, blown up most likely due to inadequate protection of their magazines. The German High Seas Fleet under Admiral Scheer duly arrived, at which point Beatty turned back to lead the German ships towards the British Grand Fleet. When the German fleet sighted Jellicoe's Grand Fleet, Admiral Scheer turned around to head for his home port and the battle that then ensued was indecisive. At one point Jellicoe turned away from a destroyer torpedo attack and, in the enveloping gloom and the approach of nightfall, the German fleet managed to escape, even passing through the British fleet in the dark, and returned to harbour. The German High Seas fleet did not challenge the blockade again and basically stayed in harbour for the rest of the war, losing condition.

There are two key aspects of the rather complicated story of Jutland to look at here: first, the clear differences it illustrates between strategy and tactics and, second, the trap of the cult of personality and the search for glory.

The strategic consequences of Jutland are quite clear. Although the Germans claimed a great victory given that they sank more ships and suffered fewer casualties than the British, the key point of any battle or any tactic is how it impinges on the overall strategy. A decisive British victory at Jutland would not have changed the overall strategic situation in Europe much at all, but a decisive German victory would have. Above all else, Britain could not afford to lose its strategic superiority. To this end, while the losses on the day were to be regretted, maintaining naval supremacy was unaltered. As Steel and Hart argue:

> Whatever specious claims can be constructed from an analysis of losses or casualties it remains a fact that *the British won the battle of Jutland*. In the end the material successes of the High Seas Fleet fade into complete insignificance in comparison to the crushing strategic success that the Royal Navy secured for the British Empire.[11]

Churchill said of Jellicoe some years later that 'he was the only man that could lose the war in an afternoon'.[12] This comment was quite correct in relation to Jutland. The best strategy for Jellicoe in the circumstances was simply to not lose, to not be risky and to maintain the British fleet superiority – and to tailor its tactics accordingly. Jellicoe's fundamental aim, even duty, was to maintain the British command of the sea.

Fortunately for Britain, Jellicoe was not impetuous – rather, he organized the Grand Fleet in the North Sea into a position where it could not be defeated. He then acted cautiously, and this tactical approach was exactly how he should have acted in accordance with overall strategy. Steel and Hart argue:

> Jellicoe was a brilliant man saddled by a poor system of command and control in conditions of appalling visibility. As C-in-C he must bear responsibility for the failures in the command structure and night-fighting techniques endemic within the Grand Fleet. Nevertheless, his natural calmness, intelligence and clear thinking allowed him to transcend these handicaps to achieve his overriding aim safely: to retain for Britain command of the world's oceans beyond the narrow confines of the North Sea.[13]

Although the Battle of Jutland is often described as inconclusive, it was not without significance strategically. While the British lost more ships in the direct battle – three battlecruisers, for a start – a number of the German ships were so damaged they took months to repair.

The blockade of Germany was unaffected and was already having a major effect on the German people and their economy. The blockade cut Germany off from its colonies in Africa and Asia and these were snapped up in the early part of the war. Supplies from overseas virtually ceased and had the longer-term effect of leading to real starvation at home as the war bogged down on the Western Front. The failure to break the naval blockade led to Germany adopting an alternate strategy based on unrestricted submarine warfare. This did have a major impact on merchant ships supplying Britain until convoys were instituted, but submarine attacks also led to the United States joining the war on the side of France and Britain. From that point on, Germany was doomed.

The second point is the cult of personality and the mistake of trying to emulate Nelson in another era while failing to understand what he had actually done. What we have is the contrasting styles of the British two admirals at Jutland. John Jellicoe was the technocrat, careful and considered; David Beatty was seen as the inheritor of Nelson, whose first instinct was to simply charge into battle. Jellicoe was criticized afterwards for being overly cautious, for turning the fleet away when there were reports of torpedo tracks. He was also criticized for allowing the German fleet to escape in the darkness, but these points should be seen for what they were; safeguarding the strategic imperatives. Beatty on the other hand almost lost the day. He was overly impetuous and could be accused of playing to the German tactics by engaging with the German battlecruisers. A disaster was only narrowly averted. Most of the British casualties were from the initial, reckless attack of Beatty's battlecruisers, most likely due to equipment failure and slipshod handling of explosives. The public wanted dash; they wanted Nelson again. Britain did not get the great victory it had achieved at Trafalgar. But times had changed, and tactics needed to change too.

Above all, the real lesson of Nelson had been misunderstood. The best naval tactic was not a mad dash for glory, but Nelson had not done this. The lessons of Trafalgar and the Battle of the Nile were that the events of both battles were set in place years earlier by training, by equipment, by the balance of probabilities. Even when the French fleet was larger in number its strength was illusory. Nelson knew that the French ships were in poor shape and that, at Trafalgar, the Spanish ships were in even worse condition. This was the result of years of neglect, badly trained crews, being stuck in harbour by blockade where skill levels atrophied. Nelson knew this and acted on it. Rather than glory it was a realistic appreciation of relative capability and the exploiting of an opportunity. As Mahan argued 20 years before Jutland:

> At Trafalgar it was not Villeneuve that failed, but Napoleon that was vanquished; not Nelson that won, but England that was saved; and why? Because Napoleon's combinations failed, and Nelson's intuitions and activity kept the English fleet ever on the track of the enemy, and brought it up in time at the decisive moment. The tactics at Trafalgar were in their main features conformable to the principles of war, and their audacity was justified as well by the urgency of the case as by the results; but the great lessons of efficiency in preparation, of activity and energy in execution, and of thought and insight on the part of the English leader during the previous months, are strategic lessons, and as such they still remain good.[14]

After the Battle of Jutland there was an unseemly war of words between the supporters of Jellicoe and those of Beatty. Jellicoe was moved to a shore posting and Beatty to commander-in-chief. In effect, Jellicoe was sidelined and Beatty rewarded, as the people seemed to want a hero. While both were given various honours and were somewhat reconciled towards the end of their lives, the reality is that Beatty may well have lost the Battle of Jutland by acting impetuously and playing to the German tactics, as well as losing a third of his battlecruisers. As a newspaper report a century later would note:

> Systemic failures were matched by tactical ones. Whitehall blundering failed to alert Jellicoe to Scheer's exact movements. More extraordinary still, Beatty failed to tell his chief where exactly the enemy was heading and at what speed – vital to interception in poor visibility – a silence that lasted from 4.45 pm to 6.06 pm. Later he would fiddle the record and suppress the official history of the battle to exculpate

himself . . . Beatty won the immediate PR war and got control of the levers of power . . . Never mind that Beatty's cruisers had been beaten by Hipper's inferior force.[15]

The British press and public wanted a Nelson-like victory that would end the war; anything to obviate the slaughter of the Western Front. But times had changed. Unlike Trafalgar, Britain would not be saved by a naval victory, no matter how monumental. The only way that Jutland could have affected the strategic balance at the time would have been from a big German victory, big enough to take away British naval superiority. As Massie argues:

> Criticism of Jellicoe for not being another Nelson and hurling himself at the enemy is unfair. Tactics are governed by strategy and Jellicoe's strategic purpose was to retain command of the sea. The destruction of the High Seas Fleet was a secondary object – highly desirable but not essential.[16]

The cult of personality in favour of Beatty and his 'Nelson touch' almost led to calamity. Simply charging at the enemy may have been seen as glorious, but it was foolhardy. Beatty may have had 'a theoretical grasp of what was required for a complete naval victory, but he did not have either the application or the brilliance to achieve it when it mattered during the battle'.[17]

Fortunately for Britain the Grand Fleet at Jutland was in the hands of an admiral in Jellicoe who knew his duty, who appreciated fundamental British strategy and tailored his tactics accordingly. But in the aftermath it was the admiral who failed most badly who was rewarded and the one who did the right thing strategically was effectively sidelined.

Tactics in the Pacific War

The tactics of any conflict need to be in alignment with overall strategy, otherwise resources and time can be wasted. As discussed earlier, the overall strategy of the Japanese in World War II was gravely, even fatally, flawed from the very start. But what of the tactics? Was not Pearl Harbor a stunning tactical victory, even given the reservations about the strategy? It is argued here that Pearl Harbor was almost as flawed tactically as it was flawed strategically and that other tactical decisions taken by Japanese forces during World War II were counter-productive with regard to either winning the war or winning the peace that must follow any conflict.

The surprise attack on Pearl Harbor early on Sunday morning 7 December 1941 did catch the American forces in Hawaii unprepared. Radar images of Japanese aircraft approaching Oahu had been picked up but were misinterpreted as being a flight of American planes that were due. Air force planes were lined up on runways for defence against illusory saboteurs, but this only made them easy pickings for Japanese aircraft. The US Pacific battleship fleet was effectively destroyed at its moorings. Superficially, then, the attack appears to be a great tactical victory, but in several ways it was no such thing.

For a start, battleships were now obsolete, as the Japanese planes were showing – but not for the first time. Such an attack had happened before, as both sides would have known. A year earlier, an attack by British carrier-borne aircraft against the Italian navy at Taranto had shown that battleships were vulnerable to air attack, including in their docks. The destruction of American battleships was no longer crucial to US naval power as the most powerful warships were now aircraft carriers. Second, none of the three American aircraft carriers stationed in the Pacific were in Pearl Harbor that day. This was a further tactical failure by the Japanese. If they had been and were damaged or sunk, this would have more effectively altered the naval balance than the attack on battleships. So long as they survived the Americans still retained effective naval air power. Third, Pearl Harbor is shallow, its depth only slightly more than the battleships drew. Most of the eight operational battleships, even if sunk as five were, only settled into the mud and could be refloated later. Only two were total losses, as was an obsolete one used for target practice. Damaged ships, including some that had been sunk, were repaired and used later in the war. Fourth, concentrating the attack on battleships meant that other targets were not harmed. If submarine bases, power stations, machine shops and, above all, oil tanks had been targeted as well as the now obsolete battleships, the US navy may have had to withdraw to the mainland. The Japanese did discuss a third-wave attack to target other facilities, but in the event this was decided against and the Japanese fleet withdrew, content with their day. As Hotta argues:

> Oil tanks, machine shops, and other fixed U.S. facilities were mostly left untouched. Japan was also unable to inflict damage on any of the U.S. submarines and aircraft carriers, which were not present in the

harbor at the time. This, along with the fact that the harbor's shallow waters made the repair of damaged crafts easier, enabled a speedy recovery of U.S. naval night in the Pacific.[18]

This failure to press home their advantage meant that the Japanese attack on Pearl Harbor was a tactical failure as well as a strategic one. It was a raid, not a prelude to invasion, and did little to damage the American navy, despite the battleship losses on the day. Within a relatively short time, Pearl Harbor was back in action, serving as the American advance base in the Pacific for the rest of the war.

There are differing opinions as to the tactical success of the attack on Pearl Harbor, even if there are few contrary views as to its strategic folly. Prange argues:

On December 7, 1941, Nagumo had his ships at the right place, at the right time, with the right equipment, the right information, and the right men in the right state of training and frame of mind. All those factors enabled the Japanese to make the Pearl Harbor attack a grand tactical success – yet in the long run a great strategical failure.[19]

To Prange, then, Pearl Harbor was a tactical success, but a strategic failure. Morison argues it was a failure of both strategy and tactics arguing:

The surprise attack on Pearl Harbor, far from being a 'strategic necessity,' as the Japanese claimed even after the war, was a strategic imbecility. One can search military history for an operation more fatal to the aggressor. On the tactical level, the Pearl Harbor attack was wrongly concentrated on ships rather than permanent installations and oil tanks. On the strategic level it was idiotic. On the high political level, it was disastrous.[20]

The overall strategic purpose was foolish in the extreme, as discussed earlier. But tactically it was little better. If tactics are to contribute to purpose, it is hard to see how the Pearl Harbor attacks assisted the Japanese purpose, itself highly problematic. The American battleships were heavily damaged but they were already obsolete. The US strategic position was little affected, but the Japanese had stirred a hornet's nest of American unity with its surprise attack. If tactics are to reinforce and assist in pursuing the overall strategy, it is hard to see how the tactics at Pearl Harbor were anything other than a failure.

Coral Sea

Five months later, another event in the same theatre points to crucial differences between tactics and strategy. In May 1942, the Battle of the Coral Sea took place between a Japanese fleet that included troopships headed to capture Port Moresby and a combined American and Australian fleet.

The Japanese operation included two seaborne invasion forces, a small one targeting Tulagi in the southern Solomons and the main one aimed at Port Moresby. These were to be supported by land-based airpower from bases to the north and by two naval forces containing a small aircraft carrier, several cruisers, seaplane tenders and gunboats. More distant cover would be provided by the big aircraft carriers *Shokaku* and *Zuikaku* with their escorting cruisers and destroyers. The US Navy had some idea of the enemy plans by superior communications intelligence, and countered with two of its own carriers, plus cruisers (including two from the Australian Navy), destroyers, submarines, land-based bombers and patrol seaplanes.

The Battle of the Coral Sea was the first naval engagement in history where opposing ships never saw each other. It was a battle of aircraft carriers. Preliminary operations on 3–6 May 1942 and two days of active carrier combat on 7/8 May led to the United States losing one aircraft carrier, a destroyer and one of its very valuable fleet oilers, plus damage to the second carrier. On the other side, the Japanese were forced to postpone their Port Moresby seaborne invasion and never revisited it. They had lower casualties from the fighting, losing a light carrier, a destroyer and some smaller ships. The carrier *Shokaku* had serious bomb damage and the other carrier *Zuikaku's* air group was badly depleted.

McQueen, an Australian historian, argues that the Japanese won the Battle of the Coral Sea.[21] And simply adding up the ships sunk and casualties there is a case to be made. But this ignores the broader point that any battle, any tactical operation, must be seen in how it relates to overall strategy. Winning or losing a battle may be an irrelevance to this larger purpose. By this measure, despite higher casualties in ships and men, the US and Australian navies won the Battle of the Coral Sea as the Japanese were prevented from achieving their main strategic purpose of landing troops at Port Moresby. As Prange argues:

> In the Battle of the Coral Sea viewed purely as a sea engagement, the Japanese had the edge . . . But strategically, any battle which fails of its purpose cannot be considered a victory, and the Japanese failed to achieve their objective – capture and occupation of Port Moresby. So, considered objectively, it was a draw – a tactical Japanese victory versus a strategic American one.[22]

In strategic terms the result was rather better than a draw for the Americans. Both forces lost a carrier, although only a small one on the Japanese side. But in addition, the two large Japanese carriers that were damaged were then not available to participate in the Battle of Midway a month later, where their presence could have made a significant difference to the outcome. An important point is that adding up the winners of particular battles is irrelevant other than in how tactical events contribute to overall strategy.

Midway

After the Battle of the Coral Sea, as well as the Doolittle raid in April where Tokyo had been bombed by carrier-borne aircraft, Admiral Yamamoto believed more than ever that the American fleet needed to be destroyed and pushed ahead with his next offensive. The plan involved the bombing and capture of the small island of Midway 1,700 kilometres to the west of Honolulu. A diversionary attack on the Aleutians was part of the bigger plan. The overall idea was to draw the US carriers out from Hawaii where they could be destroyed by – in an echo of Jutland – a powerful battleship fleet following behind. Of course, what happened was a trap in reverse. The US carriers were already at sea and waiting for the attack on Midway they knew was going to happen.

The Japanese fleet included four aircraft carriers, all veterans of the Pearl Harbor attack. There would have been six if two had not been damaged at the Battle of the Coral Sea the month before. At this early stage of the war, the Japanese planes were generally better, notably the Zero fighter. But the US had other assets. The US may have had only three carriers, but they were larger and carried more planes than the Japanese ships. They were also able to use the airfield on Midway Island, effectively giving them an additional unsinkable carrier. They had another advantage in possessing radar as well as intercepted and decoded radio messages that gave strong indications that the target was Midway. Although there were limits to the decoding the US did have very good information regarding Yamamoto's fleet, tactical disposition, and routes of approach to its target. The US carrier *Yorktown* had been damaged at the Battle of the Coral Sea, with repairs expected to take several weeks or even months. But after three days it was sufficiently ready to leave Pearl Harbor with the other two carriers, as naval intelligence had pointed towards the Japanese attack on Midway being imminent. In the immediate build-up to the battle, Midway's defences were improved, with more men and aircraft stationed there.

After the Japanese invasion fleet was sighted by a US reconnaissance plane, land-based bombers from Midway attacked but were ineffectual. Japanese carrier aircraft attacked Midway causing damage but not of a decisive nature. American torpedo bombers from Midway also arrived at the Japanese carriers, but their attack was ineffective – the planes were obsolete and easily shot down. After a US Navy search plane spotted the Japanese carrier fleet, aircraft from the *Enterprise* and the *Hornet* headed to attack but initially could not find the Japanese carriers. Torpedo bombers from the *Yorktown* and the *Enterprise* attacked the Japanese but without fighter support many were shot down. The initial tactical aspects of Midway had favoured the Japanese as the early US attacks were beaten off, with heavy casualties on the US side.

But shortly after this, while the Japanese defending fighters were still at low altitude, US dive bombers from the *Enterprise* arrived, and in some six minutes three Japanese carriers – *Akagi*, *Kaga* and *Sōryū* – were damaged and sunk, two blowing up. The fourth carrier, *Hiryū*, survived for a few more hours and was able to launch an attack against *Yorktown*, but the *Hiryū* too was located and eventually sunk. The *Yorktown* was disabled and abandoned two days later, then torpedoed by a Japanese submarine and sunk while under tow to Pearl Harbor.

At this point the tactical flaws of the Japanese plan became apparent. Yamamoto's main fleet was too far away to assist in the immediate battle and his feint towards the Aleutians a waste of resources. Also, as he was at sea and maintaining radio silence he was effectively out of contact with the other fleets. The American admiral Nimitz on the other hand was based on land in Hawaii and could coordinate and send messages as they came to hand. Yamamoto's main fleet included large battleships despite it being evident that these were no longer effective; perhaps he wanted one last fleet action using gunfire, but this was not going to happen. The Japanese plan to attack Midway was overly complicated and 'depended for success on the Americans doing exactly what was expected of them'.[23] They did not do so. The submarine trap was a failure as the US ships had already passed before the Japanese submarines got to their stations.

The result of Midway may have been regarded as luck. Perhaps it was luck that the Enterprise's dive bombers were able to follow the course of a Japanese destroyer to find the Japanese carriers; it may have been luck that bombers from Enterprise and Yorktown arrived above the Japanese carriers just when they were at their most vulnerable due to refuelling and re-arming operations taking place. But the years of training, the capabilities of officers, sailors and pilots and the prosecution of the war from Admiral Nimitz's headquarters in Pearl Harbor were not luck.

It was all over, and not only the battle. Midway can be seen as the turning point of the war in the Pacific, as Hanson argues:

> The beginning of the end for the Japanese was Midway, where they lost their best airmen and irreplaceable aircrews and the core of their carrier fleet – and, most important, in a mere three days had their confidence shattered to such a degree that they would now fear, rather than look eagerly to, engaging American ships on the horizon.

After Midway the Japanese aircraft carrier fleet was much less effective and the replacement of ships and pilots occurred at a far slower rate than that of the Americans. An additional American carrier arrived in Pearl only a few days after the Battle of Midway and another a few weeks later. Many more were built and delivered. The Empire of Japan had raced out to its boundaries in a few months and would go no further. Despite the more than three years of hard fighting that followed, the war was effectively over. The naval initiative was lost with the carriers and what remained was stoic defence of what had been taken in those heady few months.

Japanese tactics at Midway were poor; the plan itself was gravely flawed and the handling of the ships and aircraft far from ideal. They suffered from over-confidence, having previously been all-conquering. Sailing their carriers in close company may have been good in the abstract by providing mutual protection, but it offered more targets for attacking aircraft once the fleet had been located. The Americans possessed the advantages of radar, advance knowledge of the Japanese plan and superb tactical leadership from its admirals and captains.

Island hopping

The Pacific War saw the adoption of the tactic of island hopping: leapfrogging or bypassing strongpoints that could then be left to wither away, thereby avoiding heavy casualties from attacking them serially.

Japanese strategy at the start of the naval war was to gain territory to form an island chain protecting the home islands. With the US Navy no longer in the way after Pearl Harbor, Japan would 'rapidly occupy the vulnerable colonies of the Western powers, now either themselves occupied or besieged by Nazi Germany, and build an impregnable defensive perimeter on the islands at the outer edges of the empire'.[24] The territory was indeed seized at the start, but then could not be defended or supplied as the Japanese navy had insufficient resources to defend its far-flung garrisons. Even using its new possessions to supply resources became untenable once command of the sea was lost.

In July 1942 Japanese troops landed on Guadalcanal, one of the Solomon Islands, and began to build an airfield. A month later, US Marines landed on the island and seized and held the airfield, beginning a series of battles lasting for close to six months. Guadalcanal was costly in terms of casualties in men, ships and aircraft, but also marked the furthest extent of the Japanese empire into the Pacific. It began an American push towards Tokyo in two directions; through the islands of the Central Pacific by the US Navy led by Admiral Chester Nimitz and from New Guinea to the Philippines with the army led by General Douglas Macarthur.

Island hopping meant simply bypassing some strongpoints, such as the island of Truk. With the Japanese fanatically defending every inch of captured territory, bypassing could achieve US strategic goals without frontal assaults everywhere. In what was largely an air war and a naval war, islands were useful in providing airfields that could then be used to project power as far as aircraft fuel range. Capturing another island would then extend the fuel and bombing range even further. In this process, given local air and naval superiority, some enemy places could simply be bypassed and isolated. They were also increasingly difficult to supply as Japanese merchant ships were sunk by bombs or submarines.

The town of Rabaul in New Britain was taken by the Japanese in February 1942 and became their headquarters for the South Pacific. As the war turned, however, instead of attacking Rabaul, it was simply bypassed and did not surrender until the end of the war. But it was strategically out of the war long before that. It was bombed at will by the Americans, had no aircraft to fight back, and simply withered. As Renzi and Roehrs argue:

> The advantage lay with the attacker in island warfare because defenders simply could not be everywhere at once. So long as the Allies could capture seemingly insignificant islands and quickly develop and supply airfields on them, the Japanese would have almost no chance of responding in strength and with coordination of effort. The true genius of 'island hopping' was its ability to keep the Japanese off balance and constantly responding to allied initiatives. That combined with the flood of new and improved weapons at the Allies' disposal, virtually guaranteed the outcome, if not the timetable, of the war's conclusion.[25]

The initial Japanese strategy of seizing the island chain was a strategic failure. It could only have worked if the seas between islands were swept clear of enemy ships, submarines and aircraft, and this was not possible given their resource inferiority. As soon as the US established its air and naval supremacy it was then able to use the islands to strike at Japan. The refinement that island hopping added was deliberately avoiding some fortified Japanese islands and leaving them to become isolated, removed from reinforcements and supplies and left to irrelevance. This approach was also a way of dealing with the great distances in the Pacific. If there was no need to take an island, then simply leave it. And once Japan itself was in range of island-based bombers its cities quickly became ruins.

Behaviour during conflict

How combatants carry out their tasks affects overall strategy both at the time and in the future. As noted earlier, Sun-tzu refers to the idea that no one benefits from protracted war and that it will be over eventually. The behaviour of protagonists in the war might become more salient after it ends. Conditions at the Confederate Andersonville camp for Union prisoners of war were so dire that some 13,000 of its 45,000 prisoners died of disease, exposure or malnutrition[26] and its commander was executed for war crimes after the war. Agreements such as the Geneva Convention to regulate behaviour in war, including treatment of prisoners, were entered into by most developed countries in the interwar years to provide a framework for how war was to be carried out.

Sun-tzu also argues for leniency for captives as they can be 'turned'. He says, 'Treat the captured soldiers well in order to nurture them [for our own use]. This is referred to as "conquering the enemy and growing stronger".'[27] Poor treatment of prisoners can become counter-productive; soldiers are likely to fight harder if they surmise they will be mistreated or executed if captured. Good treatment of prisoners, or complying with international agreements, also increases the chances of our own soldiers being well treated in return if they end up in the hands of the other side.

During the Revolutionary War, the British and their Hessian mercenaries sometimes executed American prisoners on the grounds that they were rebels rather than soldiers. This stiffened resistance, with the apparent barbarity helping turn the larger public in America against the British. Some 10,000 American prisoners of war died in prison hulks in New York harbour, more than died in action. On the other hand, George Washington insisted that American troops treat their prisoners well; that 'Hessian captives would be treated as human beings with the same rights of humanity for which Americans were striving'.[28] American leaders believed that it was not enough to win the war. They also had to win in a way that was consistent with the values of their society and the principles of their cause.[29] As it turned out, a quarter of the Hessians who survived the Revolutionary War stayed on as settlers and still others emigrated later.[30]

By attacking Pearl Harbor without warning or a declaration of war in World War II, the Japanese set themselves outside the established ways of carrying out conflict between states. For their enemies they could not be trusted to reach or sustain an agreement. This had a strategic point in that the United States stated early in the war that the only possible outcome of war with Japan was unconditional surrender. No deal could be made with a pariah nation and its militarist leaders. Although no other result would anyway have been acceptable for American domestic politics, it also meant that the Japanese war aim of a negotiated peace was unachievable. And from the American point of view, an agreement could not be made with a country that had showed its unwillingness to follow the rules of international conflict.

To make things even worse, how the war was prosecuted exacerbated the view that Japan was now a pariah nation. Japan's setting itself outside the agreed international order did seem to mean a suspension of orderly behaviour, and on both sides. The Pacific War was quite nasty; normal rules were not always followed, particularly, it must be said, by the Japanese.

Japanese soldiers faced privations of their own, but their treatment of prisoners was by any standard cruel and inhuman, including such instances as the Bataan death march, forced labour on the Burma-Thailand railway, and the Sandakan death march where six of 2,700 prisoners of war survived. Prisoners were routinely tortured and mistreated even though, while Japan had not signed the Geneva Convention on the treatment of prisoners, it had agreed to abide by its terms. But time after time, prisoners on the ground were treated brutally, perhaps reflecting the contempt shown to anyone who had surrendered in Japanese culture, where surrender was regarded as inconceivable. After rescuing two American aircrew from a life raft and interrogating them, the Japanese on the *Makigumo* simply threw them overboard.[31] A US Navy pilot, Ensign Osmus, rescued by the Japanese during the Battle of Midway, gave up valuable information including the number of American carriers. After his interrogation he too was thrown overboard.[32]

If Japanese mistreatment of prisoners of war was appalling, no less appalling was their mistreatment of civilians in captured Asian countries. There had been little thought given to running its new colonies, and ineptitude in this had strategic consequences. As Paine argues:

> Japanese operational strategy produced strategic disaster throughout the war. By focusing on military operations, the Japanese failed to give adequate attention to the social, diplomatic, and economic repercussions. Atrocities fed animosities and conjured countervailing alliances. Unrelenting warfare undermined first the Chinese and then the Japanese economy.[33]

With greater effort it may have been possible to win over some of the leadership in other Asian societies, but the administration of new Japanese territories was poor and brutal. The treatment of people in Japan's captured territories was so bad that it continues to affect relations negatively more than eighty years later. It did not need to be like that.

The colonial regimes of East Asia were in terminal decline anyway. As the Dutch, French and British faced turmoil in Europe, their colonies could not be defended. The Japanese idea of 'Asia for the Asians' or self-determination and nationhood was attractive in the abstract; however, the reality was more often yet another even more brutal colonialism. As James argues:

> The Japanese largely failed to persuade the natives that they were sincerely dedicated to their slogan of 'Asia for the Asiatics'. The early Japanese military successes did much to dispel illusions among Southeast Asians regarding the white man's superiority . . . But as the occupation wore on, growing numbers of Indonesians, Malays, Thais, Burmese, Vietnamese and Filipinos were repelled by the oppressive, exploitative methods of the Japanese, who worked native laborers as brutally, seized raw materials and foodstuffs as rapaciously, and stifled dissent as ruthlessly as the worst of the white colonialists.[34]

Atrocities committed by Japanese soldiers in Nanjing in 1937 are not forgotten in China and still form an unfortunate but real part of the continuing dialogue between Japan and China. It is not the fact that here was a war between them at one time that is a problem – rather, it is that Japanese behaviour during that war was so extreme that true forgiveness and contrition seem elusive even eighty years later. Many people in the once-conquered nations of East Asia continue to be resentful of Japan due to its behaviour during the war, whether it is attitude to prisoners or 'comfort' women in Korea; this is true even in Indonesia, where some locals initially thought it a good opportunity to end Dutch colonialism. As Paine argues:

> Japan's gratuitous brutality transformed potential sympathizers into bitter enemies. For a short time Asians living in the Pacific theater looked upon Japan as their liberator from the colonial powers, but Japanese actions rapidly made clear their own colonial ambitions, and their oppressive rule soon outdid all powers save Russia, Germany, and China, the record setters for mass murders in the twentieth century.[35]

As Sun-tzu notes, at some point the conflict will be over, and the possibility of losing and having to account for behaviour always needs to be borne in mind. War may be war, but when it is over nations need to be able to again work with other nations. Most of the time this can happen without lingering resentments. For Japan, though, almost eighty years after the war a pall still hangs over it, affecting its relations with its neighbours. How a combatant behaves during war can be strategic in its influence on the peace that follows.

A choice of tactics: Cuban missile crisis

In late 1962, the world appeared to be on the brink of yet another war, this time a nuclear one, when the United States found Soviet missiles – presumably nuclear – in Fidel Castro's Cuba. Once fully installed, these missiles would threaten the United States, a mere ninety miles away. Such a situation was intolerable for the US. From its perspective there was a clear primary objective of removing the missiles, but it also wanted to remain at peace, if possible, and keep other conflict issues such as the fate of Berlin out of the picture. Removing the missiles from Cuba was a clear enough purpose, but there were still questions of how to achieve that purpose; the options and the tactics to use to achieve that purpose.

The US response played out over 13 days from 16 October 1962, involving lengthy meetings in the White House of the Executive Committee, or ExCom, which was composed of military people, politicians, intelligence officials and the like. The various options were debated at great length. President Kennedy chaired the ExComm but allowed free debate. Options raised included: (i) do nothing; (ii) diplomatic pressure; (iii) a secret approach to Castro; (iv) invasion; (v) surgical air strike; and (vi) blockade.

Some were quickly ruled out. Doing nothing was completely unacceptable. A message to Castro would be ineffective as the missiles were not Cuba's. Invasion or bombing was feasible but would risk the chance of full-scale war with the Soviet Union, including possible nuclear exchange with catastrophic consequences for the world. A surgical air strike could not guarantee that all the missiles would be destroyed and would inevitably cause civilian casualties. The stronger options also risked diplomatic repercussions from other countries not directly involved.

The US military chiefs argued that a full-scale attack and invasion was the only solution. They believed that the Soviets would not attempt to stop the US from conquering Cuba. Kennedy was sceptical as a full invasion was seen as logistically difficult, politically problematic and possibly inviting Soviet retaliation against West Berlin.

In his classic account of the Cuban missile crisis, Allison argues that in the end Kennedy's advisers gave him two options: 'attack or accept Soviet nuclear missiles in Cuba'. He continues:

> But Kennedy rejected both. Instead of choosing between them, he crafted an imaginative alternative with three components: a public deal in which the United States pledged not to invade Cuba if the Soviet Union withdrew its missiles, a private ultimatum threatening to attack Cuba within 24 hours unless Khrushchev accepted that offer, and a secret sweetener that promised the withdrawal of U.S. missiles from Turkey within six months after the crisis was resolved.[36]

The public deal involved a naval blockade of Cuba, with US Navy ships empowered to search ships they suspected might be carrying Soviet weaponry. The term 'naval quarantine' was used instead of 'naval blockade' as declaring a blockade could be considered an act of war. There were advantages to this course of action, as Allison argues:

> It was a middle course between inaction and attack, aggressive enough to communicate firmness of intention, but still not so precipitate as a strike . . . It placed on Krushchev the burden of choice for the next step. He could avoid a direct military clash by keeping his ships away . . . At our doorstep, a naval blockade was invincible . . . This move permitted the United States, by flexing its conventional muscles, to exploit the threat of subsequent non-nuclear steps in each of which the United States would enjoy significant superiority.[37]

The naval blockade was instituted, resulting in incidents where Soviet ships were turned around. A few days later the crisis was over.

One of the reasons that the crisis could be settled was that the US made a significant concession over its missiles based in Turkey, as close to the Soviet Union as Cuba was to Florida. Kruschchev had written to Kennedy, pointing out that American missiles in Turkey were logically similar to Soviet missiles in Cuba:

> You are worried over Cuba. You say that it worries you because it lies at a distance of ninety miles across the sea from the shores of the United States of America. However, Turkey lies next to us . . . You have stationed devastating rocket weapons, which you call offensive, in Turkey, literally right next to us . . . This is why I make this proposal: We are willing to remove from Cuba the means which you regard as offensive . . . Your representatives will make a declaration to the effect that the United States . . . will evacuate its analogous means from Turkey.[38]

The US agreed to a withdrawal of missiles from Turkey, with the proviso that this course of action not be made public at the time.

As one of the most important events of the long Cold War, the Cuban missile crisis has attracted much attention. Allison's study of decision-making at that time is rightly regarded as a classic.[39] Robert Kennedy – the president's brother and one of the participants in the Executive Committee – wrote a book about the incident – Thirteen Days – that was published after his untimely death in 1968.[40] Even if rather self-serving there is one aspect of current relevance.

The president's brother sets out several points about the Cuban missile crisis to be taken into account when negotiating. These may well have greater applicability than being merely about that particular event.

1 Take time to plan; don't go with your first impulse. A hasty decision is unlikely to be the most effective because a full assessment of the costs and benefits of the alternatives requires considerable time.
2 The President should be exposed to a variety of opinions in order to make a proper assessment of the alternatives.
3 Rely heavily on those with solid knowledge of the Soviet Union. Those who make a careful study of the USSR are best suited to assess Soviet motives, the meaning of Soviet signals, and the Soviets' needs and interests.
4 Retain civilian control and beware of the limited outlook of the military. Many members of the military during the Cuban missile crisis advocated belligerent courses of action and failed to recognize the dangers of humiliating the opponent and courting unintended escalation.

5 Pay close attention to world opinion. A congenial diplomatic climate can facilitate resolution of a crisis on favorable terms.

6 Don't humiliate your opponent; leave him a way out.

7 Beware of inadvertence – the 'Guns of August' scenario. Accidents, inadvertence, and breakdowns in command and control can lead to actions beyond the President's knowledge and control, and may result in unintended escalation.[41]

It is an interesting set of propositions, starting with the need to be considered rather than hasty. Also, exposing the president – any leader for that matter – to a variety of views is also likely to lead to better overall outcomes. Robert Kennedy points to the need to maintain civilian control over the military and their limited outlook, arguing that many of the military put forward belligerent courses of action. And not humiliating an opponent and providing a way out and taking account of international opinion are sensible. The last point – the Guns of August – refers to the seemingly inadvertent start to World War I.[42] That there was a real possibility of global war starting inadvertently or accidentally over Cuba was a consideration to be taken into account in the negotiation. This list of points could be used more widely.

For present purposes, the Cuban missile crisis shows that even when the strategy is clear, even when the overriding purpose is clear, there are still different ways or different tactics that can be employed to help to get there. The naval quarantine of Cuba was cleverly pitched. It was a proportionate response rather than an excessive one considering the higher-level ones of bombing or even invasion. Escalation beyond that point was still possible but it would have to be the Soviets who escalated.

Perhaps the other tactical choices would have worked, but this will never be known. The US was way ahead in terms of military capability at that time, but much damage could have been done. Repercussions would have been worldwide. Conflict may even have become nuclear, as many feared at the time. Fifty years after the crisis, Allison argued:

It has been said that history does not repeat itself, but it does sometimes rhyme. Five decades later, the Cuban missile crisis stands not just as a pivotal moment in the history of the Cold War but also as a guide for how to defuse conflicts, manage great-power relationships, and make sound decisions about foreign policy in general.[43]

One impressive point about the Cuban missile crisis is the way that the various options and possible tactics were considered and how decisions were made. Some decision-makers, some presidents even, would jump to a conclusion without due consideration and would not allow debate as President Kennedy did. The choice made was quite neat and allowed all parties to escape with some dignity. The naval quarantine and agreements with the Soviets about Turkey did keep the peace. Somehow what was likely to have been the best tactic was chosen.

Conclusion

Tactics are the final facet of strategy in the PCWTT framework set out here. Tactics could be considered to be action plans, as lower-level events and even missions that assist in bringing about a strategic purpose already set out. Part of the art of being a strategist is being able to select from a number of possible tactical options the one best able to achieve the desired result at reasonable cost.

Tactics need to take into account the other facets of strategy. What are the respective capabilities at the time? Are there any constraints of terrain, or aspects of terrain that can be used to advantage? Will leadership be sufficient? What is the state of morale? Can all levels be motivated to work towards the tactical goals?

Tactics also need to work with, but be subordinate to, the overall strategic purpose. This may seem jarring for a linear model where, once the purpose has been decided, the other facets follow logically enough, including the tactics to be used. In the real world, though, the process is far from linear, and tactical considerations can and should be considered by the strategic purpose in question. In other words, when deciding what to do, the subsidiary consideration of just how to do it should be included in the purpose itself. For instance, if the purpose of the Japanese attack on Pearl Harbor was to reduce the US Navy's strength in battleships in the Pacific, the tactics of bombing and torpedoing the battleships were appropriate. But if the purpose was to weaken the US Navy in the Pacific as a whole, targeting oil tanks and machine shops would have been far more useful. Moreover, the strategy of seizing and holding a chain of islands around Japan should have considered exactly how tactically the islands could be supplied and defended against Allied submarines and aircraft.

There are likely to be different possible tactical responses following from a given purpose and, ideally, various possible options can be weighed in terms of likelihood of success, possible cost, speed, even though there can be no certainty as to which tactic is going to work best. Often the best one to follow is not known in advance. In a major war there is a lot of choice around expending resources on one option rather than another. Ideally, the tactics to follow should be those that are likely to lead to the best advancement of the strategy at lowest cost. Given uncertainty, this may not be easy to achieve. Still, any tactical plan should constantly ask, first, whether it is going to assist in the advancement of that strategy, second, if it is timely, efficient, and cost-effective, and third, whether it advances the strategy in a long-term sense, not cutting across the need to make sure that its negatives do not outweigh its positives.

Washington's attack on Trenton in 1776 was a small-scale incident where an unexpected tactical deployment resulted in the capture of some nine hundred Hessian soldiers and with few casualties. But this minor tactical victory had major strategic implications, including helping to convince France to join the conflict and Americans that Europeans could be defeated. As with Sherman's march through Georgia, tactics and strategy were seamless, the one reinforcing the other.

Notes

1   Carl von Clausewitz, *On War*, edited by Anatol Rapoport (Harmondsworth: Penguin, 1968), p. 173.

2   Chas W. Freeman, *Arts of Power: Statecraft and Diplomacy* (Washington, DC: United States Institute of Peace Press, 1997), p. 71.

3   Sun-tzu, *The Art of War*, in Ralph D. Sawyer (ed. and transl.), *The Seven Military Classics of Ancient China* (New York: Basic Books, 2007), p. 158.

4   Ibid.

5   Burke Davis, *Sherman's March* (New York: Random House, 1980), p. 21.

6   Ibid..

7   Lawrence Freedman, *The Future of War: A History* (London: Penguin, 2018), p. 37.

8   Davis, *Sherman's March*, p. 299.

9   Alfred Thayer Mahan, *The Influence of Seapower upon History 1660–1783* (New York: Hill & Wang, 1957 (orig. 1890), p. 88.

10 Andrew Roberts, *Napoleon the Great* (London: Penguin, 2014), p. 374.

11 Nigel Steel and Peter Hart, *Jutland 1916* (London: Cassell, 2003), p. 424.

12 Robert K. Massie, *Castles of Steel* (New York: Random House, 2003), p. 56.

13 Steel and Hart, *Jutland 1916*, p. 435.

14 Mahan, *The Influence of Seapower upon History 1660–1783*, p. 9.

15 *The Guardian*, 29 May 2016.

16 Massie, *Castles of Steel*, p. 675.

17 Steel and Hart, *Jutland 1916*, p. 435.

18 Eri Hotta, *Japan 1941* (New York: Vintage Books, 2013), p. 287.

19 Gordon W. Prange (with Donald M. Goldstein and Katherine V. Dillon), *Pearl Harbor: The Verdict of History* (Harmondsworth: Penguin, 1986), p. 497.

20 Samuel Eliot Morison, 'The Lessons of Pearl Harbor', *Saturday Evening Post*, 28 October 1961, p. 27 in Gordon W. Prange (with Donald M. Goldstein and Katherine V. Dillon), *Pearl Harbor: The Verdict of History* (Harmondsworth: Penguin, 1986), p. 482.

21 Humphrey McQueen, *Japan to the Rescue: Australian Security around the Indonesian Archipelago during the American Century* (Sydney: Heinemann, 1991).

22 Prange, *Miracle at Midway*, p. 44.

23 Peter Padfield, *Maritime Dominion* (London: John Murray, 2009), p. 265.

24 S.C.M. Paine, *The Wars for Asia, 1911–1949* (Cambridge: Cambridge University Press, 2012), p. 183.

25 William A. Renzi and Mark D. Roehrs, *World War II in the Pacific* (London: Routledge, 2015), p. 119.

26 James M. McPherson, *Battle Cry of Freedom* (New York: Ballantine, 1988), p. 796.

27 Sun-tzu, *The Art of War*, p. 159.

28 David Hackett Fischer, *Washington's Crossing* (New York: Oxford University Press, 2006), p. 378.

29 Ibid., p. 375

30 Ibid., p. 379

31 Prange, *Miracle at Midway*, p. 254.

32 Jonathan B. Parshall and Anthony P. Tully, *Shattered Sword: The Untold Story of the Battle of Midway* (Washington, DC: Potomac Books, 2005), p. 288.

33 Paine, *The Wars for Asia*, pp. 219–20.

34 D. Clayton James, 'American and Japanese Strategies in the Pacific War', in Peter Paret (ed.), *Makers of Modern Strategy: From Machiavelli to the Nuclear Age* (Princeton: Princeton University Press, 1986), p. 714.

35 Paine, *The Wars for Asia*, p. 214.

36 Graham T. Allison, 'The Cuban Missile Crisis at 50: Lessons for U.S. Foreign Policy Today', *Foreign Affairs*, 91, 4 (2012), p. 12.

37 Graham T. Allison, *Essence of Decision: Explaining the Cuban Missile Crisis* (Boston: Little, Brown, 1971), p. 61.

38 Ibid., pp. 223–4.

39 Ibid.

40 Robert F. Kennedy, *Thirteen Days* (New York: W.W. Norton, 1969), in David A. Welch, 'Nuclear Crises', in Graham T. Allison, Jr., Robert D. Blackwill, Albert Carnesale, Joseph S. Nye, Jr. Robert P. Beschel, Jr. (eds), *A Primer for the Nuclear Age*, CSIA Occasional Paper No. 6 (Lanham, MD: University Press, 1990).

41 Paraphrased in ibid.

42 Barbara Tuchman, *The Guns of August* (New York: Macmillan, 1962).

43 Allison, 'The Cuban Missile Crisis', p. 16.

7

CONCLUSION

Earlier chapters argued that strategy can be conceived as the interaction of five facets – purpose, capability, will, terrain and tactics – and examples have been put forward to illustrate these. By analogy, this framework may be used in other situations than warfare. Even if strategic issues in business or other settings are unlikely to be as crucial or life-threatening as those facing the armies during the American Civil War, for instance, analysis of such events can still provide useful insight.

PCWTT may be an awkward acronym, but it is argued that the words that form it do represent the key aspects of strategy. Any strategy needs purpose; any consideration of action against adversaries needs comparison of capability. A strategy takes place in an environment, a natural environment – here under the heading of terrain – that can affect the strategy either positively or negatively. Tactics include those subsidiary actions that assist in prosecution of the strategy, while will is about deciding whether or not to move ahead with an action, which includes aspects of leadership and the interactions between people that tend to make strategy more of an art than a science.

The approach here of looking at real instances in conflict situations does raise questions of applicability to less violent arenas. At best there may be analogy, but studies of strategy are replete with analogy. The tale discussed earlier (chapter 4) of Cortés and the supposed burning of the boats at Vera Cruz is much referred to in popular culture as a way of fortifying the spirit of subordinates by taking away any option of retreat. It seems that this event did not happen as usually described – that is, Cortés appears to have run the boats on to the shore rather than burning them, and for different reasons than those usually given – but does this mean that the story is wrong and should not be used? In one sense it does not matter as it is only a story and a real or fictional story can be used for analogy. But at least in this case it would be better to have an appreciation of what is more likely to have happened, and if a lesson is to be drawn then to use that lesson instead of the myth. In many circumstances, a better strategy when facing someone with superior resources is to avoid battle or war altogether rather than risk losing everything. Cortés conquered Mexico eventually by enlisting allies disillusioned with Aztec dominance, by marshalling resources and by calculation, not by risking everything in a quixotic search for glory by removing the possibility of retreat.

There are lessons to be drawn from each of the five facets, and these add colour and movement to events and also food for thought for future projects. But the PCWTT model does not provide a complete answer to understanding strategy. Even if there are similarities between strategies, or strategic situations, each one is also likely to be unique, with its own mix of facets.

The model in five facets

The five facets of strategy – purpose, capability, will, terrain and tactics – have been argued to be the key aspects of strategy; they are all mission-critical, as it were. They may be interdependent and in some circumstances one or other facet can be more important than others. For instance, terrain – particularly the weather – was particularly important in the Alaskan conflict in World War II. While the ferocious weather was never overcome – an impossibility – it was better tolerated by the superior resources deployed by the United States, which the Japanese were unable or unwilling to match. Terrain and capability were therefore closely linked in this case.

The American Civil War and the two world wars were won by the sides with the superior resource capability, although all the facets were certainly present.

Purpose

Purpose is without doubt the most crucial part of strategy; it is why we do something, it's the ultimate goal. Purpose is clearly higher than 'mission', more about fundamentals, more about the very *raison d'être* of an organization, venture or situation. Setting purpose should be a considered, analytical exercise, weighing options, working out scenarios, setting out possible risks. Questions about purpose should include: is this a fundamental purpose; are there impediments sufficient to detract from the purpose outlined; is the purpose realistic; does the purpose make unrealistic assumptions about the will or motivation of possible protagonists?

Without purpose the other facets make little sense. Purposeless strategy does seem to be a contradiction in terms, even if it may occur from time to time. Instances in earlier chapters of lack of purpose, unrealistic purpose, esoteric purpose or illogical purpose tend to end in tragedy. And although there are, in warfare, examples of purpose driving strategy, there are other examples where purpose was unclear or even absent.

Even though purpose is the most crucial facet of strategy, it is also the one that has proved most problematic. There are several instances where purpose was ignored, bypassed or not even considered, and this in major conflicts costing millions of lives. It would be assumed that nations are strategic and go to war in a considered way, for good reason. Clausewitz believed this. In reality, though, it is 'rarely (if ever) the case that the decision to go to war is a pure function of threat assessments . . . and of clear political war aims'.[1] Clear purpose may be a Clausewitzian ideal, but it should still be an aim.

Capability

Capability refers to the assets held by a protagonist that can be deployed in a contest and what can be done as a consequence of having and holding these assets. What are my resources compared to those of another or others with respect to the articulated purpose? Aspects of capability include infrastructure, assets both actual and potential, human capability including education, training, organization, administrative skills, and information, intelligence and analytical abilities. Capability also needs to include what might be potentially available or may be brought to bear in a relatively timely way.

Overall capability is one thing, but more to the point is capability related to the specific strategy. During the Vietnam War, for instance, the US military capability as a whole was far greater than that of its Vietnamese adversaries, but it was neither able nor willing to deploy all its resources, many of which, in any case, were unsuited to that particular conflict.

Even if strategy should be an iterative process involving all five facets, capability is usually second only to purpose as the most important of them. Capability should be an early and intimate part of any planning in an iterative process; indeed, the purpose should be contingent on a realistic assessment of the available capability to be allocated for that purpose. In practice it is quite difficult to measure capability in an unbiased way; there may be tendency to overstate one's own capability and discount that of others. Information may not be available and intelligence is too often insufficient for making an assessment; even when available it may be poorly analyzed. It appears that making inferences from any information is a common failing.

Will

Will is about decision-making – deciding to take, or not take, action. It involves the ability to move and the leadership of others in order to move. Will involves having the strength of character, the firmness, the decisiveness, to undertake an action. It is about commitment, deciding to proceed or not, both individually and collectively. The other facets of strategy may all be present, but without the will to move ahead an organization is not going to move at all. Will involves some of the more personal aspects of strategy, including leadership as the manifestation of will. This facet is difficult to assess, though it is crucial in rounding out the facets of strategy. If will is not present nothing will happen and the other facets are moot.

Will is harder to quantify than capability, where categories of, say, money, numbers of people, training, heavy equipment, light equipment, infrastructure are more measurable and able to be compared with those of an adversary or adversaries. Purpose and capability are usually overt and clear, while will is more vague and esoteric. Will turns on motivation, on leadership, on perceptions of relative moral strengths and on processes of decision-making. These are tenuous by nature and innately hard to measure other than quite subjectively. The will of an opponent can be foolishly disparaged or discounted in a comparison with one's own side. Napoleon disparaged Wellington as a mere 'sepoy general,' referring to Wellington's time in India. And, as argued earlier, the Japanese belief in both their superior will and the axiomatically inferior will of their opponents proved disastrous in a longer war. Will alone could not overcome the vastly superior resources of the United States in an industrial-scale war.

Terrain

Terrain refers to the field, area or arena on which a contest is to take place, and also to constraints or opportunities imposed by the natural environment. In most contexts thinking about terrain involves factors that are relevant but beyond human control such as geography or physical conformation, the land and the sea, the elements, the seasons and the weather. Terrain is undoubtedly important but can be overcome by deploying greater resource capability. Terrain would have been more salient before technology provided greater means for moving mountains or bridging rivers that were once impassable. Issues of terrain must be included in planning, but the possibility of being supplanted by greater resources also needs to be taken into consideration. An impressive aspect of the building by Wellington of the Lines of Torres Vedras in the Peninsular War is that they were built to be just impassable enough for the size of army and equipment that the French were likely to deploy against them. Also, Wellington's army was able to move and was not held static behind the lines; the terrain was useful but never everything in the strategy.

Tactics

Tactics are day-to-day or lower-level actions that aggregate in order to carry out an overall purpose. Tactics could be in the form of action plans or some other kind of subsidiary initiatives, events or actions that assist in bringing about the larger agreed purpose. Tactical actions that are inconsistent with purpose may cause delay and may cut across a desired strategic outcome.

An obvious issue is that of choosing the set of tactics to be deployed from many possibilities. Each one undertaken consumes resources that could be used elsewhere. This means that tactical planning needs substantial strategic thinking of its own, even if the overall strategy is unchanged. Tactical planning therefore requires through examination of capability, will and terrain in order to decide what may be the most effective tactics for pursuit of the overall strategy. Tactics are probably more important for an outcome than terrain, even though terrain is an important consideration in planning overall and for tactics in particular.

Interactions of facets

Some of the instances and examples used in previous chapters involve more than one of the five facets of the PCWTT model, albeit of varying strength. George Washington's strategy during the American Revolution was used earlier as an exemplar of clear purpose and maintaining focus on that purpose throughout the various trials and tribulations he went through. Washington maintained a high level of will, but this could not be said of those around him or his superiors in the Congress, some of whom were fractious and less than fully supportive. Capability was not of a high level, particularly early on. His army was often weakened by desertion and by rivalries between even high-ranking officers. Similarly, the supply of resources was often quite poor in the early stages. But the use of terrain – retreating into the interior – was masterful, while the tactics were entirely appropriate given the resources and terrain.

Wellington in Portugal was also able to overcome weakness in capability through superior use of terrain. The armies ranged against him were typically much larger than his, but Wellington was able through alliances with Portugal and Spain to supplement the numbers and at times gain local advantage. And, as the British navy maintained command of the sea, Wellington was well supplied through Lisbon; his soldiers were better fed, armed and clothed than those of the French. In addition, the tactic of rendering the resources of the countryside unavailable through a scorched earth policy made life difficult for the French army camped in front of the Lines of Torres Vedras. Faced with terrain it could not overcome, without much food or forage and in the midst of a hostile population that made supply from France difficult, Masséna's army withdrew, having suffered heavy casualties mostly through starvation and disease. Wellington's use of terrain was masterful.

All five facets of strategy were highly significant in the Pacific War. For the Japanese the purpose was clear enough, even if, as argued earlier, unrealistic – so unrealistic as to defy rationality. The leadership, society and military possessed very high levels of will – albeit often self-destructive – to the extent that they disparaged the will of anyone outside. But will, even if superior, cannot overcome major deficiencies in capability. As an instance, six Japanese aircraft carriers attacked Pearl Harbor in December 1941. The loss of four of these at Midway a mere six months later turned the Japanese advantage in this class of ship to an instant and lasting disadvantage. As it generally took several years to build even one such ship, the US advantage was not going to be surrendered given its far greater industrial capacity. The Japanese use of terrain and tactics were often poor. Successful surprise attacks early in the war could not be sustained and captured territory could not be held or supplied given naval and civilian maritime incapacity. Tactics used after the initial wave of conquests were often predictable, and the combining of individual acts of bravery with poor resources led to high and unsustainable casualty rates. Additionally, the way the war was carried out and the treatment of captive countries, civilians and prisoners was counter-productive and led to long-lasting enmity in the region. The venture was not thought through.

However, in the same arena of the Pacific, the United States rates very highly on all five facets. The highest sense of purpose in their cause was gifted to them by the Japanese attack on Pearl Harbor. The act of being attacked meant that the war was just, and that the attack occurred without warning only added to the American response being both righteous and fully supported by the public. Most of the isolationists, so prominent in the previous decade, changed sides immediately.

If purpose was high, so too were capability and will. Resources did take some time to become fully available, but the US had started rearming a few years earlier so had something of a start. And once its factories and shipyards were operating fully they produced enough to supply the US and its allies in both Europe and the Pacific. The will to prevail was certainly present in what was later seen as the last good war, while leadership at the political and military levels was outstanding. The terrain of the Pacific was challenging given its extent, but this was countered by the US by using its resource capability to build more and better aircraft, ships and equipment, construction of all kinds, including bases pointing towards the Japanese home islands. Tactics too were tailored to the resource advantage, with machines deployed and unnecessary casualties avoided as far as possible.

In general, purpose, capability and will occur prior to action, while terrain and tactics impinge more on how an action is carried out once it has been decided upon. But even if terrain and tactics occur later, a viable strategy still needs to take them into account in the early stages of planning. Perhaps the Japanese in the Pacific War thought that purpose and will could overcome any deficiency, but as the war developed they were unable to overcome disadvantages in capability, terrain and tactics. Purpose may be the most important facet, but it does depend on the others. Capability affects purpose for obvious enough reasons – that is, even considering a course of action requires an assessment of capability. Terrain and tactics similarly affect purpose. They are related to each other to an even greater extent than the other facets. Both are subsidiary actions once the decision to commit has been taken. As for tactics, once there is an armed conflict it is best dealt with quickly, at least cost in resources and lives, and without lasting resentments given that the default status should be peace so that ordinary people can go about their business without fear.

Final thoughts

History may not repeat itself exactly, but there are still lessons that can be drawn from it. Some events are so long ago that there cannot be certainty ascribed to motives or behaviours, and it is inevitable that the past is looked at from a present-day lens. But the present is also constructed of the past; any society today is an amalgam of its culture, its present and its past. The searing experience of being unprepared at Pearl Harbor has driven US grand strategy for the eighty years since. An article of faith among all subsequent administrations has been that never again would the US be caught by surprise.

There is an obvious issue that wars have been set in train for what could be seen – not only with hindsight but also at the time – as irrational reasons. This does not mean, however, that all wars can or should be avoided and that unilateral pacifism provides universal benefit. As long as the world is organized into nation-states and national governments, rivalries will arise; defending the nation and its people is one of the key responsibilities of any government. It is always possible that a rogue regime will arise, as in Germany and Japan before World War II, with the express aim of war for expansionary reasons, and such a possibility needs to be considered by likely adversaries. In specific circumstances there may be a benefit to be gained from war, or at least recourse to war as a last resort. Even if it is hard to discern a realistic purpose in Japan's Pacific War, there was no doubt in the response of the US and other countries. They were attacked without warning and not only responded but did so with the full force of public opinion behind them.

The notion that war is calculable, that it can be carefully analyzed and assessed, does not often apply in the real world. Wars have been entered into for all kinds of reason; requiring carefully assessment beforehand flies in the face of much actual practice. Even if purpose is crucial to military strategy there are many instances where purpose is not apparent – World War I – or wildly unrealistic – Japan in World War II –, and in either or both of these wars subsequent events led to the deaths of millions of people. A clear analysis of Japan's position prior to the Pacific War would not have led to war.

Purpose, capability, will, terrain and tactics may be applied to other situations than war, even though terrain or tactics may not be issues for all strategic circumstances. There are limitations, however. One limitation is that other kinds of strategy are non-lethal, with the downsides of failure not as dire as in war. Military strategy tends towards being zero-sum in that there will be a winner and a loser, or even, as in World War I, negative sum with all the main participants worse off. In business, both parties may sometimes win. Trade, for instance, is usually a non-zero-sum game as both parties can gain. In other corporate circumstances there may be only one winner, but even then the punishment for failure is unlikely to be lethal. For all that non-military strategists may wish to emulate the great works of great generals, the reality is that the stakes are far higher in war.

The most important facet of strategy is purpose, but as has been seen, there are instances where purpose was unclear or even missing. Perhaps any attempt to find clear purpose is doomed to fail in some instances. It could be argued that there should be more analysis and more calculations of costs and benefits, including longer-term consequences, before going to war, but then this is what some of the theorists used here have argued.

As noted earlier, Sun-tzu argues that 'Warfare is the greatest affair of state; the basis of life and death, the Way [Tao] to survival or extinction. It must be thoroughly pondered and analyzed.'[2] Strategy or war should not be resorted to lightly, on a whim or without reason. It is always potentially risky. As Sun-tzu notes, 'Those who do not thoroughly comprehend the dangers inherent in employing the army are incapable of truly knowing the potential advantages of military actions.'[3] Recently, Colin Powell has argued that

> War should be the politics of last resort. And when we go to war, we should have a purpose that our people understand and support; we should mobilize the country's resources to fulfil that mission and then go in and win.[4]

War and strategy by extension are serious and should not be entered into without clear analysis. Strategy may be a logical process in the ideal case, but the ideal case may not be that relevant in a world of brawling for all kinds of reasons.

The aim here has been to provide answers to a set of related questions: what is strategy, how can it be illustrated and does examination of some past events through the five facets – purpose, capability, will, terrain and tactics – provide a useful lens with which to look at strategy? Using a series of examples to illustrate each of these facets, it is argued that the five facets do provide a set of conceptual lenses with which to view the world. But the story is incomplete. Any strategy must be adapted to its own reality even as it draws from past lessons. If there is a general lesson it is that strategy needs to be approached with care.

Notes

1   Beatrice Heuser, *The Evolution of Strategy* (Cambridge: Cambridge University Press, 2010), p. 489.
2   Sun-tzu, *The Art of War*, in Ralph D. Sawyer (ed. and transl.), *The Seven Military Classics of Ancient China* (New York: Basic Books, 2007), p. 157.
3   Ibid., p. 159.
4   Eliot A. Cohen, 'Playing Powell Politics: The General's Zest for Power', *Foreign Affairs*, 74, 6 (1995).

INDEX

Printed in the United States
By Bookmasters